PATERNOSTER THEOLOGICAL MONOGRAPHS

The Apathetic God

Exploring the Contemporary Relevance of Divine Impassibility

PATERNOSTER THEOLOGICAL MONOGRAPHS

The Apathetic God

Exploring the Contemporary Relevance of Divine Impassibility

Daniel Castelo

Foreword by Thomas G. Weinandy, O.F.M., Cap.

WIPF & STOCK · Eugene, Oregon

Wipf and Stock Publishers
199 W 8th Ave, Suite 3
Eugene, OR 97401

The Apathetic God
Exploring the Contemporary Relevance of Divine Impassibility
By Castelo, Daniel
Copyright©2009 Paternoster
ISBN 13: 978-1-60899-100-6
Publication date 10/1/2009
Previously published by Paternoster, 2009

This Edition published by Wipf and Stock Publishers by arrangement with Paternoster

Series Preface

In the West the churches may be declining, but theology—serious, academic (mostly doctoral level) and mainstream orthodox in evaluative commitment—shows no sign of withering on the vine. This series of *Paternoster Theological Monographs* extends the expertise of the Press especially to first-time authors whose work stands broadly within the parameters created by fidelity to Scripture and has satisfied the critical scrutiny of respected assessors in the academy. Such theology may come in several distinct intellectual disciplines—historical, dogmatic, pastoral, apologetic, missional, aesthetic and no doubt others also. The series will be particularly hospitable to promising constructive theology within an evangelical frame, for it is of this that the church's need seems to be greatest. Quality writing will be published across the confessions—Anabaptist, Episcopalian, Reformed, Arminian and Orthodox—across the ages—patristic, medieval, reformation, modern and counter-modern—and across the continents. The aim of the series is theology written in the twofold conviction that the church needs theology and theology needs the church—which in reality means theology done for the glory of God.

Series Editors

Oliver Crisp, Lecturer in Theology, University of Bristol, UK

Trevor A. Hart, Head of School and Principal of St Mary's College School of Divinity, University of St Andrews, Scotland, UK

Anthony N.S. Lane, Professor of Historical Theology and Director of Research, London School of Theology, UK

Anthony C. Thiselton, Emeritus Professor of Christian Theology, University of Nottingham, Research Professor in Christian Theology, University College Chester, and Canon Theologian of Leicester Cathedral and Southwell Minster, UK

Kevin J. Vanhoozer, Research Professor of Systematic Theology, Trinity Evangelical Divinity School, Deerfield, Illinois, USA

To Kimberly Gwen

Contents

FOREWORD

There was a time, not too long ago, when many, if not most, contemporary theologians confidently boasted that finally, after almost two thousand years, the notion of divine impassibility had been forever chucked into the waste bin of passed theological aberrations. Having indisputably demonstrated that divine impassibility was not in accord with the biblical revelation of a loving and compassionate God, but rather the alien and disfiguring remnant of Greek philosophy, these theologians boldly and assertively argued that God was affected by the horrendous strife and evil inflicted upon the innocent and the just, and so suffered in mutual solidarity with them. Their theological sound-bite was: If God is loving and compassionate, and surely he is, then he too must compassionately suffer in love.

However, those days of confident boasting are now over. There is a growing theological literature that is more biblically sound, more philosophically astute, more historically accurate, more theologically sophisticated, and more spiritually satisfying which demonstrates that divine impassibility belongs to the very essence of a loving and compassionate God, especially as expressed within the doctrines of the Trinity, the Incarnation and the saving actions of Jesus. Dr. Daniel Castelo's book, *The Apathetic God: Exploring the Contemporary Relevance of Divine Impassibility*, is a welcome contribution to the retrieval and development of this biblical Christian truth that God is impassible not because he is not loving and compassionate, but precisely because he is all loving and compassionate.

Dr. Castelo provides a strong biblical defense and understanding of God's impassibility. He gives a clear and accurate account of the Patristic literature, and he is especially helpful in explaining the writings of the Protestant Reformers. He offers a thoughtful analysis and perceptive critique of Jürgen Moltmann's theology of a suffering God showing it to be biblically, historically and philosophically naïve and so theologically indefensible. Moreover, Dr. Castelo provides a very clear and compelling soteriological presentation of the Incarnation and the importance of the Communication of Idioms, where the Son of God, while not suffering within his divine nature, does indeed truly suffer as man. Lastly, because the Christian biblical tradition is at the heart of Dr. Castelo's study, this book is spiritually rewarding and pastorally sensitive.

It is heartening to find new scholars who are not taken in by the theological fads of the moment, but seriously, creatively and systematically address contemporary philosophical and theological issues from within the context of the Bible as well as from within the context of traditional Christian doctrine.

Thomas G. Weinandy, O.F.M., Cap.
Capuchin College
Washington, D.C.
March 2009

Acknowledgements

My work on divine impassibility started one summer in the basement of Perkins Library at Duke University where I began reading Jürgen Moltmann's *The Crucified God*. Given my sympathies with ancient Christian sources, I was startled by both Moltmann's presentation and dismissal of the patristic witness, thus initiating my journey in researching and contemplating the role of divine impassibility within Christian theology. The culmination of this interest led to my PhD dissertation, "Only the Impassible God Can Help: Moltmann and the Contemporary Status of Divine Impassibility". Even then, however, I wanted to offer a work that spoke to the issue at large. Although the present endeavor does not cover every issue of interest surrounding the role of divine impassibility within the contemporary discussion, the presentation itself is broader and more general than its predecessor.

In the interim between the dissertation's defense and the completion of this work, a couple of articles were published that treated some of the themes considered here. Chapter 2 is a reworking of "A Crisis in God-talk? The Bible and Theopathy", *Theology* 110.858 (November/December 2007), pp. 411-16. Chapter 4 appeared in shorter form as "Moltmann's Dismissal of Divine Impassibility: Warranted?", *Scottish Journal of Theology* 61.4 (2008), pp. 396-407. I wish to thank the editors of these journals for their permission to use some of the material in these earlier items within the present work.

From an academic standpoint, I would like to thank my teachers and friends at the Church of God Theological Seminary. Specifically, Cheryl and Jackie Johns, John Christopher Thomas, and Steven Land have supported me, both verbally and in tangible ways. I have valued both their academic output and their friendship over the years. At Duke, my doctoral advisor, Geoffrey Wainwright, offered a helpful eye and a supportive spirit to the dissertation's composition. Others on the dissertation committee, including Stanley Hauerwas, Reinhard Hütter, Willie Jennings, and Warren Smith, offered important suggestions along the way. The present work, of course, is different from the one they originally supervised; errors and omissions are solely my own.

I have also been blessed with the opportunity to work at Seattle Pacific University. My colleagues have been a great gift to me and my family, and I am grateful that they were willing to accept me into their company. I especially want to thank the Center for Scholarship and Faculty Development for a Faculty Research Grant awarded to me for the 2007-2008 academic year, Doug Koskela for reading the bulk of the work and offering very helpful comments, Steve Perisho for his professional assistance in obtaining library resources, and Luke Reinsma for his help in the editorial task. I would also like to express my gratitude to my teaching assistant, David Lippold, for his detailed work on this manuscript.

Finally, I would like to recognize my family for believing in me and what I am doing. My parents, Cornelio and Annette Castelo, have supported my work in theology in a committed and dedicated manner. I would not have been able to continue along this path had it not been for their subvention. My wife, Kimberly Gwen, has been in the trenches with me during this entire process. It is a great gift from God to have a companion in life with whom one can have a serious theological discussion! Even more so, I appreciate her desire to serve God and her sense of humor. Our daughter, Kathryn Elisabeth, came to us the day after I gave birth to the original dissertation. What a wonderful joy it has been to have her in our lives, reminding us in the midst of hardship and trials that God is forever the giver of life and the source and end of our hope.

And on that note, may this work serve its purpose in rendering to God that which we can. *Soli Deo Gloria!*

Daniel Castelo
Seattle Pacific University
March 2009

Introduction

Why would anyone be interested in a book that entertains the notion of an "apathetic" God? Is not an apathetic God simply a misrepresentation of the God revealed in Jesus Christ, the one who suffered and died on a cross? Furthermore, in the Christian way of thinking, God's very nature is love, and obviously love is contrary to apathy: Love seeks out the beloved while apathy is removed from the fray. It would seem that only abstract, metaphysical conceptions, like those of the Stoics and other philosophical schools, could offer an ideal such as an "apathetic God", for in these cases, affective language is dismissed on specific grounds particular to their commonly held commitments.

The suspicions and assumptions of the preceding paragraph govern the hermeneutical practices of many who read ancient Christian sources that extol the value of divine *apatheia* (Greek) or *impassibilitas* (Latin). Since *apatheia* means "apathy" and *impassibilitas* implies "not passionate", some figures, including a number of respected authorities, denounce the picture of God that many in the ancient world held. These connotative assumptions – ones that are difficult to identify and problematize because they appear to be so "obvious" – suggest a more difficult notion, namely that the contemporary Christian articulation of who God is and what he is like stands in deep tension with previous views native to different epochs. Since the philosophical conventions of any given era have been used (both intentionally and unintentionally) throughout Christian history as "spoils of the Egyptians", this tension is, of course, part and parcel to the study of Christian theology.

The startling difficulty associated with divine impassibility, however, is that many scholars regard this linguistic phrasing, with its detectable heritage within the Greek philosophical tradition, not as a legitimate expression of a particular setting but a blatant, unwittingly accepted error. For many, divine impassibility provides the exemplary test case for showing how Christianity went too far in adopting the discourse of a given epoch. The argument one often encounters in these discussions is that the "Greek conception of God" stands in stark contrast to the biblical God who repents in the Old Testament and who suffers and dies in Christ within the pages of the New.

But the assumption that divine impassibility is incompatible with Christian faith is itself incompatible with the fact that many early Christians found this maxim to be helpful not only in their theological grappling but also for their everyday piety. That many scholars cannot appreciate this particular use of divine impassibility suggests a two-tiered mistake – both historical and theological. In light of the first consideration, other than specialists in historical theology, few have demonstrated sufficient hermeneutical generosity with early Christian sources to allow these to determine their own boundaries and ways of narrating the God of their beliefs and convictions. Because of modernity's desire to categorize and fit all phenomena within systems, schools, and tendencies, divine impassibility was prominently raised as a symptom of Christianity's inability to liberate itself from the grip of Hellenistic philosophy. In fact, P. L. Gavrilyuk labels the narration associated with these historical readings as the "Theory of Theology's Fall into Hellenistic Philosophy".[1] Begun in earnest in its modern form by Adolf von Harnack, the theory suggests that the early church uncritically appropriated divine impassibility from its native Hellenistic context and in so doing formulated a biblically unfounded view that has been termed "classical theism". Many today uncritically promulgate this narrative of theology's "fall" and believe they are doing theology a service by rescuing contemporary God-talk from this pagan captivity. Arguments against "classical theism" abound in contemporary theology, and the triumphalism on the part of its despisers is rampant.

The linguistic assumption associated with rendering *apatheia* as "apathetic" is a theological problem because with this move there is a loss as to what theological work the term did in the first place. In other words, because the mere mention of an "indifferent God" is anathema to the contemporary reader, the linguistic connotations for *apatheia* in its native contexts are lost as well as the theological value the original use of the term was aiming to achieve. Moderns often assume that the early church was so wedded to Greek philosophy that it could not see how contradictory such concepts were to the biblical portrayal of God. But a closer reading of many ancient sources suggests that many early figures were in fact largely more biblically conversant than their modern counterparts and that their use of *apatheia* aimed at preserving a vital feature of the biblical witness.

The present work is thus guided by certain commitments. This book assumes that divine *apatheia* as a theological maxim was theologically significant for the early church. Although the term itself is unquestionably derived from Hellenistic sources and while it is true that a Hellenistic context inevitably makes its use easier to justify, taken on its own, *apatheia* largely did not mean "indifference" to the early church when used in relation to God. On the contrary, the early church used *apatheia* in an attempt to safeguard the divine transcendence in an apophatic manner, especially within those contexts in which the notion of "suffering" was gaining acceptance as a category to be used in relation to the godhead.

And it is this function, of safeguarding the divine transcendence apophatically, that is gravely needed in contemporary theological discourse. At a time when it is easier for Christians to fathom the crucifixion than the resurrection, God's transcendence is in continual need of being reconsidered and revitalized through alternative metaphysical and epistemological

---

[1] P. L. Gavrilyuk, *The Suffering of the Impassible God* (Oxford: Oxford University Press, 2004), p. 5.

categories. Divine *apatheia*, a notion that from the onset is unnerving and apparently non-justifiable to the contemporary observer, provides the opportunity for such a reconfiguration. The challenge at hand is to investigate if divine impassibility can be retrieved and formulated in ways that can contribute to the contemporary theological climate.

In offering a rationale for the need to give up and retrieve that which is necessary for a rehabilitated notion of divine impassibility to be operative in contemporary theological discourse, this work does not advocate the dismissal of divine passibility; however, given the way so many theologians and believers today assume it unquestionably, divine passibility has to be checked and qualified in order that it does not become overly sentimentalized or domesticated. The notion of a "suffering God" has some truth to be preserved when considered in a very specific, christological sense, and this work attempts to honor that feature of God-talk.

The affirmation of the value of both divine impassibility and passibility, however, will not result in an entirely objective and nonpartisan representation of the issues involved. After all, the contemporary climate unquestionably tends to one side of the divine (im)passibility debates. Therefore, although this text attempts a *via media* of sorts, the emphasis will be on justifying the role of divine impassibility in order that a greater balance can ensue within these two alternatives in contemporary God-talk.

To begin the task, one must first understand the current situation in which divine passibility is integral to mainstream God-talk, both for the academy and the pew. Chapter 1 will look at some of the contributing factors to the present situation that favor divine passibility in order to illuminate why divine impassibility is so maligned by contemporary thinkers. This section will also seek to suggest in a more programmatic way what a qualified account of divine impassibility could look like. Chapter 2 will analyze the matter from a biblical viewpoint. Many biblical scholars, especially those in the field of Old Testament studies, have chimed in on these debates, stating that the biblical text suggests for those within systematics to render within their work a view of God's passibility. The chapter will aim to show that the biblical text does not simply call its readers to divine passibility, for past reading practices have pointed to the text itself in order to affirm a qualified view of divine impassibility. Chapter 3 will look at the testimony of the early church in order to problematize the claims made by proponents of the "Theory of Theology's Fall into Hellenistic Philosophy", all the while citing a number of examples that can inform the process of retrieval. Chapter 4 will consider trinitarian issues using Jürgen Moltmann's work as a starting point for a discussion about the trinitarian implications within the divine (im)passibility debates. Turning its attention to the christological debates, Chapter 5 will look to Chalcedon and its interpretations over the years as they relate to (im)passibility. Finally, Chapter 6 will look into the realm of Christian discipleship with the aim of narrating *apatheia* as key to a Christ-shaped embodiment in which suffering is not simply avoided but undertaken voluntarily as a sign and practice of God's redeeming work.

All in all, by highlighting the difficulties that today's assertion of divine passibility creates, the text will attempt to show divine impassibility's relevance to the contemporary scene. In this regard, the work itself will push against the mainstream opinion in a way that is not entirely inconsonant with the Christian mystical tradition. Such a path is not coincidental: When one engages such a difficult theme as suffering, the realms of rationality and proof are pushed to their limits, creating the need for other appeals and resources. The aim of this book is to offer an account of God and suffering that suggests both solace and hope. In depicting a God who is both passible and impassible, the vision being entertained is not only of a God who is in solidarity with us but also of a God who can redeem us.

CHAPTER 1

The State of the Question Today

A. Speaking of God and Suffering This Side of Auschwitz

One of the ongoing challenges to faith is the relationship between God and suffering. Since the global community now has technological access to information and images that repeatedly remind it of the horrors of evil, people today are constantly made aware of the pain and suffering in the world. Terror attacks, tsunamis, floods, civil wars, genocide – all are examples of unmitigated suffering that the world has witnessed. The question of God's relationship to all of this lived reality is perpetual and non-ending.

The Shoah (Holocaust) remains perhaps the quintessential challenge to a belief in God on a number of levels. Images, documentaries, and the gradual passing away of the survivors remind the worldwide community that this event cannot and should not be dismissed from the collective conscience of the world. Not only was the Shoah in and of itself a terrible atrocity, resulting in the systematic genocide of millions of Jews, but the matter is further compounded by the fact that the Jews are understood by themselves and others as the chosen people of God.[1] The Shoah, therefore, was not simply an affront to the sensibilities of humanity but also to theology and its object of study in general.[2] The Shoah was a historical tragedy that also had religious significance, thereby elevating this moment as a difficult one in the scheme of how one reconciles faith in a good God alongside a hurting and dying world. That tragedies of mass exploitation and destruction occur is painful; that God's chosen people are continually the targets of persecution and systemic annihilation *because of* their

---

[1] This association changes the matter significantly; as R. L. Rubenstein remarks, "There is one aspect of the Holocaust which is absolutely different from all other programs of extermination and mass destruction in the modern period: *The fate of the Jews is a matter of decisive religiomythic significance in both Judaism and Christianity*" (*After Auschwitz* [2nd ed; Baltimore: Johns Hopkins University, 1992], p. 161).

[2] A direct development from these implications is the sub-field of "Holocaust theology"; for a general survey of the field, see D. Cohn-Sherbok (ed), *Holocaust Theology: A Reader* (New York: New York University Press, 2002) and S. K. Pinnock, *Beyond Theodicy* (Albany, NY: State University of New York Press, 2002); other, shorter pieces within the field include J. F. Moore, "A Spectrum of Views: Traditional Christian Responses to the Holocaust", *Journal of Ecumenical Studies* 25.2 (1988), pp. 212-24 and S. R. Haynes, "Christian Holocaust Theology: A Critical Assessment", *Journal of the American Academy of Religion* 62.2 (1994), pp. 553-83.

religious identity has the added dimension of being harmful to one's faith.[3]

Given the evidence of human suffering, it is no surprise then that many people, including many Jews, have resorted to atheism as the only religio-philosophical alternative. The instantiating problematic within this context usually takes on a form of reasoning similar to what one sees in the Humean line of questioning that has an Epicurean background: "Is [God] willing to prevent evil, but not able? then is he impotent. Is he able, but not willing? then is he malevolent. Is he both able and willing? whence then is evil?"[4] The kind of atheism that resulted from these questions has been denominated as "protest atheism".[5] This view basically suggests the denial of belief in God not so much on philosophical as moral grounds *inherent to* the belief of God itself,[6] thereby resulting in a "metaphysical rebellion" of sorts "in the name of moral value".[7] In other words, belief in God is denied because it is proclaimed that the notion of God fails on its own terms.

The most-cited example of this alternative is a fraternal exchange between Ivan and Alyosha in F. Dostoevsky's *The Brothers Karamazov*. At one point in the engagement, Ivan raises the question of God and suffering and suggests that there is no explanation for the suffering of children. Ivan does not shy away from the element of human culpability – that often people behave worse than animals in torturing their own progeny. Yet, innocent children cannot be said to deserve in any way the afflictions and suffering they sometimes endure. Is redemption possible for their tears? In a poignant moment, Ivan suggests, "'And if the suffering of children goes to make up the sum of suffering needed to buy truth, then I assert beforehand that the whole of truth is not worth such a price.'"[8] In perhaps the most famous line of the work, Ivan goes on to state, "'I'd rather remain with my unrequited suffering and my unquenched

---

[3] Rubenstein's own, non-traditional response is to discount the biblical portrayal of God and his covenant with and election of Israel, leading some to label his project a Jewish form of "death of God" theology. What one finds in the expanse of varied Jewish theological reflection is a questioning of long-held views about God, a development that has its parallels with certain currents in Christianity. A case in point is the work of H. Jonas, who rejects the view of an omnipotent God because of a controlling understanding of God's goodness; see "The Concept of God after Auschwitz: A Jewish Voice", *Journal of Religion* 67.1 (1987), pp. 1-13.

[4] D. Hume, *Dialogues and Natural History of Religion* (Oxford: Oxford University Press, 1998), p. 100.

[5] For a brief discussion of the major tenets of this form of atheism, see W. W. Willis, Jr., *Theism, Atheism and the Doctrine of the Trinity* (Atlanta: Scholars Press, 1987).

[6] J. J. O'Donnell attempts to clarify this distinction when he remarks that "methodological atheism" rejects God on the basis that the term is unverifiable whereas "protest atheism" rejects God in the name of God himself. See *Trinity and Temporality* (Oxford: Oxford University Press, 1983).

[7] A. Camus, *The Rebel* (trans. A. Bower; New York: Vintage, 1991), p. 55.

[8] F. Dostoevsky, *The Brothers Karamazov* (trans. R. Pevear and L. Volokhonsky; New York: Farrar, Straus, and Giroux, 1990), p. 245.

indignation, *even if I am wrong*. Besides, they have put too high a price on harmony; we can't afford to pay so much for admission. And therefore I hasten to return my ticket. . . . It's not that I don't accept God, Alyosha, I just most respectfully return him the ticket."[9] Simply put, there is no justification or excuse available to God for allowing suffering. Within such a depiction, suffering has a non-negotiable value and so "precedes thinking"[10] and all forms of rational evaluation.

Theologians, of course, find these claims to be serious challenges to the Christian faith, and in many ways it is their burden to negotiate the claims of the gospel with the demands made upon it by the wider world. The strategy of choice for modern theologians has been to efface the divide between God and suffering in order to show that God is not oblivious to human suffering but that he is involved in it in some way. Thus, theologians began to offer a theology "of"[11] or "after"[12] Auschwitz as a strategy for achieving a certain contemporary relevance within a culture of dissatisfaction regarding traditionally formulated answers.[13] Auschwitz was often cited because this concentration camp came to represent all the horrors associated with the Shoah. Unfortunately, the widespread reference to the camp was so vast and frequent that at times there were detectable inaccuracies between how it was portrayed and what in fact happened.[14]

A prominent account associated with the horrors of the Shoah and cited repeatedly by theologians is E. Wiesel's *Night*. At one point, two Jewish men and a youth are hung, begging the question of God's presence in the midst of these events. Wiesel notes that he heard a voice internally as he observed this event, a voice that suggested God was to be found hanging on the gallows as well.[15] The story itself, often mistakenly attributed to Auschwitz when in fact it

---

[9] Dostoevsky, *The Brothers Karamazov*, p. 245.

[10] Such a remark echoes J. Moltmann's paraphrase of L. Feuerbach in "The 'Crucified God': A Trinitarian Theology of the Cross", *Interpretation* 26.3 (1972), p. 280.

[11] U. E. Simon, *A Theology of Auschwitz* (London: Victor Gollancz, 1967).

[12] J. B. Metz on occasion has mentioned that the theological landscape today is one "after Auschwitz"; see "Suffering unto God", *Critical Inquiry* 20 (1994), pp. 611-22; and *The Emergent Church* (New York: Crossroad, 1987), pp. 17-33.

[13] Moltmann also uses Auschwitz as a paradigmatic case when he states, "God in Auschwitz and Auschwitz in God – that is the basis for a real hope which both embraces and overcomes the world, and the ground for a love which is stronger than death and can sustain death" (see *The Crucified God* [trans. R. A. Wilson and J. Bowden; Minneapolis: Fortress, 1993], p. 278; hereafter *CG*).

[14] With legitimate warrants, M. Sarot believes that Christian theodicists should remain silent when employing the stories of Auschwitz because of the tendencies by these theorists to avoid the Jewishness of the camp in claiming it as a moment of "severe and innocent suffering" and succumbing to the apparently irresistible temptation to apply a christological reading to these events; see "Auschwitz, Morality and the Suffering of God", *Modern Theology* 7.2 (1991), pp. 135-52.

[15] E. Wiesel, *Night* (trans. M. Wiesel; New York: Hill and Wang, 2006), p. 65.

occurred in Buna, has been used at least thirty times within different theological works,[16] thereby taking on a life of its own, reminding the theological community that theology can no longer be endeavored in the abstract.

The Shoah and similar tragedies have contributed to the recasting of the theodicy project itself. In the words of Sarot, "The question how we are to square the dreadful fact of evil with the existence of an omnipotent, omniscient and morally perfect God has been somewhat recast, so as to change it into the question how a morally perfect God can remain unaffected by the suffering of the human beings He has created?"[17] The shift in focus is clear: Past articulations assumed that suffering had to be accommodated to the given premise of a good or omnipotent God whereas today the direction of the accommodation is reversed.[18] In this portrayal, the category of "suffering" comes to have a non-negotiable value all unto its own so that one's doctrine of God subsequently requires modification in some significant way. If theodicy is constructed in this way, then one cannot help but sympathize with the view that God did indeed hang on the gallows. Ultimately, only a powerless God or a "suffering God" could be viable to those victims who experience and witness events like Wiesel's.

Many of these modern theodicists have pitted their options against a view often called "classical theism", which to them is the Hellenistic conceptuality of the divine nature that includes such tenets as simplicity, perfection, immutability, impassibility, eternality, and the like. This conceptual apparatus is deemed to be a pagan philosophical importation into Christian God-talk, and given its origin, it is an unfaithful interpretation of the God associated with Christian belief. They contend that this conceptualization of God began to take its hold on the early church when it embarked upon an apologetic turn in its history. Although this framework has exerted its influence within Christianity for centuries, scholars have recently aspired to release the grip that Greek ontotheology has exerted on Christian theology for so long.

These theological "revolutionaries" or "pioneers" who have attempted to rewrite Christian theism have found amenable certain philosophical tendencies commonly called "dynamic ontologies". In contrast to a purported "static" form of being, these "dynamic ontologies" look at reality in more fluid terms, suggesting interactions of influence and degrees that across time vary and to an extent are therefore unpredictable. Two major influences in this regard are the

---

[16] Sarot, "Auschwitz, Morality and the Suffering of God", p. 135.

[17] Sarot, "Auschwitz, Morality and the Suffering of God", p. 135.

[18] The influence of modern sensibilities cannot be downplayed here; K. Surin's assessment of modernity's approach to evil is telling: With the onset of modernity, three tendencies are detectable: 1) the rise of a historical condition in which evil can no longer be intellectually considered, 2) the view that evil can no longer be abstracted from concrete human experiences, and 3) the questioning of human reason because of the apparent irrationality of evil. See "Theodicy?", *Harvard Theological Review* 76.2 (1983), pp. 225-47 and his more extensive treatment in *Theology and the Problem of Evil* (Oxford: Blackwell, 1986).

legacy of G. W. F. Hegel[19] and the modern work of philosopher A. N. Whitehead.[20] Within this conceptual sensibility, it is viable to suggest that, since God and the world are not so much contrasting entities as ones that interact and are interdependent with one another, God does in fact suffer. With these developments in the wider philosophical community, it seems to many that the Hellenistic hold that apparently was upon the Christian doctrine of God is starting to lessen, thereby providing believers with a more viable and respectable conceptual apparatus with which to think about and speak of God.[21]

However, the shift is not simply within the field of philosophical theology; scholars in biblical and historical studies have started to dismantle the once-perceived hegemony that God does not suffer. Old Testament scholars have offered a biblically-informed account of God in which interaction and engagement provide the conceptual parameters for subsequent issues such as (im)passibility. Historical studies have begun to problematize the view that the early church was uniform in its affirmation of an impassible God, both by offering counter-examples to this hegemony as well as showing the extent to which prior voices owed their methodological preferences to the dominant Hellenistic culture at large. The difficult examples such as that of Augustine, who would go so far as to state that there is no such person as an "innocent sufferer",[22] are mentioned time and again in order to show the degree to which some of the fathers were captivated by Platonic-Stoic paradigms of value and meaning. For these historians, the assumed corruption of a biblical, pre-Constantinian faith was excessively severe to the point that suffering, pathos, and the like were negatively conceived by believers with regard to the human and divine realms.

In light of these developments, a proposal has gained currency, one in which a startling divide of its own is entertained: either one believes that God does not suffer (thereby subscribing to a pagan form of thought, suggesting

---

[19] The influence of Hegel is especially detectable among those who are trained in continental European settings.

[20] Theologically, the influence of Whitehead has been most prominent in the movement known as process theology. Unsurprisingly, the themes of evil and of theodicy in general are frequently treated within the movement. See D. R. Griffin, *God, Power, and Evil: A Process Theodicy* (Philadelphia: Westminster, 1976) and *Evil Revisited* (Albany, NY: State University of New York Press, 1991).

[21] Another movement worth mentioning in this collage of theological persuasions is "openness theism". Interestingly, this movement has been promulgated in more conservative camps; for some works in this field, see C. Pinnock, *Most Moved Mover: A Theology of God's Openness* (Grand Rapids: Baker, 2001) and C. Pinnock, R. Rice, J. Sanders, W. Hasker, and D. Basinger (eds), *The Openness of God* (Downers Grove, IL: InterVarsity, 1994).

[22] One can see this trajectory of argument chiefly in Augustine's *On Free Choice of the Will*; for an extended discussion of this work as well as a critical engagement along the lines of the innocent sufferer, see J. E. Thiel, *God, Evil, and Innocent Suffering* (New York: Herder and Herder, 2002).

apostasy/heresy) or that he does (thereby adhering to sound, biblical belief). The former alternative, despite its long history, is seen to be theologically and philosophically short-sighted and antiquated: this god is the god of the philosophers (in short-hand, Aristotle's "Unmoved Mover") rather than of Abraham, Isaac, and Jacob. From both a biblical and philosophical-cultural perspective, a suffering or possible God is depicted as the only alternative. What results from this convergence of voices and authorities is a shift of significant proportions where the hegemony within the academy shifted to the other side of the impassibility-passibility spectrum. Some observers have been shocked by the rapidity of the shift, leaving many to wonder how it occurred.[23] Historical narrations of the shift have ensued with the purposes of establishing some sort of continuity with the received tradition, but interestingly enough, the assessment of the change has occurred *post factum* to divine possibility's establishment as the biblical and conceptual norm. In other words, the impulse to affirm a "suffering God" was often applied to rather than generated from the inquiry itself, thereby skewing the ensuing historical findings and reconstructions. Given the implications such changes have for the development and articulation of the Christian doctrine of God, the (im)passibilist debates are of significant importance for the contemporary shape of Christian God-talk.

B. An Appreciation of J. K. Mozley

Because of their rapidity and scope, all of these transitions seem to be overwhelming, but history shows that the issue of God's (im)passibility has been seriously debated for centuries. Although it may be true that more people today than ever before would say that God does suffer, it is interesting to note that Christianity, by the inherent claims of its christology (particularly the incarnation), has always had a self-subverting principle that would resist any conceptually unmitigated overture to Aristotle's "Unmoved Mover". The claims of the gospel are such that simple "either-or" answers are not available to a Christian, who believes that the Son of God took on human flesh and suffered and was tempted in all the ways humans are. Because of the incarnation, then, Christians do not have the luxury of opting for one pole of the (im)passibility spectrum in their God-talk.

As significant as the current debates are concerning God's (im)passibility, it is worth noting that some of the most important and heated debates regarding this issue culminated in Great Britain at the turn of the 20th century. The mood in the air was reflected by A. M. Fairbairn when he stated, "Theology has no

---

[23] Some of the more accessible accounts of the shift are R. Goetz, "The Suffering God: The Rise of a New Orthodoxy", *Christian Century* 103.13 (1986), pp. 385-89 and R. Bauckham, "'Only the Suffering God Can Help': Divine Passibility in Modern Theology", *Themelios* 9.3 (1984), pp. 6-12. Despite the tone of these pieces, it is important to note that the shift itself (more so than its popular acceptance) has been taking place for some time.

falser idea than that of the impassibility of God."[24] Similarly, D. White could say, "The doctrine of the impassibility of God, taken in its wide sense, is the greatest heresy that ever smirched Christianity."[25] The matter became so controversial that the Archbishop's Doctrinal Commission at that time charged J. K. Mozley to write a monograph on the subject, subsequently titled *The Impassibility of God*. Mozley too found the shift from the impassibilist to the passibilist perspective to be quite swift in his own day: "Of this tradition [of divine impassibility] the truth is not unchallenged to-day. But whereas it is usually possible to trace stages in the development of a reaction against a particular doctrine or tradition . . . that is by no means the case with the present subject."[26] Until recently, Mozley's monograph has been unsurpassed in its comprehensiveness in English,[27] making its longevity and usefulness regarding the subject unparalleled. Even those contemporary endeavors that advance on the theme are quick to point out the value of Mozley's work for today.[28] Why does this text continue to have such value and importance for the conversation regarding divine (im)passibility?

The quality in question may be related to what E. G. Selwyn mentioned posthumously of Mozley in the latter's *Some Tendencies in British Theology*. In conversation with Mozley, Selwyn believed "the deepest or most tangled issues were often illuminated in a sentence or two".[29] This illumination was due to "[Mozley's] vigorous intellect and force of character [that] were alike salted with wit and sweetened by an abounding charity; no mean or unfair word crossed his lips, for no such thought was allowed to lodge in his mind".[30] In reading his work, one knows where Mozley's sympathies lie, and yet he was

---

[24] A. M. Fairbairn, *The Place of Christ in Modern Theology* (New York: Charles Scribner's Sons, 1899), p. 483.

[25] D. White, *Forgiveness and Suffering* (Cambridge: Cambridge University Press, 1913), p. 84.

[26] J. K. Mozley, *The Impassibility of God: A Survey of Christian Thought* (Cambridge: Cambridge University Press, 1926), p. 127.

[27] In addition to Gavrilyuk's book, a couple of works that rival Mozley's breadth of consideration include T. G. Weinandy, *Does God Suffer?* (Notre Dame: University of Notre Dame Press, 2000) and A. G. Nnamani, *The Paradox of a Suffering God* (New York: Peter Lang, 1995).

[28] Weinandy remarks that Mozley's monograph has been "immensely important and influential" (*Does God Suffer?*, p. 3, n. 8). K. J. Woollcombe believes that Mozley's work is "one of the most invaluable guides to our present thinking" on the subject ("The Pain of God", *Scottish Journal of Theology* 20.2 [1964], p. 136). Even a figure like Moltmann, who is unquestionably on the side of divine passibility, esteems Mozley's work as being "the classic and most comprehensive treatment on the subject" (*The Trinity and the Kingdom* [trans. M. Kohl; Minneapolis: Fortress, 1993], p. 21, n. 2; hereafter *TK*).

[29] Selwyn's Preface to J. K. Mozley's *Some Tendencies in British Theology* (London: SPCK, 1951), p. 7.

[30] Mozley, *Some Tendencies in British Theology*, p. 7.

meticulous in giving the historical and theological contexts of the many figures and issues he considered. Unfortunately, in his own day – as in ours – few people outside of historical theologians attempted to speak of divine (im)passibility in such carefully qualified terms. In a balanced and genuine way, Mozley remarks, "Much harm results from inattention to the historical background [of the term *apatheia*]. Whether the idea of a 'suffering God' be true or false, exponents of this conception would have been well advised to discuss it in the light of the Christian tradition."[31]

The premise of Mozley's work, therefore, is to give a thick historical description, meticulous in its method and yet expansive in its scope. Mozley was able to show that, taken on their own terms, many prior impassibilists were attempting within their God-talk to safeguard certain elements, ones that, given their own commitments, passibilists are burdened to underwrite. Mozley criticizes strongly those who would discount the testimony of the early church fathers simply because they affirmed an impassibilist perspective: "To suppose that Christian thinkers carelessly passed over all that seems to us involved in our belief in God's loving care, His fatherly providence, and His moral purposefulness, would be the greatest injustice both to their words and to their thought."[32]

Against these cursory treatments, Mozley suggests that both passibilists and impassibilists have something important to bring to the conversation, that each group can contribute in a vital way to how one should go about relating God to suffering. According to Mozley, the advantages of the impassibilist perspective include 1) the affirmation of the divine transcendence, 2) the belief that God's life is ultimately a blessed one, and 3) the explicit attempt to avoid anthropomorphism in its unhelpful iterations.[33] On the other side, passibilists can 1) emphasize that God is love in suggestive ways, 2) affirm that God suffers alongside a suffering world, and 3) claim the cross, with the Son obviously suffering for the world, as indicative of the eternal, divine nature.[34]

Fittingly, Mozley ends his text with "six necessary questions" he believes must be considered before any treatment of a "suffering God" can begin to take a historically informed and contemporarily relevant shape; in abbreviated form, these questions relate to the following themes: 1) the complexity involved in affirming both an absolute and personal God, 2) the imperative of narrating God's relationship to his creation, 3) the place of eternity and time in the life of God, 4) the semantic range of affective language and its distinctions (if any) when applied to God and humans, 5) an adequate assessment of whether there is any religious value secured by the assertion of impassibility, and 6) the relationship of the cross to the divine nature, especially because of the former's

---

[31] Mozley, *The Impassibility of God*, p. 1.

[32] Mozley, *The Impassibility of God*, p. 46.

[33] Mozley, *The Impassibility of God*, p. 173.

[34] Mozley, *The Impassibility of God*, pp. 175-76.

historical particularity.[35] Some scholars have attempted to give a systematic and workable reply to Mozley's questions,[36] but obviously these matters are so extensive and broad that they continue to be with us today. Given the contemporary philosophical mood, the shape of contemporary replies lean to the affirmation of divine passibility, thereby begging the question as to how balanced and informed the current state of the debates is.

C. Are We in a Satisfactory Place?

Given the reflection of the contemporary church on suffering, the state of philosophy today, and the apparent biblical imperative, the issue would seem to be settled, that divine passibility is the most helpful alternative. Most would agree with D. Bonhoeffer in suggesting that, "Only the suffering God can help."[37] In fact, some like J. Y. Lee have even claimed that, "The concept of divine suffering is not only the core of our faith but the uniqueness of Christianity."[38] And yet, in fact, a number of concerns question this apparent modern hegemony regarding the relationship of God and suffering.

First, it would seem quite difficult to maintain that a sudden reversal in Christian thought would be warranted simply because today's sensibilities have changed from past ones; in other words, the logical consistency of God-talk across the span of time is questioned when figures say that the majority of theological voices in the past had the issue wrong and that today we are more biblical and so more theologically sound when speaking of God and suffering. This kind of modern historical chauvinism is unhelpful, especially when Christianity is depicted as an ongoing conversation about the one in whom the church has placed its faith. That is not to say that doctrinal development does not occur across time, but one ought to be careful when generalizing about history, for what could happen at these moments is not so much an accurate assessment of past voices but the unintentional imposition of the present voice upon prior ages; as biblical scholars would say, the danger lies in doing "eisegesis" rather than "exegesis", thereby creating anachronistic expectations and fostering modern criteria of assessment.

Second, it is worth asking just how much value there is in saying that God suffers, for suffering remains even if he does so. In other words, if we suffer

---

[35] These questions are extensively considered in Mozley, *The Impassibility of God*, pp. 177-83.

[36] These endeavors include Woollcombe, "The Pain of God", and L. J. Kuyper, "The Suffering and the Repentance of God", *Scottish Journal of Theology* 22.3 (1969), pp. 257-77.

[37] D. Bonhoeffer, *Letters and Papers from Prison* (New York: Touchstone, 1997), p. 361.

[38] J. Y. Lee, *God Suffers for Us* (The Hague: Martinus Nijhoff, 1974), p. 1. Along these lines, see also W. McWilliams, *The Passion of God* (Macon, GA: Mercer University Press, 1985), pp. 16-24.

and God suffers alongside of us, suffering is still a problem. Saying that God suffers may make the suffering more tolerable and may suggest that God is less guilty than he would be if he were simply standing on the sidelines, but the basic configuration of the problem is still present in that suffering is still a reality that all encounter and endure. It is questionable then just how much the affirmation of a "suffering God" really advances the issue posed by modern theodicy.

In fact, despite the hegemony present within the theological guild regarding God and suffering, the debates continue as to how to approach this issue, suggesting not only that the matter is far from being resolved but that the hegemony itself is unsatisfactory. Interestingly enough, although it seems quite in vogue to say that God's impassibility is a nonviable conceptual alternative, few Christians would go so far as to suggest an unbridled form of God's passibility; in other words, divine passibility is not entirely adequate to solve the dilemmas at play. The casual Christian, then, finds the passibilist possibility most appealing but certainly not entirely satisfactory, a situation that suggests that the issues have to be probed and extensively analyzed in order that the nuances of the debate can come into the fray and so that thoughtful Christians can give an account of the one in whom they believe. A *via media* within the debates seems to be the only way forward.

D. The Issue of Language

One of the most complicating features in these debates is the issue of language. There is so much disagreement concerning the key terms involved in these debates that it is no wonder that the questions and concerns regarding divine (im)passibility are ongoing; therefore, if a "middle way" is to be attempted in which the thorny questions that Mozley raises are to be considered with any hope of headway, securing the language is of the utmost importance. Certainly, diversity in the connotations associated with each term exists (and arguments against the way this work will proceed could be raised), but there is no hope for clarity in these issues if the terminology itself cannot be stabilized.

D.1. Apatheia and "Impassibility"

As mentioned earlier, most Christians would find the suggestion of an "apathetic God" to be untenable in that the word "apathetic" in today's context suggests "indifferent", "detached", and so forth. Only a faith in a god who was *not* the God of Abraham, Isaac, and Jacob, who was *not* the God revealed in Jesus Christ, could accommodate in any way the brutal and insensitive possibility that a divine being is somehow not "affected" by the world's ongoing suffering. On the surface, the very title of this book would appear to be not only unbiblical but nothing short of heretical.

Yet when ancient writers spoke of God's *apatheia* in glowing and favorable terms, they did not envisage a detached and unapproachable God. On the contrary, for many writers and thinkers, God's *apatheia* suggested the opposite: that God was so distinct from and transcendent to the world's occurrences that his presence and actions could carry meaning and significance. The assumption that God was beyond the ever-fluctuating circumstances of a hurting and dying world actually brought hope to believers. The contrast could not be greater from the intuition of today: for many believers in the past, God's *apatheia* meant something altogether different from what we today would think an "apathetic God" to be. The title chosen for this work intentionally places the question of language at the forefront of the discussion, for all too often debates of God's (im)passibility are sidetracked or derailed by assumptions surrounding the language used.

The same assumptions are at play when moving to the Latin cognates. When one reads of God's "impassibility", one is led to think that God does not have *passio* – the term behind the English word "passion". To affirm the impassibility of God, then, is to suggest that God does not have passions or emotions, thereby suggesting an impersonal God, a being beyond approach and understanding. Of course, that picture contradicts the biblical accounts of God's dealings with Israel and of the God revealed in Jesus Christ, who for Christians is divinity in the flesh and who endured immense pain and anguish during the ordeal commonly known as the *via dolorosa*. The biblical God is a personal and approachable God, which by all human accounts suggests that he is "passionate" or "*pathe*-tic".

When one considers in a systematic and ordered way the language used in these debates, one senses the daunting difficulty of making any headway in these discussions. R. Creel senses this linguistic confusion when in his philosophical work on the subject he remarks:

> After working my way through many [writers] without getting a clear sense that the dispute over divine impassibility had a center of gravity, I came to realize why that is so. The issue of impassibility has four distinct aspects to it, but some authors are oblivious to some of these aspects, and other authors confuse the different aspects with one another. As a consequence some authors generate confusing statements about impassibility because they use "impassibility" to refer now to one aspect of impassibility, now to another, all the while thinking they are speaking of one and only one thing.[39]

What inevitably results from such definitional conflations is scholars and

---

[39] R. E. Creel, *Divine Impassibility* (Cambridge: Cambridge University Press, 1986), p. ix.

thinkers speaking past one another in an endless conversation about what everybody seems to think is the same thing when in fact it is not. Creel points to four general aspects – nature, will, knowledge, and feeling – and offers eight operational definitions for divine impassibility: 1) "lacking all emotions" (excluding "bliss" given patristic practice), 2) "in a state of mind that is imperturbable", 3) "insusceptible to distraction from resolve", 4) "having a will determined entirely by oneself", 5) "cannot be affected by an outside force", 6) "cannot be prevented from achieving one's purpose", 7) "has no susceptibility to negative emotions", and 8) "cannot be affected by an outside force or changed by oneself". [40]

According to biblical revelation and the Christian confession of God, some of these definitions naturally do not apply to God without qualification. In Creel's estimation of the tradition of "classical theism", the first definition is too narrow and the final two definitions, viewed in conjunction, mix the notions of divine impassibility and immutability. [41] Through different examples, Creel concludes that the second, third, fourth, sixth, and seventh definitions prove to be species or corollaries to the fifth, namely that one "cannot be affected by an outside force". [42] The fifth definition, therefore, suggests a center of operational connotative power by which to continue forward.

For purposes of this study, the operational definition of divine impassibility assumed will be that God "cannot be affected against his will by an outside force". [43] It is assumed that this definition applies to God alone and that it carries the additional implication of "perfect moral freedom". [44] Stating the matter in such a way does not mean that God is incapable of relating to the world nor of showing love, two of the more common critiques leveled by passibilist thinkers against impassibility; rather, divine impassibility understood in a way informed by the biblical and patristic testimony allows for a creative and challenging balance (that may include qualification and the use of metaphor) in which God can be understood as a transcendent being who

---

[40] See Creel, *Divine Impassibility*, p. 9 for these definitions.

[41] A strong relationship between divine immutability and divine impassibility does exist, "for if God cannot change then he cannot experience pain and sorrow" (K. Surin, "The Impassibility of God and the Problem of Evil", *Scottish Journal of Theology* 35.2 [1982], p. 97). This present work assumes divine impassibility to be a thematic subset of issues within the broader category of divine immutability, but it does not attempt to consider divine immutability on its own terms, which has been a very important conversation in and of itself, one that has witnessed cantankerous debates between process theologians and Thomists. For a survey of this debate, see S. Sia, "The Doctrine of God's Immutability: Introducing the Modern Debate", *New Blackfriars* 68 (1987), pp. 220-32.

[42] Creel, *Divine Impassibility*, p. 11.

[43] I have added to Creel's definition the phrase "against his will" because of the conceptual possibilities provided by the incarnation of Christ.

[44] G. L. Prestige, *God in Patristic Thought* (London: SPCK, 1952), p. 7.

nevertheless can relate to his creation. As G. L. Prestige remarks, "Impassibility means not that God is inactive or uninterested, not that He surveys existence with Epicurean impassivity from the shelter of a metaphysical insulation, but that His will is determined from within instead of being swayed from without".[45] With such a definition, it is possible to affirm both a God who is impassible and a God who is love, and it is this kind of vision that informs the present study.

D.2. "God", "Suffering", and "Emotion"

As a further extension of the language problem, one has considerable difficulties in considering further the terms "God" and "suffering". On the surface, speaking of God would seem unproblematic since all seem to have a general sense of what God is like and so on. This study assumes quite differently, that speaking of God is problematic because doing so tends to lead to "explanation" rather than "understanding". In other words, the present work operates from the assumption that truthful and legitimate knowledge of God has been revealed in history, principally by God's Word and Spirit, but this revelation does not preclude the category of "mystery" that is so important in safeguarding the transcendence or "otherness" of God. Although the matter will come to the fore more extensively later in this study, it is assumed that cataphatic and apophatic methodologies are viable within the speech practices involved in God-talk. As examples of these methodologies, categories like the "economic" and "immanent" Trinity are viable not because they introduce a disjunctive discourse but rather because they safeguard and secure the language at play in such a way that the category of mystery can do theological work throughout the more affirmative moments of conceptualization.

This safeguarding is crucial, especially when it comes to affectional language and the divine essence, because Scripture itself is multivalent in its affirmations of "God's emotional life". On the one hand, one senses that in the Hebrew scriptures God is very much a passionate God, for he becomes angered, saddened, and frustrated by the many events that occur in the world, especially the actions of his chosen people. There is, however, the counter-testimony that in God there is "no shadow of turning" – that in a sense God is beyond pathic language. In a deep and oftentimes disturbing sense, our talk of the relationship between God and the emotions or God and suffering demonstrates just how domesticated and conventional contemporary God-talk has become. It is at this point that apophatic considerations can be very helpful.

The issue of what constitutes "suffering" itself is another deeply contested matter. The question of suffering is very much tied to divine impassibility because suffering by nature seems to be linked to the emotions. In human

---

[45] Prestige, *God in Patristic Thought*, p. 6.

terms, the assumption is that if one has emotions, one can suffer, and vice versa. Most people seem to assume that suffering is something that needs no explanation: when one is in pain, one suffers. But then there are the questions of what constitutes suffering (physical, emotional, or spiritual pain), what conditions are at play in a given situation (unavoidable or self-inflicted), and the degree and extent of suffering experienced (an isolated incident or a lengthy ordeal). When people throw around the suggestion, then, that "God suffers", what in fact is really meant? As assuring as the statement could be initially, when pursued, the suggestion that God suffers could be deeply problematic. Does he suffer because he cannot help it, or does he suffer voluntarily? If voluntarily, does God's suffering have a purpose in itself or does it point to something else?

The question of the relationship of sin to suffering is also important. Many in the early church saw suffering as a sign that something had gone horribly wrong in what was originally considered a "good" creation, so suffering more generally came to be associated with the fall. This line of reasoning suggested to Augustine that there are no innocent sufferers since he operated from his robust account of original sin. This position has been significantly questioned today, and the tendency now among theologians is to disassociate sin from suffering. On the one hand, Augustine's claims are hard to justify today in that it moves from the general to the particular in ways that are unpalatable to today's sensibilities. And yet the link between sin and suffering is important to maintain in that suffering is not a good and so not part of God's original intentions for humanity. Although there is some value to say that suffering is part of the human condition, one should not dismiss the claims of the gospel that suggest humanity is in need of being redeemed from its fallen, broken, and painful state.

Finally, one faces the difficulty of estimating the value of "affectional" language or language relating to the "emotions". In today's pop-psychology, one hears repeatedly the need for acknowledging one's feelings, of having "emotional integrity" or "cathartic moments" in which one releases the weight of emotional baggage in order to achieve personal wholeness and congruity. At the same time, our society views "excessive" emotion with deep suspicion; for instance, people (especially males) who display deep and long-lasting emotions are often looked on as weak. This ambiguity concerning emotional language leaves us with a difficulty: which emotions are valuable and to what degree? In today's culture, one could say that anger is viewed uneasily at times because of political correctness whereas guilt, anxiety, and depression are assumed to be part and parcel of the pressures surrounding modern-day existence.

Although more will be said later on the subject, suffering and the emotions are very much related, and as the biblical portrayal shows, God is related to both. Many of these connotations can be used in relation to God, but one should travel this road with significant trepidation and care. Given the vast differences between creator and creation, it is worth noting that precaution should be taken as to how appropriately or completely such human language can be/should be applied to God.

E. Methodological Presuppositions

These many complicating factors have resulted in endless debates on the question/issue of divine (im)passibility. And as long as there are varied judgments and evaluations of God's relationship to the world and the implications that this exchange has both for God-talk and theological reflection, *this conversation is, has been, and will continue to be interminable.*

Such realism, however, does not preclude one from maintaining the hope that conceptual clarity can be pursued, that there is a means for probing further within this issue. Faced with the reality of mortality and the endless cycle of birth and death we see all around us, the question of God's relationship to suffering is a vital one that can destroy faith but also build it up.

The present study attempts to approach the subject in such a way that the best of both the passibilist and impassibilist alternatives can come to light. Given the current situation, however, this balancing act will tend to emphasize more extensively the impassibilist position since the current debate has tipped the scales to the passibilist side. The general premise in this work is that both impassibility and passibility are not only viable within the Christian narrative *but essential to one another.* Divine passibility and impassibility have to be maintained in tandem in order that a vision of God can be biblically faithful and theologically coherent in the way it incorporates metaphors, linguistic patterns, and practical considerations.

E.1. Why Divine Impassibility is Needed

Despite the triumphalistic tone of some authors, it is the contention of this investigation that divine impassibility is *not only possible* but *desirable* for contemporary God-talk because of several operational premises. First, the tenet of divine impassibility helps establish a certain epistemic distance as an orientation for contemporary theologians to have in relation to their own metaphysical and theological habits. The apparent disgust of many recent theologians for the tenability of God's *apatheia* says a great deal about how different the present situation is from prior ages. As D. B. Hart notes, "It is nonetheless striking that, in the course, say, of the great disputes of the fourth and fifth centuries concerning trinitarian dogma and Christology, divine impassibility was a principle that all parties concerned accepted without serious reservations, even though it was a principle that, on the face of it, better served the causes of what came to be viewed as the heterodox schools of thought."[46] If present-day thinkers are not dislodged from their contemporary presumptions surrounding acceptable God-talk, their own biases can detrimentally taint their hermeneutical orientation.

Second, this disorientation from the present allows contemporary theologians to interpret in a more amplified manner the tradition of Christian theological reflection. Many wish to appropriate trinitarian and christological advances made in the early church, but such appropriations inevitably become tainted if they are not attentive to the underlying premises of these articulations. Such biased readings create opportunities for reconfigured heretical tendencies to appear as constituents of a "modern orthodoxy". In light of the experiences of older voices within the tradition, the axiom of divine impassibility provides an opportunity for theologians to reconsider basic questions and conventions surrounding long-held tenets of the theological enterprise. Such a reconsideration/reevaluation creates, in turn, a conversation that neither ignores nor dismisses possible continuities and parallels within the area of Christian theological reflection.[47]

Third, the axiom of divine impassibility is a theological *desideratum* because it grants believers an alternative to the conventional responses to the crises of the age. By creating a rumbling within the conceptual scaffolding that brings into greater focus the underlying premises of past theological articulations, divine impassibility creates the opportunity for believers to reconfigure the terms of the contemporary debate in order to offer a more amplified account of what it means to believe in the triune God. This particular axiom creates the conceptual space for the cross *and* the resurrection, for promise *and* fulfillment, for suffering *and* victory, for death *and* life. Many proponents of a "suffering God" believe theirs is a hopeful alternative, but they fail to see how God's *apatheia* essentially is an axiom of hope, one that envisions an important dissonance between God and experienced reality.

E.2. Method and Outline

The argument that divine impassibility is a worthwhile consideration in contemporary God-talk requires a sustained and expansive methodology. The Bible will play a pivotal role for the present study since much of the debates center on key canonical moments and expressions. Many passibilists claim that

---

[46] D. B. Hart, "No Shadow of Turning: On Divine Impassibility", *Pro Ecclesia* 11.2 (Spring 2002), p. 186.

[47] As M. Steen notes, "'Apathy' as it used to be understood, is not necessarily identical to what is understood by it now" ("The Theme of the 'Suffering' God", in J. Lambrecht and R. F. Collins (eds), *God and Human Suffering* [Grand Rapids: Eerdmans, 1989], p. 86).

the Bible could not be any clearer in its affirmations of a "suffering God", and yet it would seem that the matter is more complex given that both Jews and Christians in the past have affirmed impassibilist possibilities in light of the scriptural testimony. As Mozley remarks, to suggest that past thinkers were blind to the Bible's testimony because of their cultural and philosophical commitments is to assume too much, but it is also true that the Bible, when speaking of God's relationship to the world, suggests images and metaphors (some of which are quite scandalous) that would challenge the impassibilist alternative. Chapter 2 will venture an assessment of the scriptural heritage.

An assumption of this study is that there is more to the patristic warrant for divine impassibility than what many passibilists would care to consider. What ensues from this history is a complex tale about how divine impassibility has been a motif within both orthodox and heretical schemas; seeing how this is so is a beneficial activity for those interested in these questions, and Chapter 3 will attempt a summary of this rich account.

One of the ongoing factors leading many to affirm a passibilist alternative is the doctrine of the Trinity as it is specifically articulated within certain trinitarian construals of recent memory. Perhaps the most influential of these proposals stems from the pen of Jürgen Moltmann, who in *The Crucified God* and *The Trinity and the Kingdom* argues that passibility is a natural conclusion of a vibrant trinitarianism. Interestingly enough, the Cappadocians, who are largely responsible for our current trinitarian speech practices, could account for a trinitarian God who is also impassible. Given the influence that Moltmann's account has had over the years, it is important to engage his account as a counterpoint to a trinitarian notion of impassibility, a task which will be the focus of Chapter 4.

In speaking of "the crucified God", one is reminded about not only the doctrine of God as it relates to impassibility but also the specific question of Christ, who is spoken of in orthodoxy as "God incarnate". Christians would generally affirm that in Christ we have the truest and most accessible portrait of who God is and what God is like, and obviously Christ suffered significantly. Christ's suffering, interestingly enough, is not limited to the violence associated with the crucifixion in the depictions of the gospels but it is also extended to other important moments: the pericope narrating his anguish in the Garden of Gethsemane, the cry of dereliction, and so on. It would seem that Christ is anything but impassible! Nonetheless, I maintain in Chapter 5 that impassibility is theologically important within those conversations that attempt to generate meaning and significance from Christ's life and work.

The final chapter will attempt to give an account of divine impassibility that can inform and form the shape of Christian discipleship. It would seem that an account of God's impassibility would have implications for believers, and I intend to pursue this path while depending upon the notion that as Christians we are called to follow and imitate Christ in the power of the Holy Spirit. The contention in this chapter will be that Christians are called to be "apathetic" in a similar way to how God is "apathetic"; therefore, the chapter suggests that the general arguments for divine impassibility are not simply ones that remain at a conceptual level: they also require embodiment and performance by Christ's followers today in the form of what could be termed an "apathetic discipleship".

CHAPTER 2

The Battle for Biblical Support

A. The Quest for a Biblical Doctrine of God

Any Christian view of God would undoubtedly have argumentative leverage if it could count on biblical support. For most Christians, a biblical basis for any Christian notion of who God is and what he is like would be paramount, if not essential. As mentioned previously, the Scriptures have been involved in the modern shift from impassibility to passibility within God-talk in that certain biblical scholars have found the tension quite resolvable given what seems to be overwhelming textual evidence for God's passibility. Two important groupings of texts have become important in these discussions: 1) Old Testament[1] passages that portray God in anthropomorphic terms so that he is "angered" or "grieved", and 2) the passion narratives in which Christ is depicted as forsaken by the Father as he dies the cruel death of crucifixion. In what follows, emphasis will be placed on the former category since the latter category will be considered more fully in Chapter 5.

A.1. The Old Testament Witness

When the issue of divine (im)passibility arises, one would think that moving to Scripture would answer some of the basic questions. Outside of certain obvious etymological constraints (including that the term *apatheia* or anything remotely similar in Hebrew is not attributed to God in the Bible), the matter is in fact quite problematized by the Bible. As Woollcombe remarks, "We cannot dodge the problem of Impassibility or Immutability by retreating into a kind of Biblical/Theological fundamentalism for the very good reason that the Bible itself poses the problem."[2] The biblical presentation reconfigures the terms in question by offering a view of who and how God is that challenges some of the assumptions that go along with (im)passibilist language. The textual evidence

---

[1] Many vials of ink have been spilt on the question of what to call the ancient Jewish scriptures, especially among Gentile Christians. Rather than concretizing the issue, I prefer to mix the names for these writings, as each title conveys something slightly different and yet true concerning their identity; therefore, I will be using such names as "Old Testament", "Hebrew scriptures", *Tanakh*, and "First Testament" interchangeably.

[2] Woollcombe, "The Pain of God", p. 131.

for divine possibility appears to be ample, but as I will later argue, such evidence requires a broader narrative framework as a necessary context for interpretation.

Undoubtedly, a number of passages in the First Testament suggests God as acting and becoming involved in the affairs of the created order, and within these encounters God is depicted as deeply personal. Person-to-person relationships are very human undertakings, ones that show readily the deep vulnerability and conditionedness of human selves, and the biblical witness does not shy away from employing this kind of logic in narrating the divine-human relationship. In other words, God comes across as very "human" in the way he is portrayed as relating to the world. Although such intimacy suggests that God is passible in some sense since he is affected by the world in some way, apparently the biblical authors do not have a problem with the potential dangers of such language.

One such passage that has an extensive *Wirkungsgeschichte* is Genesis 6. Specifically, Genesis 6:6 has been cited repeatedly within the (im)passibilist debates because of its dual word use: "And the Lord *was sorry* that he had made humankind on the earth, and it *grieved* him to his heart" (emphasis added).[3] The first word of interest, "he was sorry" (rt. – *nacham*), has God as its subject thirty times in the Old Testament and can mean either "repentance" (in the niphal) or "to have compassion or pity" (in the piel)[4], both connotations that suggest God as personal in a human sense and therefore passible. As for the second word, the kind of "grieving" considered here (rt. – *atsav*) is attributed to God in two other instances,[5] and it is also used of other biblical figures who are facing particularly distressing situations.[6] Such examples as Genesis 6:6 and others have been denominated in the past as generally "anthropomorphic", but more specifically they could be said to be "anthropopathic" since they suggest that God has an affectional life similar to that of humans, especially when such a life is demonstrated in human relationships.

Many contemporary biblical scholars would want to continue to maintain the category of anthropomorphism in that unquestionably God does not literally have hands, feet, a back, and so forth. The question of "anthropopathy" is a bit trickier, however, for many scholars speak of God as truly having an affectional or emotional life. After all, how else could God relate to the created order in a legitimate and genuine way? Whereas the terms "anthropomorphic" and

---

[3] Throughout the present work, the NRSV will be used for biblical citations.

[4] L. J. Kuyper, "The Repentance of God", *Reformed Review* 18.4 (1965), pp. 3-16.

[5] These passages are Ps. 78:40 and Isa. 63:10, both of which speak of God's state when dealing with rebellious and sinful Israel.

[6] These examples include: the state of 1) Dinah's brothers upon hearing that Shechem had raped her (Gen. 34:7), 2) Jonathan when he discovered that his father intended to kill David (1 Sam. 20:34), 3) David upon hearing of Absalom's death (2 Sam. 18:33), and 4) a wife who has been abandoned (Isa. 54:6).

"anthropopathic" imply a differentiation in that they assume etymologically that they are referencing human realities that only subsequently are provisionally used in reference to God, the difference is often softened when speaking of God's emotions. When commenting on the passage of Genesis 6:6, J. Goldingay remarks, "God's feeling emotion suggests that possessing emotions is one of the respects in which God and humanity are *fundamentally alike*. God is not without passions, as Christian doctrine has sometimes reckoned. As the First Testament will go on to show, God has all the emotions human beings have, and has them in spades" (italics added).[7] Obviously, the differentiation between divine and human emotion is not emphasized in the preceding quote, and the similarity that is emphasized tends to cloud any conceptual demarcation that may be deemed necessary at some point when the similarity is no longer helpful.

Perhaps the Old Testament scholar most often associated with the passibilist camp is T. Fretheim. Early in his monograph *The Suffering of God*,[8] Fretheim acknowledges the importance of admitting both similarity and difference in the use of metaphor. In one of his more judicious moments, he considers the notion of God's repentance in this way: "To speak of God as one who repents, with the basic ideas of reversal and change, does have some basic points of continuity with the way God actually relates to the world. Yet, there is no one-to-one correspondence between the way people and God repent."[9] He even makes one of the key claims of the present work when he remarks, "At the same time, God does not suffer in exactly the same way as humans do, and to try to get at that is important."[10] Unfortunately, it is questionable just how important Fretheim considers the point. Although perhaps more balanced than some of his peers within the biblical guild, Fretheim develops God's passibility in a particular way that presents certain difficulties for maintaining God's impassibility. First, he begins with the assumption that any relationship of integrity implies limitation and the giving up of certain rightful claims; for this reason, "God will have to give up some things for the sake of the relationship. Thus, God will have to give up some freedom."[11] From this starting point, Fretheim narrates the need for affirming a "vulnerable" God. In fact, throughout his *oeuvre*, "vulnerable" becomes Fretheim's preferred term for narrating divine passibility.[12] With the notion of vulnerability, it is no stretch of

---

[7] J. Goldingay, *Old Testament Theology* (2 vols; Downers Grove, IL: InterVarsity, 2003), I, p. 168.

[8] T. Fretheim, *The Suffering of God: An Old Testament Perspective* (Philadelphia: Fortress, 1984).

[9] Fretheim, *The Suffering of God*, p. 8.

[10] Fretheim, *The Suffering of God*, p. 8.

[11] Fretheim, *The Suffering of God*, p. 36.

[12] See B. C. Birch, W. Brueggemann, T. E. Fretheim, and D. L. Petersen, *A Theological Introduction to the Old Testament* (Nashville: Abingdon, 1999), p. 42 and pp. 110-12.

the imagination to say that God is caught up in the affairs of the world to the point that, "in some respects God will never be the same again".[13] Within such a framework, it appears that the alternative to a "vulnerable" God is a God with *potentia absoluta*, and naturally, the former appears more accessible and so more relatable than the latter.

A more difficult portrayal is the one suggested by W. Brueggemann in his *Theology of the Old Testament*. He believes that within the First Testament one finds "Israel's core testimony" that rings true for Jews and Christians alike in that themes such as God's constancy and faithfulness are on display. Accompanying this witness is what Brueggemann calls "Israel's countertestimony", those passages of Scripture that portray God in difficult ways: as a neglected husband, a warrior, and so forth. This "countertestimony", Brueggemann believes, depicts Yahweh as a god who operates within a principal of self-contradiction.[14] He can make this claim on the basis of several assumptions, including the suggestion that the theme of testimony is generally regarded as revelatory[15] and that within his work he believes he can thematize but not systematize his readings.[16] Brueggemann's contrasting core and

---

[13] Fretheim, *The Suffering of God*, p. 112.

[14] This point is repeated throughout W. Brueggemann *Theology of the Old Testament* (Minneapolis: Fortress, 1997); a few examples should demonstrate the theme's prominence: "*The substance of Israel's testimony concerning Yahweh, I propose, yields a Character who has a profound disjunction at the core of the Subject's life*" (p. 268, italics in original); "we must take this as evidence, in the testimony of Israel, that Yahweh has an intense self-contradiction between norms and yearning" (p. 366); "through the life of Israel, Yahweh is beset by competing, conflicting inclinations" (p. 367); and "There is a profound irrationality about Yahweh, which Yahweh enacts peculiarly against Israel" (p. 383).

[15] Brueggemann, *Theology of the Old Testament*, p. 360. This point is a challenging one on a number of levels. Certainly, it is quite difficult to entertain a differentiation between "testimony" and "revelation" since through Israel's testimony God reveals himself. Nevertheless, it would seem vital within this arrangement to take the testimony seriously as to what it considers important, and in this regard, I think Brueggemann is right to label his first major segment as Israel's "core" testimony. One could assume that the privileging implied by the word "core" suggests that it retains a more determinative quality for Israel's self-understanding of what they are testifying to than does a largely marginalized "countertestimony". The latter is valid as it makes its way within the pages of Scripture, but one is left to wonder if its relegation as a "countertestimony" does not have implications also for how significant of a role it plays in narrating the character of Yahweh in Israel's proclamation and worship.

[16] "But I do not intend [the word *thematization*] to claim too much, for it is a much more modest term than *systematization*. Thematization, unlike systematization, aims only at a rough sketch and not close presentation. It allows slippage, oddity, incongruity, and variation, and does not propose to arrive at closure. If one succeeds in presenting a persuasive thematization of Yahweh, a further systematization may be undertaken, perhaps by an ecclesial community (systematic theology) or by a critical community

countertestimonies are helpful in that they illuminate a level of diversity that many are not willing to acknowledge within the text. The difficulty in this reading, however, is that Brueggemann promotes the tension in a short section in his book without taking the next *theological* (as opposed to *hermeneutical*) step of making that tension do theological work. In other words, a dialectical understanding of God is not simply generated by placing two portrayals side by side (thus suggesting that these two portrayals are sufficiently on par with one another in their theological *gravitas* to warrant the comparison – a questionable notion in Brueggemann's case). The tension has to be probed and gauged as to its complexity, strength, and scope in ways that shape the readings of those key passages themselves. Since this section of Brueggemann's work is preceded by massive parts devoted to the individual testimonies themselves,[17] the effort to "maintain the tension" would require more than a simple addendum of a few pages if such a task were to be taken seriously.

Such endeavors within biblical studies have led to a more concerted account of God's possibility, largely because the operative assumption by many Old Testament scholars is that for centuries people had been reading the Hebrew scriptures with Hellenized eyes. Such an operational premise admittedly has to be at least partially true given that Western civilization relies more on Athens than Jerusalem in its philosophical proclivities and cultural tendencies. With a Hellenized background regarding all things metaphysical, Western interpreters could justifiably ask of certain Old Testament texts: "How could God lament or regret or be angered when in fact we are speaking about *God*?" The expectations that surround certain tendencies in God-talk would seem to preclude precisely that which one finds in the biblical text: a God who seems to be very human in his portrayal. The critique by these biblical scholars cannot be avoided because substantial examples prove the point: Hellenized forms of thought do not coincide well with the way the Old Testament depicts the God of Abraham, Isaac, and Jacob.

One of the most glaring examples of the Hellenized mindset's inability to deal with *Tanakh*'s portrayal of God is the way the Septuagint (LXX) translated (or, one could say, misconstrued) certain passages in the Old Testament witness. C. T. Fritsch remarks in his key text that, "Ever since the beginning of

---

(historical or literary criticism). But thematization, as I attempt it here, intends to stop short of such systematizing closure, for it is in the nature of the Subject of the thematization to resist such closure" (Brueggemann, *Theology of the Old Testament*, p. 268). Brueggemann undoubtedly shows his operational sensibilities here in that he assumes that engaging Yahweh in an act of thematization can be separate from an ecclesial or critical community, when in fact such a move inevitably betrays allegiance to a particular community of interpretation. In other words, Brueggemann is striving to resist closure, an act that is a certain kind of closure itself (and an unfortunate species of closure indeed in that it strives to be defined otherwise as such, thereby privileging itself above other forms of closure).

[17] Brueggemann, *Theology of the Old Testament*, pp. 400-403.

the scientific investigation of the Greek Old Testament, scholars have noted that the translators sought to remove or moderate many of the human qualities and emotions attributed to God in the Hebrew Old Testament."[18] Further affirming that "every translation is an interpretation", the Septuagint clearly demonstrates a "tendency towards anti-anthropomorphism and anti-anthropopathism" in the way that certain passages are rendered.[19] The theme of repentance is key in these considerations. Naturally, one assumes that repentance runs counter to the notions of God's omniscience and providence: if God knows and guides all things, there would be no need for his subsequent repentance. In the case of Genesis 6:6, the LXX translates God's repentance by suggesting that God "reflected" or "was concerned".[20] The second verb form, the one suggested above as rendering the notion of God "grieving", is rendered by the LXX as "he thought it over".[21]

As Fritsch notes, sometimes the translations are rendered through lesser anthropopathic suggestions – perhaps reverting to "anger" instead of "repentance" – but at other times, the translations clearly dismiss all possibilities of God having an affectional life. One such example is Genesis 18:30, which can be rendered from the Hebrew, "'Oh do not let the Lord be angry if I speak.'" Clearly, the term "anger", although allowed at times by the Septuagint translators,[22] is an anthropopathic term in the vein of God's repentance; the LXX has for this passage, "'Let it be nothing, O Lord, if I speak.'" The implication is clear: Because the translators responsible for the Septuagint could not accommodate the testimony of Scripture within their conceptual commitments regarding what can be said fittingly about God, the resulting dissonance is intentionally diminished or eradicated, making the passage tamer and so inconsonant with its original shape. Other examples perpetuate the pattern.[23]

Such aberrations within the LXX demonstrate that the ancient Hellenized

---

[18] C. T. Fritsch, *The Anti-Anthropomorphisms of the Greek Pentateuch* (Princeton: Princeton University Press, 1943), p. 3.

[19] Gavrilyuk, *The Suffering of the Impassible God*, p. 39.

[20] Fritsch, *The Anti-Anthropomorphisms of the Greek Pentateuch*, p. 17.

[21] Fritsch, *The Anti-Anthropomorphisms of the Greek Pentateuch*, p. 18.

[22] As Fritsch notes, "there is no consistent policy in the LXX" as to why the translators misconstrued some but not all of the canonical moments in which God is portrayed as having emotions (*The Anti-Anthropomorphisms of the Greek Pentateuch*, p. 20). Clearly, though, the fact that the translators did alter renderings at times shows that the language was problematic for them, especially in light of how such passages called into question Hellenistic metaphysical sensibilities.

[23] According to Fritsch, the LXX not only mistranslates passages that speak of God "being refreshed" (Exod. 31:17), "fearing" (Deut. 32:27), and being "furious" (Deut. 3:26) but also in other instances avoids the issue of divine repentance altogether (Exod. 31:14, 32:12; Num. 23:19). See *The Anti-Anthropomorphisms of the Greek Pentateuch*, pp. 17-20.

world had great difficulty in maintaining certain aspects of the biblical witness since these clashed with what was perceived to be proper ways of speaking and thinking about God. One sees this tendency perpetuated among early writers and thinkers of the ancient world, including those who would have a lasting impression upon the early efforts at theologically systematizing the Christian faith.

A.2. The Case of Philo of Alexandria

Genesis 6:6 received significant attention by the Middle Platonist Philo of Alexandria in his treatise *On the Unchangeableness of God*, which was the first of its kind to consider its topic. Not only was Philo a contemporary of Jesus (20 BCE – 50 CE) – thereby elevating the importance of his writings in the minds of many Christian scholars for its sociological and historical merits – but he was also one of the most influential thinkers during the emergence of early Christian thought. J. Hallman suggests, in fact, that Philo was "the single most important resource for early philosophical reflection on God's nature".[24] Given that his treatise dealt with divine immutability, what did Philo make of Genesis 6:6, with its claims of God's sorrow and grief, suggesting that God is anything but unchangeable? Philo believes that it would be foolish to take this passage literally, for "what can be a greater act of wickedness than to think that the unchangeable God can be changed?"[25] When Scripture speaks of God in such ways, it does so "for the sake of admonishing those persons who could not be corrected otherwise".[26] For Philo, passages such as these serve a pedagogic function; they are simply means to certain ends and say nothing about the divine nature per se. Philo can make such claims because of his belief in the radical difference between God and the world, a difference that he believes must be affirmed prior to any consideration of anthropomorphic references in Scripture. This dichotomy is perhaps stated no more clearly by Philo than when he affirms: "For it is the peculiar property of human weakness to be disquieted by any such feelings, but God has neither the irrational passions of the soul, nor are the parts and limits of the body in the least belonging to him."[27]

As inflexible as such statements appear, one must look at the examples Philo

---

[24] J. Hallman, *The Descent of God* (Eugene, OR: Wipf and Stock, 2004), p. 23. J. N. D. Kelly seems to concur with this assessment of Philo's importance for the emerging field of Christian theology; see *Early Christian Doctrines* (revised edition; San Francisco: HarperCollins, 1978), pp. 7-11.

[25] Philo, "On the Unchangeableness of God", V. The English translation of Philo's works used here will be *The Works of Philo: New Updated Edition* (trans. C. D. Yonge; Peabody, MA: Hendrickson, 1993).

[26] Philo, "On the Unchangeableness of God", IX.

[27] Philo, "On the Unchangeableness of God", IX.

employs in order to justify his views, especially this particular hermeneutic surrounding pathic speech for God. God is not fickle, he writes, while humans tend to make enemies or strangers of friends for no reason except simply the passing of time.[28] Additionally, God does not change his opinions whereas humans do because of their desire for conformity among their acquaintances.[29] In both cases, Philo is speaking about those characteristics of human change that are inconsistent and thus irrational. In opposition to this form of "human mutability", Philo speaks of God as "dwelling in pure light"[30] and as having all things visible before him in his constancy, purity, blessedness, and imperishability. Clearly, the "change" that Philo has in mind is associated with the limitations and irrationality of human beings. Philo is deriding a particular kind of change in light of concrete precedents in human experience, a variability that humans themselves would acknowledge as unbefitting a rational and virtuous person. This teasing out of the matter, however, begs the question: Does one have to suggest that the language found in passages like Genesis 6:6 should be explained away because of reservations similar to Philo's? Are Philo's conclusions not excessively brash? Is pathic language helpful only to the degree that it is instructive or pedagogical?

A.3. When Hermeneutics is Unhelpful

A similar hermeneutical move is detectable in those voices that interpret such difficult passages through the notion of "accommodation" or "condescension". Rather than emphasizing that such language is pedagogical, these figures stress that the eternal and transcendent God "accommodates" his self-revelation by assuming provisional metaphors in order that humans may relate him to their experience. As a case in point: Against the Anthropomorphites, who took such divine-corporal language literally, J. Calvin could state: "Thus such forms of speaking do not so much express clearly what God is like as accommodate the knowledge of him to our slight capacity. To do this he must descend far beneath his loftiness."[31] The assumption is that because of inherent human inabilities, God has to use a certain discourse that is amenable in some way to human cognitive capacities.

In the cases of Philo and Calvin (as well as many others who follow their cues), the hermeneutical assumption is that one should begin from the vast distinction that exists between God and humans before proceeding to engage what subsequently can be labeled as anthropopathic language. The assumption

---

[28] Philo, "On the Unchangeableness of God", VI.

[29] Philo, "On the Unchangeableness of God", VI.

[30] Philo, "On the Unchangeableness of God", VI.

[31] J. Calvin, *Institutes of the Christian Religion* (2 vols; ed. J. T. McNeil; trans. F. L. Battles; Philadelphia: Westminster, 1960), I, p. 121.

seems to rest on the view that, like anthropomorphisms (in which God is said to have "hands", "feet", etc.), instantiations of anthropopathic terminology cannot be taken literally and so there is no way that God could have an "affectional life".

The danger with such moves is that if one seeks to explain away these passages with the arguments for pedagogy or accommodation (and both are related to one another), the force of such expressions is subsequently diminished. Their rhetorical impact is abated because from the beginning the hermeneutical premise is one of disjunction between God and humans. On this reading, the "logical" or "rational" starting point is that, of course, one cannot say that this language literally applies to God. If one begins with the vast difference between creator and creation, it makes no conceptual sense to say that God can have emotions such as anger, jealousy, and sadness.

And yet a remarkable feature of the biblical text is that the tensions that interpreters constantly face are already inherent to the text itself. A case in point is 1 Samuel 15: In verse 11 God says, "'I regret that I made Saul king, for he has turned back from following me, and has not carried out my commands'" only to be followed by Samuel's remark that the "Glory of Israel will not recant or change his mind; for he is not a mortal, that he should change his mind" (v. 29). Within the same pericope, the affectional language associated with God is problematized only a few verses later, making the point that affectional language affirms both continuity and discontinuity when used in relation to God. Additionally, for all of the theopathic speech patterns found in Genesis and other Pentateuchal sources, one also sees limiting cases such as Numbers 23:19 ("God is not a human being, that he should lie, or a mortal, that he should change his mind") and Psalm 110:4 ("The Lord has sworn and will not change his mind"). In sum, the Bible reflects some of the same tensions found in the historical and modern debates surrounding propriety in God-talk.

Given the surveyed patterns of biblical interpretation above, it appears that past voices have gone to great lengths to discount the value of affectional language when used in relation to God's dealings with the created order. Such a hermeneutic is unfortunate as it demonstrates more a commitment to certain assumptions about affectional language and metaphysical propriety than to the "plain sense" of Christian Scripture. At the same time, it appears that the largely unqualified contemporary embrace of such language is an equally problematic move that blurs the distinction between God and humans. Recalling the point made by Fretheim, one is reminded of how biblical revelation is inherently metaphorical and as such affirms both continuity and discontinuity. For this reason, affectional language when used in reference to God retains a level of both legitimacy and provisionality; such language is suggestive and descriptive, although not in some kind of comprehensive or exclusive way.[32]

Given that Scripture presents God-talk in such a tension-laden fashion, is there a biblical way of making these passages do theological work? In other words, can one formulate a conceptual framework from the canon itself that can suggest greater clarity for the use of affectional language in contemporary God-talk?

B. The God of the Covenant

One of the difficulties inherent in the arguments concerning God's (im)passibility is the tendency to isolate God as an entity to be described in his own terms, i.e., as an individual entity that can be probed and prodded intellectually and conceptually at an abstract level. Perhaps this is a tendency of the Greek mindset that sought to categorize everything under its appropriate genus. Whatever the intellectual background, the move is anti-biblical. What one finds in the Bible is not a systematic theology nor is God's portrayal an abstract collection of attributes and properties (such as immutability or impassibility) distinct from any connection or relationship to the world. On the contrary, what one finds in the Bible is a depiction of God as one who is thoroughly *relational*. Before Genesis 1:1 concludes, the reader is introduced to two constants: 1) The "givenness" or "prevenience" of God and 2) the notion that God is a creating god. Apart from this activity of creating, God's existence is not explained or rationally justified, nor is God's nature abstractly considered.

Given such a background, it is no wonder then that Weinandy claims that "the Bible tends to speak in terms of how God and persons function and interrelate rather than what they are ontologically in themselves", suggesting that God is known primarily by the "types of relationships [he] has with the created order".[33] In speaking of the prophets, A. Heschel could also state, "They did not offer an exposition of the nature of God, but rather an exposition of God's insight into man and His concern for man. They disclosed attitudes *of* God rather than ideas *about* God."[34] These suggestions probably appear

---

[32] These points fall in line with what Fretheim initially suggests quite judiciously about metaphors in *The Suffering of God*, pp. 7-11.

[33] Weinandy, *Does God Suffer?*, p. 41. Such a manner of proceeding suggests perhaps a dichotomy between the metaphysical/absolute and the personal/relative as these categories are used to describe the attributes of God. Although these distinctions serve a purpose, it is also important to attend to the biblical witness; as J. Webster points out in relation to holiness, the biblical testimony considers "the language of personal agency and historical relation" as ultimately irreducible (see *Holiness* [Grand Rapids: Eerdmans, 2003], p. 42, n. 25).

[34] A. Heschel, *The Prophets* (2 vols; Peabody, MA: Prince, 1999), II, p. 1.

counter-intuitive for most Western readers, but it is a point not lost on major theological traditions in the East: Persons are known in and through their relationships with others, and given that Scripture depicts the God of Abraham, Isaac, and Jacob as a thoroughly *personal* God,[35] it follows that knowledge of this God ensues from the relationships that this personal God has with other persons.[36] Obviously, the persons in question are not on the same ontological plane: God and humans are not within the same genus, so to speak. But the expanse that exists between the two, however great, is already bridged by virtue of the doctrine of creation; simply by being creatures of the Most High, created in his own image no less, humans stand in some relation-constituted condition with God.

Through such passages as those mentioned above, the Bible itself presents its readers with the tension of God's impassibility and passibility and does not seek to resolve or obliterate the paradox. J. Pelikan considers this tendency in relation to divine immutability: "In Judaism it was possible simultaneously to ascribe change of purpose to God and to declare that God did not change, without resolving the paradox; for the immutability of God was seen as the trustworthiness of his covenanted relation to his people in the concrete history of his judgment and mercy, rather than as a primarily ontological category."[37] The terminological shift should not go unnoticed: Pelikan moves from an ontological term like "immutability" to a relational term like "trustworthiness" in giving an account of the Hebrew patterns of God-talk. A similar observation could be made of divine impassibility: The affectional language used of God's relationship with his people suggests something vitally important about the legitimacy and genuineness of his relationship/covenant with Israel. At the same time, talk of God's passibility or impassibility apart from this narrative history would be quite untenable and foreign to Hebrew sensibilities.

While these patterns of God-talk within the Hebrew Scriptures prioritize relational over ontological terms, it is also important to recognize another facet of this broader, biblical framework. At the risk of oversimplification, the limits and possibilities of God-talk within modern, conventional sensibilities and those detected in *Tanakh* can be illustrated by the adjective of choice used in describing God. When pushed, modern Christians would tend to conclude the phrase "God is . . ." with the predicate adjective "love". This tendency is largely due to the contemporary favoring of the Johannine witness as well as

---

[35] Part of this personal portrayal is substantiated through the revelation of God's name. See W. Eichrodt, *Theology of the Old Testament* (2 vols; trans. J. A. Baker; Philadelphia: Westminster, 1961-1967), I, pp. 206-208.

[36] Perhaps the figure most responsible for raising issues of personhood in systematics is J. D. Zizioulas; see his *Being as Communion* (Crestwood, NY: St. Vladimir's Seminary Press, 1993) and *Communion and Otherness* (New York: T & T Clark, 2006).

[37] J. Pelikan, *The Christian Tradition* (5 vols; Chicago: University of Chicago Press, 1971-1989), I, p. 22.

certain cultural presumptions about viable and healthy relationships. One could argue quite convincingly, however, that the Old Testament portrayal suggests different adjectives, many of which are difficult for interpreters to understand today. Certainly, one finds the theme of "love" in the Old Testament, but it is not as prominent as in the New Testament in that it is usually accompanied with other notions when used.[38]

For whatever one wants to make of the passibilist passages in the Old Testament, this strand of testimony makes up only one facet (and a non-dominant one at that) of a more general Jewish understanding of God that tends to privilege God's majesty, glory, transcendence, holiness, and otherness. Yahweh and Israel are two intimately linked covenant partners, but within its intimacy this relationship does not ignore the vast difference that exists between them. After all, it is Yahweh who both *initiates* and *sustains* the covenant relationship. Israel, on the other hand, constantly breaches and calls into question the covenant, suggesting that at points in which the narrative reaches a tense and critical moment, God not only is but shows his righteousness, holiness, and mercy.

B.1. An Important Test Case: Heschel

This general sentiment of how the OT depicts God is often overlooked by those attempting to "retrieve" a biblically passibilist understanding of God. In fact, those who advocate a passibilist alternative sometimes neglect instances and passages that would destabilize their agendas. This outcome has happened repeatedly with the case of Heschel.[39] For many "retrievalists", Heschel is a very important figure who gives a monumental theological reading of the Prophets. With thinkers such as Jehuda Halevi, Maimonides, Spinoza, and Philo no less, Heschel had his own group of authorities who would counter any notion that the God of Scripture is a "pathic" god. Yet, Heschel persevered, and in his much revered work *The Prophets*, he reclaimed a *"pathos-laden"* language that has invigorated the reading of the prophetic voice in Scripture.

Heschel thereby provides the conceptual space for such a category as the "divine *pathos*", a notion that has received much support because of its departure from conventional ways of reading the Prophets in the academy. Heschel's program is thought to be constructively revolutionary as it employs Martin Buber's famous notion of the "I-Thou" relationship for the purpose of showing how God reacts to human history. Contrary to the disjunction of considering God *in se* before God *pro nobis*, Heschel suggests that God is very

---

[38] See L. J. Enron, "You Who Revere the Lord, Bless the Lord!", *Journal of Ecumenical Studies* 18.1 (1981), pp. 67-68.

[39] I am indebted to Weinandy's reading of Heschel for these points (see *Does God Suffer?*, pp. 64-68).

much a God involved within the history of his covenant partner Israel; by no means is God portrayed in the Prophets as static; he is, rather, a God who is thoroughly involved within Israel's identity and life. In proceeding this way, Heschel insists on the viability and importance of affirming such a category as the "divine *pathos*".

It is important to note, however, that Heschel is very intentional in how he talks about the "divine *pathos*". At one point he says that it is "functional rather than a substantial reality; not an attribute, not an unchangeable quality, not an absolute content of divine Being, but rather a situation or the personal implication of His acts".[40] Another moment of intentional restraint or chastening regarding this kind of logic is his remark that "the divine pathos is not an absolute force which exists regardless of man, something ultimate or eternal. It is rather a reaction to human history."[41]

This intentionality and its form are often lost on those persons who rush to affirm an affectional life for God. Heschel is just too important of a figure for many of these passibilists to qualify their use of his work on the grounds of his own carefully stated restraints. One sees this tendency especially in Moltmann when he makes the case for God's passion.[42] Whereas many in the passibilist camp would state that Heschel makes a formidable argument for the "divine *pathos*", one ought to remember that Heschel approaches Scripture as a Jew and that this identity brings along with it certain hermeneutical tendencies. The dynamism of the interactions of the covenant partners is situated in light of the vast expanse between God and human beings, and as was the case previously, there is no need here to resolve the apparent paradox. In other words, Heschel clearly distinguishes between divine *pathos* and human *pathos*: "In the prophetic mind there was a dissociation of the human – of any biological function or social dependence – from the nature of God. Since the human could never be regarded as divine, there was no danger that the language of pathos would distort the difference between God and man."[43] Although one may agree with Weinandy that Heschel could have made the point a bit stronger in his elaborations,[44] the point is still valid: Heschel never lost sight of the difference between human and divine *pathos*. In spite of the fact that *The Prophets* was largely arguing for the possible parallels between the two, the hermeneutical formation implicit in his identity as a Jew would not allow Heschel to say all that he does about the "divine *pathos*" without some sort of qualifier in the process to keep the language theological and thus defiant of possible captivity to the anthropological.

---

[40] Heschel, *The Prophets*, II, p. 11.

[41] Heschel, *The Prophets*, II, p. 5.

[42] A key moment in Moltmann's corpus for this line of logic can be found in *TK*, pp. 25-30.

[43] Heschel, *The Prophets*, II, p. 50.

[44] Weinandy, *Does God Suffer?*, p. 67.

B.2. The Revelatory Implications of
Two Vastly Different Covenant Partners

One notices from this foray into the testimony of the First Testament that God is portrayed both immanently and transcendentally in relation to his covenant partner Israel. God is related to Israel via the covenant he has made with his chosen people. For all the pronounced use of anthropomorphic and anthropopathic imagery in the biblical text, when God's immanence comes to the foreground, his transcendence is not too far in the background. Within this arrangement, transcendence serves to check what can be said faithfully about God within the give-and-take dynamic implied by covenant relationship. This difference is imperative to acknowledge continually as God is always the one faithful to Israel, whereas Israel often fails in its faithfulness to him. God's transcendence helps to show how it is always God who comes back and restores the brokenness and fragmentation of the covenant bond.

In light of this relationship-in-disparity, what can one say about *Tanakh*'s depiction of God as suffering, lamenting, and the like? What can one generate from the complex testimony of Scripture regarding God's affectional life?

First, even to try to assign God terms such as passibility or impassibility would be counter-intuitive to the patterns of God-talk found in the Old Testament. As noted, the Bible does not employ the kind of language that makes neat divisions between God in himself and God for us. Clearly, the language of (im)passibility rests on the former, whereas the language of faithfulness or trustworthiness rests on the latter. Given the way that God is portrayed in the Hebrew scriptures, the case can be made that the language of covenant relationship ought to be prior to and determinative of speculative endeavors. That is not to say that the language of (im)passibility is entirely inappropriate or unfitting for the theological task, but its implications are significantly demarcated by the vision of God suggested by the biblical witness.

Second, the pattern of Scripture suggests that in every significant moment of God's self-revelation there is also an accompanying concealment. In other words, every act of God's divine disclosure has an accompanying facet of closure or hiddenness involved. In the case of Moses, for example, we see the notion sustained at several moments: the revelation of the divine name, which is considered a name but an awkward one in that it rests on two forms of the Hebrew verb "to be" (Exodus 3:14); Moses seeing the "backside" of God, which implies that at the moment in which Moses "grasped" him, God was already moving away (Exodus 33:23); and the time in which God spoke to Moses within a dark cloud (Exodus 33:9). The immediacy of God's presence implied by the Exodus and its aftermath does not obliterate the way the biblical portrayal emphasizes that the revelation was not "exhaustive" or "comprehensive" of who God is and what he is like.[45]

Third, it is important to note that precisely within the covenant relationship with Israel we usually see pathic attribution made to God.[46] God's anger or lament within this relationship shows that God is an active and personal covenant partner. He is not a removed entity who willfully chooses to remain hidden from Israel but rather an agent who is very much involved in the midst of Israel's life. In other words, God is "personally self-invested" in the fate of the Hebrews as a people; therefore, when Israel fails in its covenant obligations, God is moved by this set of circumstances. Within this context, Heschel's remarks concerning the "divine *pathos*" as reactive are appropriate: God's "affectional life" within the covenant partnership vitalizes and invigorates the relationship itself. Given this framework, when one wishes to speak of God as having "emotions", it is imperative that the divine drama, the grand narrative of God's covenanting with Israel, is maintained as a significant check when moving to talk about God's very being. Speculation ought to be tempered by the shape of revelatory history.

Fourth, despite what appears to be an overly personal depiction of God's nature in the Hebrew scriptures, one must remember that the "concept of the holiness of God is a central concept in the Old Testament".[47] A quick perusal of *Tanakh* shows that holiness is not simply a character trait or one idea among many, but in a vital and orienting way, it is the very "essence" of God. Jewish God-consciousness is permeated by the view that God is holy and majestic. As Weinandy remarks, "Holiness, within the Hebrew scriptures, then, is not just one of many divine attributes, but rather characterizes Yahweh's very identity."[48] Similar statements by both Jews and Christians alike have been made in association with the First Testament's portrayal of God.[49]

Within its connotative spectrum, holiness implies at least two things: 1) the fullness of the divine being, as one sees with the chanting of the seraphim both in the OT (e.g., Isaiah 6:3) and in the NT (e.g., Revelation 4:8) in continual

---

[45] These first two points have their parallels in B. Childs, *Old Testament Theology in a Canonical Context* (Philadelphia: Fortress, 1985), p. 41.

[46] Fretheim mentions that a threefold schema as to why God suffers in the Old Testament is available, namely that God suffers "*because* of the people's rejection of God as Lord, *with* the people who are suffering, and *for* the people" (*The Suffering of God*, p. 108). Of the three categories, the first is quite striking, given its preponderance within Scripture and the way it presents affectional language functioning within the covenant bond.

[47] J. D. Gammie, *Holiness in Israel* (Minneapolis: Fortress, 1989), p. 197.

[48] Weinandy, *Does God Suffer?*, p. 50. Eichrodt remarks, "'Holy' is the epithet deemed fittest to describe *the divine Thou whose nature and operations are summed up in the divine Name*; and for this reason it comes to mean that which is distinctively characteristic of God, that which constitutes his nature" (*Theology of the Old Testament*, I, p. 274).

[49] See Heschel, *The Prophets*, II, pp. 7-8.

worship and 2) the distinction between God and the mundane (as suggested in the Hebrew root *quesed* – "to cut off"). These two facets imply both a positive and negative aspect to the term, one of fullness and one of separation.[50] Therefore, holiness functions quite helpfully as a theme or motif that can maintain both the immanence and the transcendence of the triune God.[51] Gammie summarizes the matter quite helpfully; on the one side, "Holiness in Israel was not first and foremost something for human beings to achieve, but rather that characteristic of ineffability possessed only by God, the Lord of Hosts, the Holy One of Israel."[52] And yet, this holiness is a summoning presence, one that "summoned Israel to cleanness." In other words, "holiness requires purity."[53]

Finally, it is within God's relationship with Israel that his holy otherness is manifest. Interestingly, the theme of separation is tied to the divine presence; as Fretheim speaks of God's holiness, "The transcendence of God is thus manifested by the *way in which* God is present among his people."[54] Eichrodt, in speaking of God's personal nature, ties the notion to the revelation of the divine name, and yet the name itself requires that it not be misused, a command which is essentially an education in having a personal relationship with God.[55] In other words, Israel and followers of the Name are called to learn how to think, speak, and relate to this Holy One, and this task is integrally related to the modality of worship.

C. Conclusion

Hopefully, this brief excursus into the biblical materials has demonstrated the inherent difficulties associated with relating moments within the biblical

---

[50] These qualities are analogous to what Otto and others have talked about in the attraction and repulsion of the holy, or as Eichrodt mentions, the "*oscillation between repulsion and attraction*, between *mysterium tremendum* and *fascinans*" (*Theology of the Old Testament*, II, p. 269). A better way to think about holiness would be C. Gunton's suggestion that holiness "is both action and attribute, both relative and absolute, and is, moreover, derived more from the Bible than from philosophical theology, despite Rudolf Otto" (*Act and Being* [Grand Rapids: Eerdmans, 2002], pp. 24-25).

[51] To relate this point, Weinandy remarks that within biblical revelation the immanence of God takes "epistemological precedence" whereas his transcendence takes "ontological precedence" (*Does God Suffer?*, p. 50). Such language could be potentially problematic because of its disjunctive tidiness. Perhaps a more fitting alternative would be Heschel's assertion of a "transcendent relatedness" (*The Prophets*, II, p. 7).

[52] Gammie, *Holiness in Israel*, p. 195.

[53] Gammie, *Holiness in Israel*, p. 195.

[54] Fretheim, *The Suffering of God*, 70.

[55] Eichrodt, *Theology of the Old Testament*, I, p. 207.

testimony to the evolving and ever-emerging Christian doctrine of God. The relationship between written text and proclaimed witness is continual and ongoing. Thankfully, within today's academic climate and culture, it is more acceptable to affirm the complexity of the biblical voices when they depict God as having an affectional life. Unlike prior ages, thinkers, and even translations, today's climate can accommodate the view that God can be said to suffer in some way. It is also important to ask what themes or issues are easily trivialized or ignored because of the cultural conventions of any given context, including our own. In light of the way the contemporary ethos unquestionably and quite naturally assumes divine passibility, one ought to ask what is missing from the contemporary discourse surrounding God-talk. It could very well be the case that the notion of God's passibility has been so conventionalized that it now occludes important features of a dynamic and suggestive theological discourse.

Part of the goal of this chapter has been to show a biblically informed strategy for the shape of such a correction regarding God's (im)passibility. However, it would be remiss not to mention that to a degree the reaction against divine impassibility itself was warranted and valid. As in the case of Philo and others, the text was often misshaped and misinterpreted in light of cultural conventions regarding the value of the emotions. Passibilists are right to react to these moments of biblical interpretation and those stages of theological discourse that adamantly reject a priori the notion that God suffers in some way. At the same time, a notion of God's transcendence was and continues to be vital for conceiving God's relational self.

Unfortunately, this balance was obscured throughout Christian history not only in the way texts were interpreted but also in how theological reflection was envisioned to be undertaken adequately and fittingly, leading to the question: What has happened in the course of Christian history that for so long has complicated the multivalent account of the biblical narrative regarding God-talk? Are there accounts of divine impassibility that are workable within the early Christian sources that do not entirely undercut the biblical understanding of God? These questions, largely situated within the realm of historical theology, will be explored in the following chapter.

CHAPTER 3

A Heretical *and* Orthodox Divine Attribute

A. The Difficulty of Claiming Support within the "Tradition"

Perhaps one of the few academic realms in which divine impassibility is seriously considered today is the field of historical theology, for this area of study attempts to take seriously the testimony of past voices in an effort to understand inherited tendencies and proposals. Unfortunately, in the area of systematic theology, if the theme of divine impassibility does happen to be mentioned, it is usually in the form of derision, usually with the evaluation of past sources as inadequate or overly wedded to past conceptual tendencies. With such approaches, thinkers try to resolve or improve these sources rather than entertain or engage them on their own terms. Sadly, a "hermeneutic of generosity" that is so paramount for the study of history is often put to the side by those more oriented to the constructive task of theology.

Often, as this study has noted, the dismissal is phrased as a rejection of "classical theism". This phrase is a catch-all category, suggesting that previous voices within the tradition operated by means of a unified account of metaphysics that has as its orienting concerns Hellenistic philosophical categories. Usually, the term is operative within a broader framework that has been referred to as the "Theory of Theology's Fall into Hellenistic Philosophy".[1] The theory often takes the shape of suggesting that theology eventually succumbed to Greek metaphysics early on in its history as it sought a place within the broader culture, a move that relinquished much of its distinguishing features, including its Judaic background. Although there are many aspects to this issue (and these will be considered extensively throughout this chapter), "classical theism" is used repeatedly within these broad historical surveys as a way to suggest that previous voices were captive to a unified mindset that only now is being questioned and deconstructed. Naturally, the biblical testimony is said to be pitted against this alternative, and in supposedly moving back to the Bible, many attempt to bypass the "Babylonian captivity" of the doctrine of God that for too long has been determined by Hellenistic (and so pagan) thought forms and categories. As a consequence of this portrayal, divine impassibility is left by the wayside as excessively aligned to this Hellenistic past, and so it is marked as irrelevant for the present task of theological reflection.

---

[1] See Gavrilyuk, *The Suffering of the Impassible God*, p. 5.

This narrative is both comforting and helpful when contemporary observers have to wrestle with the fact that for many in the ancient church the axiom of divine impassibility was prominent in their God-talk. This linguistic and conceptual feature can be explained away as an accident of history rather than a category that was used intentionally and in a qualified way by many within the early church. The narrative of "classical theism" is a convenient way of sidestepping the difficulty that is involved in speaking about historical constructs that address the relationship between God and suffering. Is it no wonder, then, that so many individuals assume this grand narrative? It helps make sense of why divine impassibility is such a prevalent theme in a number of authors and writings centuries removed from our own.

Obviously, historical reconstruals such as these always tend to the general, and in the case of how the specific narrative of Gavrilyuk's "Fall" applies to divine impassibility, any clarity that can be gleaned from this background story is largely overridden by the inaccuracies that it promotes. Given that "classical theism" is an anachronistic category of convenience for labeling different and distinct voices under one heading, the term fails to account for the multivalent ways in which divine impassibility functioned for numerous ancient writers and thinkers, especially those who were able to affirm both divine impassibility *and* the legitimacy and value of the incarnate Christ who suffered in the flesh.

What follows is *not* a comprehensive treatment of the theme of divine impassibility from the vantage point of the church fathers; plenty of historical studies already serve that function, and many have been cited and used within the present text. Rather, this chapter aims to give vignettes of divine *apatheia* present within Christian sources in order to problematize the prevalent assumptions by many contemporary theologians concerning the theme's form in Christian antiquity. Through several examples, the chapter attempts to make the category of "classical theism" nonviable for contemporary systematics in order to suggest that divine impassibility, when framed in a specific way, has been and can continue to be an important feature of doctrinal orthodoxy.

A.1. The Philosophical Background

Theology is never undertaken in a vacuum, and when one looks at any theological work, inevitably signs and indications of the context of the writer's *Sitz im Leben* appear. The case is no different for the contexts and proponents associated with divine impassibility.

Given the confluence of cultural identities in the first-century Mediterranean world (including the way in which Jewish identity was significantly Hellenized), one cannot deny that knowledge of Greek culture, including its philosophical expression in relation to a generalized *Weltanschauung* and specific moral matters, existed among the educated elite. Plato and other philosophers undoubtedly informed the way these individuals saw and interpreted the world. Such matters naturally led to the promotion of certain tendencies within metaphysics in general and to issues such as divine impassibility in particular. Although the matter becomes much more systematized in later iterations, one initially can see that the roots of impassibility lie within several strands of Hellenistic philosophy.

If one were to begin the history of Western metaphysical speculation, one could start with the so-called "problem of the One and the Many". In brief, the problem consists of "identifying the ultimate reality (the One) that underlies all things (the Many) and of explaining the relation between them or how the Many derives from the One".[2] Because this problem was very important for the pre-Socratics, it has been pivotal for all subsequent Greek, and therefore Western, philosophical speculation. Whereas the notion of the Many was apparent enough through experience, the notion of the underlying One was a bit more complex, involving what can be termed "metaphysical intuition".[3] The conviction that a principle of unity exists behind all reality is characteristic of Greek metaphysics, and a number of theorists hypothesized as to what this principle was. Thales and Heraclitus, for example, thought it had to do with substances or essences (such as water or fire, respectively); others such as the Pythagoreans thought in terms of structural or numerical order. Because the One was usually set in juxtaposition to the Many, variability and changeableness were relegated to the latter category and excluded from the former; hence, one finds the introduction of the "principle of simplicity" at this particular juncture since the logic would suggest that the One is perfect, immutable, and not made of parts like the sensible world. Because the world of the Many was constantly in flux (and considered by some to be illusory), the One was given priority for the speculation of what was ultimate reality.

Tied to the problem of the One and the Many was the elevation of reason by the Greeks. The concept of reason, generally associated with the term *logos*, came to predominance among many ancient thinkers as the ideal category for their varied speculations,[4] a move that was directly opposed to the prior tendencies of explaining reality through religio-cultural myths. Human beings also were said to have an element of the rational in themselves, thereby partaking in microcosmic form of that which governs the universe. With this operative anthropology, reason was elevated and the apparently irrational devalued, and the latter category came to include those aspects of human experience normally associated with particular acts and emotional states. Simply through inference, many thinkers believed human emotions "possessed"

---

[2] E. L. Miller, *Questions that Matter* (4th ed; New York: McGraw-Hill, 1984), p. 59.

[3] F. Copleston, *A History of Philosophy* (9 vols; New York: Image, 1993-1994), I, p. 76. According to Copleston this move "constitutes [the Greeks'] glory and their claim to a place in the history of philosophy" (I, p. 76).

[4] Speculation regarding the term *logos* can be found in the thought of Heraclitus, the Stoics, and others (Copleston, *History of Philosophy*, I, pp. 43-44).

human beings against their wills, and these external forces were inconsistent, irrational, and unintelligible (characteristics in line with their association with the realm of the Many); therefore, the affections were to be disregarded/diminished at worst or disciplined at best in order that humans could strive to embody that which was most noble within them: namely, reason.

Following the lead of the pre-Socratics, Plato (427-347 BCE) engaged in a number of reflections about varying topics, and at times his thoughts extended into the metaphysical. His work promoted certain tendencies and themes that influenced Hellenistic philosophy in ways that subsequently had repercussions for the category of divine impassibility. Plato at times hints at important issues regarding impassibility within some of his later works, including the *Timaeus*, which is the Platonic work that exhibits more religio-mythic qualities than any other and the one that has had the most long-lasting influence upon Christian thought because of its importance during the Middle Ages.

Before considering the *Timaeus*, however, one can see an important contribution to the impassibility discussion with the *Phaedo*. In this dialogue, one finds the body-soul distinction in which the latter is elevated in value and is said to acquire refinement through the disciplining of the former. Naturally, this schema is grounded in Plato's distinction of the realms of Being and Becoming since the soul is that part of the human composition that stems from the world of Being. The body, on the other hand, is an impediment to true knowledge and is susceptible to change. As he states, "The soul of the true philosopher thinks that this deliverance must not be opposed and so keeps away from pleasures and desires and pains as far as he can."[5] Evidently, any form of emotional display is looked down upon by Plato, who claims it as inconsistent with the true, good, and beautiful world of Ideas.

In moving to the references of an ordering deity in Plato, one sees the *Timaeus* as Plato's most expansive elaboration of the theme. In this dialogue, Plato depicts a "creator" god, one who molds the eternal matter according to a predisposed plan, thereby insinuating the rationale for considering the universe as intelligible and good. Consistent with Plato's general claims, the distinction between Being and Becoming is maintained, and the world is only a secondary reality in a chain of causality; therefore, the cosmos has come into being by some primary cause, which Plato does not hesitate to call a "maker", "father", "god", and "framer".[6] This Demiurge, who had no particle of envy, designed the universe after himself and "implanted reason in soul and soul in body, and so ensured that his work should be by nature highest and best".[7] From describing this cause of the universe in such lofty ways, Plato moves in the *Timaeus* to speak of human beings, and on one occasion, he states what has become obvious in the Platonic worldview: In speaking of the soul's

---

[5] Plato, *Phaedo*, 83b; quotes are from *Five Dialogues* (trans. G. M. A. Grube; Cambridge: Hackett, 1981).

[6] Plato, *Timaeus*, III, 29 and IV, 30; quotes are from *Timaeus and Critas* (trans. D. Lee; Middlesex: Penguin, 1983).

[7] Plato, *Timaeus*, IV, 30.

"incarnation" into the body, the soul would have to be subject to "desire and its mixture of pain and pleasure, and fear and anger with the accompanying feelings and their opposites; mastery of these would lead to a good life, subjection to them to a wicked life."[8]

Despite its apparent parallels with the Christian tradition, the Platonic *corpus* is not without its important differences in its depiction of ultimate reality. The *Timaeus* does not portray an omnipotent god (because "creation" is not depicted as *ex nihilo* but as preexistent matter that requires a "shaping" or "molding") nor a personal god who is worthy of worship. Rather, the god portrayed in Plato's writings (and in the *Timaeus* more than the others) is simply an induction from the intelligibility of the universe, a working hypothesis for the apparent causation of what appears to be. With the overriding distinction between the worlds of Being and Becoming, it is clear where Plato believes the passions reside, and this estimation marks a significant moment in the historical development of divine impassibility.

Coupled with Platonism, the philosophical school of Stoicism was the dominant viewpoint of the early Roman Empire at a time when Hellenistic influences pervaded the emerging *Pax Romana*.[9] The attitude of the educated elite "might be described as either a Platonizing Stoicism or a Stoicizing Platonism".[10] In the case of Stoicism, one finds a philosophy centered primarily on conduct, on building character and growing in the virtues; for these reasons, it has been called an ethical philosophy. The influence of Stoicism has been quite considerable in the history of theology, especially in forming the popular morality of early Christianity. Because *apatheia* is a moral term that arose within Christianity largely because of Stoicism,[11] it is worth examining this school for its general claims about the ideal life.

The goal for the Stoics was for the individual to live "according to nature",

---

[8] Plato, *Timaeus*, X, 42.

[9] Although Plato's intellectual successor in Athens cannot be neglected, Aristotle's (383-321 BCE) influence among Jewish and Christian thinkers became more pronounced at a later period. Certainly, Aristotle had much to contribute to the impassibility debates, especially in his *Metaphysics* where he speaks of the "Unmoved Mover" in his deliberations about causation. This eternal, unmovable substance, the First Mover and the Final Cause, is pure actuality and is a logical necessity within Aristotle's project; as with Plato, one finds no indication that this First Mover is personal, and certainly, this being is free of desires and appetites given that it is the object of these. See *Metaphysics*, 1071b-1073a. For a specific gesture towards impassibility, see 1073a.

[10] Kelly, *Early Christian Doctrines*, p. 19.

[11] As Hart states, "*Apatheia* entered Christian thought not only as an attribute to be ascribed to God, but as a virtue to be pursued and, in this latter acceptation, the term was borrowed primarily from the Stoics, for whom it signified chiefly a kind of absolute equanimity, an impassive serenity so fortified by prudent self-restraint against any excesses of either joy or sorrow as to be virtually indistinguishable from indifference" ("No Shadow of Turning", p. 193).

which meant living in conformity to reason, i.e., *logos*.[12] The Stoic ethic considered such emotions as fear, pleasure, and sorrow as unnatural and therefore irrational.[13] According to the Stoics, the wise person was to be free from all passions that inhibit the ideal life in favor of a life of *apatheia* or impassibility. By achieving *apatheia*, one could reach true moral freedom and independence (as the passions represent external forces) and be a good citizen of the world since such activity would approximate more closely the *logos* within all human beings. In later iterations, achieving *apatheia* required a number of stages, schemas which inevitably included within their pronouncements the need to order the desires according to reason.

Although this interpretation falls in line with standard generalizations of the Stoic school that are normally promulgated, the passions and the notion of *apatheia* are much more complex concepts for classical Stoicism than one is inclined to believe. For individuals like Zeno, a distinction existed between a passion and an emotion, the former being defined as "an unnatural movement of the soul, a once natural impulse which is now out of hand"[14] whereas the latter term was, in the healthy person, not contradictory but in line with reason. The goal of *apatheia* therefore was juxtaposed to the former but not to the latter. In fact, one can say that the Stoics advocated for the wise person the condition of *eupatheia* if these "good emotions" were the "rational emotions" of joy, wishfulness, and a sense of precaution.[15] These qualifications demonstrate that the Stoics were not so naive as to advocate an emotion-less existence, but they did advocate *apatheia* when the *pathe* in question were unreasonable and out of hand – "pathological" passions that weakened and corrupted one's self.

From these forays into the Hellenistic mindset, one can see that the tenets generally thought to be constitutive of "classical theism" are found in their primitive form here, including the notion of impassibility as a metaphysical and ethical concept. Undeniably, one cannot avoid the influence of such figures as Plato and the Stoics in the history of Christian thought, and implicit within this trajectory was an estimation of what constituted the good and the beautiful, the eternal and the true.

Although what is claimed to be "classical theism" was greatly influenced by this context, one cannot assume that early Christian theologians carelessly used

---

[12] Copleston, *A History of Philosophy*, I, p. 395.

[13] "Anger is contrary to nature" (Seneca, "On Anger" in *Moral Essays* [ed. J. Henderson; trans. J. W. Basore; Loeb Classical Library, vol. 1; Cambridge, MA: Harvard University Press, 2003], p. 123). Although a representative of a later Stoicism, Seneca falls in line with many of the Stoic ideals.

[14] J. M. Rist, *Stoic Philosophy* (Cambridge: Cambridge University Press, 1969), p. 29. *Pathe*, therefore, were seen by early Stoics more as "diseases" or "pathological disturbances of the personality" than mere emotional states (p. 27). The distinction is important in that one sees the Stoic goals within a more realistic and compelling fashion.

[15] Rist, *Stoic Philosophy*, p. 25; see also Gavrilyuk, *The Suffering of the Impassible God*, pp. 27-30.

these resources for their elaborations. Given the evidence, the claims under consideration, and the methodological tendencies of the fathers, "a more differentiated judgment is necessary".[16] At stake is how these early thinkers managed the tensions between their cultural ethos and the scriptural narrative, and in this regard the following questions must be raised: Which perspective, biblical or philosophical, proved to be dominant in the early church, or which framework adjusted to the other's conventional style and conceptual tendencies? For such questions to be answered, the fathers will have to speak for themselves, which is the purpose of the next major section following another brief excursus into the thought of Philo of Alexandria.

A.2. Philo of Alexandria (Again)

Philo was already mentioned in Chapter 2 as a figure of great importance for early Christian theology. As a Hellenistic Jew, his influence as a figure both versed in *Tanakh* and culturally educated for his day is important. Given his reading of such passages as Genesis 6, many have suggested that Philo's work epitomizes "classical theism" in a primitive, pre-Christian form.

As mentioned, though, Philo's reservation about Genesis 6 rests on a particular understanding of "change", i.e., a human form of fickleness that would not be applicable to God. Some have investigated the thought of Philo in order to see whether his generalizations apply to all forms of change, and some studies have shown that a certain form of variability does indeed appear within Philo's understanding of God, although it is one that Philo would not characterize with the word "change". This kind of variability turns on the notion of God's mercy. When considering another of Philo's works, *De plantatione*, Hallman states in light of Philo's views concerning God's reaction to evil and good: "The biblical doctrine of divine moral constancy implies God's ability to respond to changing circumstances of reward or punishment. The biblical doctrine of divine responsiveness has broken through Philo's philosophical insistence that God cannot change God's will because all is foreknown."[17] In light of this observation, one can temper the generalizations Philo makes with regard to biblical anthropomorphism with a certain notion of God's responsiveness due to his justice and mercy when dealing with his creation. Certainly, this kind of "mutability" is *prima facie* more fitting to a creator God than the examples of human change that Philo mentions in "On the Unchangeableness of God".

Even with a figure like Philo of Alexandria, one who is often said to be a key representative of early forms of "classical theism" since he seemed to

---

[16] W. Pannenberg, *Basic Questions in Theology* (2 vols; trans. G. H. Kehm; London: SCM Press, 1971), II, p. 178.

[17] Hallman, *The Descent of God*, pp. 28-29. It should be mentioned that Philo's remarks on this score are brief enough to clarify the directional thrust of Philo's sympathies.

embody a bridge between the Hebrew scriptures and the philosophical climate of his day, one still detects a *qualified* notion of God's immutability. Admittedly, some features are generally agreed upon by commentators regarding his work: His is a strongly apophatic theology, one in which there is little room for the variance and change implied by the "irrational passions" found among human beings. Yet, in the midst of these traditional categories, the biblical testimony creates the conceptual space for the notion of God's mercy, a term that harkens back to the relational (as opposed to the ontological) qualities considered vital for a relationship with a covenantal God. Philo is just one of many thinkers who defy the categorization of the "classical theist" in one or more ways. Rather than assuming that all individuals fit within the designation commonly known as "classical theism", one could pursue the more helpful possibility of thinking of a continuum, one in which there are different levels between the "thoroughly passibilist" and "thoroughly impassibilist" perspectives, both of which have been said to be unsuitable for contemporary belief. Although Philo unquestionably tends to the latter category, given his commitments to the biblical text, one occasionally finds moments of variance within his *corpus*.

In fact, it is questionable if any orthodox Christian theologian of ancient antiquity would fit entirely within the 'thoroughly impassibilist' perspective. There are certainly different levels, and some thinkers would be much closer to the ideal than others would be comfortable acknowledging, yet a vast group of orthodox Christian thinkers in the early church were maintaining an impassibilist view of God while simultaneously affirming the incarnation and its passibilist implications. That they were engaging in these kinds of negotiations between revelatory history and their cultural ethos suggests that the label of "classical theism" inaccurately and inadequately reflects this lively exchange. A more cautious and careful engagement requires a closer look at certain key figures of Christian antiquity, not for the purposes of giving a thorough account of these debates in the past but to make the point that the dominant readings of many of these figures occlude the complexity and significance of their *critical* appropriations of their culturally bequeathed philosophical conventions.

B. The Testimony of the Early Church

In addition to the Jewish understanding of God, early Christian God-talk depended upon the confession of faith in the Son of God who had come in the "flesh". God incarnate, a concept that was untenable within the Hellenistic metaphysical categories associated with the origins of "classical theism" mentioned above, was a belief that was of the utmost importance to the emerging faith. One sees in countless ways (Thomas' encounter with Jesus, the Johannine preoccupation of fighting against what seem to be pre-docetic tendencies, and other instances) how the New Testament wishes to affirm that Christ *really* suffered, leaving no room for dismissing this phenomenon via

some philosophically more respectable way. With the emerging claims of
Christ's divinity leading up to and after the Arian controversy (and perhaps, for
the purposes of this study, culminating in the Fifth Ecumenical Council's
declaration that "one of the Trinity suffered in the flesh"), such an
understanding reconfigured in a more radical way the personalist terms in
which God was understood in the Old Testament.[18] God's transcendence still
played a part in the general understanding of God,[19] but God's immanence was
allocated to God's self-revelation in the incarnate Son. Therefore, early
Christians had to grapple with their Jewish heritage, their Hellenistic culture,
and their faith in the revealed Son of God who suffered and died at the hands of
the Roman authorities. All of these influences led to a complex belief system,
one that adapted and reconfigured various terms and strategies from a number
of sources to convey in a compelling and relevant way the implications of the
gospel. A key voice in this development was the testimony of the Apostolic
Fathers.

B.1. A Christ-Centered Divine Impassibility: Ignatius of Antioch

The Apostolic Fathers were those figures who endured significant persecution
as Christianity was attempting to make inroads into the dominant Roman
culture of the second century. These individuals were second- and third-
generation followers of the disciples who were given the unenviable task of
representing Christianity to a culture that found the former's truth claims to be
inconsonant and competitive with its own; therefore, one finds a number of
martyrs during this time period, and although their theological claims were not
the most sophisticated or developed within the history of Christian reflection,
their conviction certainly was without question.

One such figure is Ignatius of Antioch, a martyr of the early second century
who demonstrates in a particular way the manner in which the term
"impassibility" began to gain currency among early Christian writers. Ignatius
finds it important to underwrite Christ's impassibility from the very start of any
consideration of his salvific ministry: "Be on the alert for him who is above
time, the Timeless, the Unseen, the One who became visible for our sakes, who
was beyond touch and passion, yet who for our sakes became subject to
suffering, and endured everything for us."[20] Moving to the other side of Christ's
work, Ignatius, who perhaps was fighting off quasi-docetic tendencies among

---

[18] At this juncture, one can assume that the personalist understanding of God in the Old
Testament carried through to the New Testament period (Mozley, *The Impassibility of
God*, p. 5).

[19] This transcendence usually was granted with the acknowledgement of the "Father", a
notion that will receive more attention in Chapter 4 below. General theistic passages in
the New Testament that have been used to affirm divine impassibility are rare; the most
prominent of these are 1 Tim. 6:16 and Jas. 1:17.

[20] Ignatius, *To Polycarp*, iii, 2.

his addressed communities, can speak of his desire to imitate the passion of his God in his zeal for martyrdom,[21] all the while acknowledging that Christ's suffering – his *real* suffering[22] – was endured by the "physician who is at once fleshly and spiritual, generate and ingenerate, God in man, true life in death, born of Mary and of God, first passible then impassible, Jesus Christ our Lord".[23] This kind of terminology is remarkable in that it includes explicitly the notion of "impassibility". Apparently, Ignatius was operating in this passage with an understanding of Christ's impassibility that was directly related to his resurrection from the passion and death of the cross.

Given the example of Ignatius at this early date,[24] divine impassibility could be applied to God within a christological framework in which God was "passible" in the life, work, and death of Christ. Both before and after these events, however, impassibility could be applied to the Son, thereby affirming a transcendent element within a christological (and therefore economic) framework. In this way, the logic of salvation history as suggested by the Son's descent, life, death, and resurrection determines the parameters for the use of (im)passibilist language.

That Ignatius could affirm divine impassibility within a context of fighting quasi-docetic claims is all the more remarkable, for the truth of God's transcendence did not require elimination within an argument for God's incarnation. The relative time frame of Ignatius is also important because, as a figure who lived in the early second century, he proves that the term "impassible" was one that was in use by Christians long before any subsequent "Hellenization of Christianity" in formal Christian theological reflection could purportedly take place.

---

[21] Ignatius, *To the Romans*, vi, 1.

[22] Ignatius, *To the Smyrneans*, ii, 1.

[23] Ignatius, *To the Ephesians*, vii. Interestingly, M. W. Holmes translates a variant of *apatheia* as "beyond [suffering]" in this passage (*The Apostolic Fathers in English* [3rd ed; Grand Rapids: Baker, 2006], p. 98), a rendering that perhaps is more palatable to contemporary sensibilities but also one that complicates the rehabilitation of a workable understanding of divine impassibility. Given the translation, one would never know that *apatheia* was originally used even though Holmes in fact has translated the term in a way that is sympathetic with the aims of the present work.

[24] Other Apostolic Fathers do not explicitly make use of the term "impassibility" within their elaborations. This lack of support may make Ignatius an exception to other narrations of the tradition that would support divine passibility, but one must temper such an objection with at least two qualifications: 1) the dominant mindset at the time, due to the Platonic/Stoic philosophical lineage elaborated above, favored impassibility over passibility in formal theological discourse, and 2) possibility was attributed to God only in christological form at this particular time period.

B.2. Negotiation or Capitulation? The Apologists

Following the lead of Philo, a group of Christian thinkers emerged who were more inclined than the figures of the apostolic period to find parallels between the dominant Hellenistic culture and the Christian gospel. These Apologists were attempting to walk the fine line of staying faithful to the Christian gospel while narrating this message in the terminology of Hellenistic discourse, and the success of each is an issue significantly debated up to the present day. Since these thinkers considered Hellenistic culture to be more amenable to a Christian narration than their predecessors, the issue of divine impassibility came to be more and more a part of the discussion; therefore, these individuals are usually criticized as beginning the "Hellenization of Christianity", but one must remember that Christianity emerged within a Hellenistic context, inevitably leading to teachings and understandings that were phrased in terms of the dominant culture. Therefore, Hellenization did not happen after a nascent Christianity since early on (even in the NT) one notices Hellenistic features.

Certainly, the Apologists demonstrate methodological preferences that were distinctive of their times; however, not all allowed such a framework to absorb the biblical narrative entirely; on the contrary, many were much more selective in their elaborations than some interpreters would care to admit, demonstrating that calculated judgments regarding what was and was not appropriate in the process of communicating and defending the gospel in the cultural vernacular of their times were made on a number of different occasions.

Although each Apologist has his own distinctive methodological characteristics and aims, certain elements are common to most. In the first place, the Apologists' theology was strongly apophatic. This method of theological speculation carries Platonic overtones, thereby inclining some figures to move in ways that would appear inconsistent with some biblical understandings.[25] For example, the Apologists employed terms and conceptualities generally associated with Hellenistic metaphysics,[26] including the term "impassible" on a number of occasions. That the Apologists would proceed in this manner is not at all surprising, for they were attempting in their works to prove that Christianity was the one true philosophy; therefore, elements that they found worth keeping from Greek metaphysics were used to explain the nature of the godhead *in se*. With such a strong apophaticism, some

---

[25] Perhaps one of the more startling examples of this tendency can be found in Justin Martyr when he states: "But to the Father of all, who is unbegotten, there is no name given" (*Apology*, 2, vi, 1). Naturally, this opinion appears to be in contradiction to the revelation of God's name in Exodus, making Justin a figure who is perhaps more inclined to Hellenism than the general tenor of most of the Apologists. One sees a similar program in the work of Pseudo-Dionysius or Denys the Areopagite, a figure who will be considered more extensively below.

[26] The example of Athenagoras proves significant here: "We acknowledge one God, uncreated, eternal, invisible, impassible, incomprehensible, illimitable, who is apprehended by the understanding only" (*A Plea for the Christians*, x).

were inclined to speak of cataphatic elements in the sense of God's works. A typical exemplar is Theophilus, who states: "All things God has made out of things that were not into things that are, in order that through His works His greatness may be known and understood."[27] For Theophilus, the attributes of God that can be known are those that are revealed through his works, and here one can find slight traces of the Hebrew understanding of God's self-revelation through his covenanting with Israel.[28]

Such a strong apophaticism was not only in line with Greek metaphysical speculation (and not altogether divorced from the transcendent element of God's self-revelation in Scripture), but it also served the Apologists in distinguishing the God of the faith from the pantheon of gods and goddesses of the day.[29] In the epics and myths that constituted a part of the cultural knowledge of the typical Greek and Roman, the gods and goddesses acted in ways unbecoming to virtuous mortals, much less immortal deities. The Apologists tried to show how such views were inconsistent with the lofty claims that must be made of an all-powerful deity who was the source and end of all things. In this regard, they distinguished God's impassibility from the lustful and fickle gods and goddesses of the cultural myths familiar to their audience.[30]

Many of the Apologists did not remain content with this view of apophaticism because of the central claims of the gospel, namely that the Son of God came in the flesh for the redemption of humankind. In this regard, the Apologists turned to another aspect popular within Greek philosophy and advanced it in ways that were beyond the parameters of its native source. This application involved the term *logos*, which has been surveyed throughout this study in the non-Christian forms of the Stoics and Philo. The Apologists appropriated and altered this term to describe how one could speak of a positive understanding of God's activity within the world without compromising their apophaticism. Although moments exist in which one wishes that the Apologists would have been more forthright in their elaborations of "the Logos" as the Son

---

[27] Theophilus, *To Autolycus*, 1, iv.

[28] Another remark in this vein suggests the divine character: "You will say, then, to me, 'Is God angry?' Yes; He is angry with those who act wickedly, but He is good, and kind, and merciful, to those who love and fear Him; for He is a chastener of the godly, and father of the righteous; but he is judge and punisher of the impious" (Theophilus, *To Autolycus*, 1, iii). Given Theophilus' strong apophaticism, this statement is quite remarkable, showing that this thinker was not altogether uncritical of Hellenistic metaphysics.

[29] Examples here are sundry, including Justin Martyr, *Apology*, 1, xxv; and Athenagoras, *A Plea for the Christians*, xxi.

[30] This particular line of argumentation aligned the Apologists with the earlier efforts by the Greek philosophers of questioning the viability of the myth gods. Such a process occurred from the figure of Xenophanes up to Zeno, the founder of Stoicism. For an introduction to the theology of the early Greeks, see W. Jaeger, *The Theology of the Early Greek Philosophers* (trans. E. S. Robinson; Eugene, OR: Wipf and Stock, 2003).

of God, one does detect hints in the Apologists' reflections of how the Logos was distinct and yet equal with God. A remarkable example is Tatian's reference in a passage on the Logos to the "suffering God" when speaking of souls that are obedient to wisdom.[31] Athenagoras is more in line with the Apologists' understanding when he states: "But the Son of God is the Logos of the Father, in idea and in operation; for after the pattern of Him and by Him were all things made, the Father and the Son being one."[32]

In brief, rather than being a group who "sold out" the faith to the cultural conventions of their day, the Apologists were largely a group of committed Christians who were attempting to narrate the faith in ways that would make sense to their intended audience. Such a concern certainly forced them to stray away from themes or popular uses that have been standardized since their time, yet their efforts are not without their merits. That many of them did not adopt entirely and without question their cultural preferences when it came to parameters for fitting God-talk is a *prima facie* indicator that they maintained an underlying commitment to the scriptural witness and apostolic testimony of God's self-revelation. They used such terms as "impassibility" and "immutability" when speaking of God's transcendent being while maintaining simultaneously that the Son of God, the Logos of the Father, provided an alternative conceptuality for configuring the implications of an incarnate God. That they did not explicitly state the implications and material consequences of this incarnation is perhaps indicative of their overall task; due to their laborious endeavor of entertaining opposing viewpoints, however, one cannot deny that the setting is in place for such subsequent discourse.

B.3. Advancing the Christological Center: Irenaeus of Lyons

Moving from the Apostolic Fathers and the Apologists, one continues to find in pre-Nicene theologians the use of divine impassibility in ways that were consonant with its usage in the past. With many of these theologians, the threat of heresy was a considerable one, and divine impassibility played a role in these contexts. As Pelikan states, "The early Christian picture of God was controlled by the self-evident axiom, accepted by all, of the absoluteness and the impassibility of the divine nature."[33] Ironically, the heretics whom these theologians countered were also of the same mind when it came to divine

---

[31] Tatian, *Address to the Greeks*, xiii.

[32] Athenagoras, *A Plea for the Christians*, x.

[33] Pelikan, *The Christian Tradition*, I, p. 229. Extending this same observation, C. Grant remarks: "In the controversies through which Christian orthodoxy was fashioned, nothing was so assured as the assumption that God was characterized fundamentally by a self-sufficient imperviousness. Whatever the differences between the two sides in the major controversies, Trinitarian and Christological, the protagonists on both sides tended to be equally convinced about the divine aseity" ("Possibilities for Divine Passibility", *Toronto Journal of Theology* 4.1 [1988], p. 3).

impassibility, thereby making the question not one of whether impassibility was viable but rather how extensive its application could be in light of the gospel claims of God coming in the flesh. The diversity of opinion regarding this issue came to spawn some of the more pronounced heresies in the history of Christianity, thereby influencing Christianity's shape for centuries.

One such figure worth considering within this context is Irenaeus of Lyons, whose principal opponents were the Gnostics. The heresy of Gnosticism was a considerable one, threatening Christianity at a number of angles by countless espousers because of its syncretistic tendencies. In his *Against the Heresies*, Irenaeus outlines the tenets of the gnostic cosmological myth, which is complicated by the number of intermediate beings, or aeons, that exist between the material and spiritual worlds. Unlike the Gnostics, Irenaeus argued that God was a creator God, and this quality establishes both his transcendence and relationship to the created order.[34] From this vantage point, Irenaeus could engage the erroneous gnostic views of impassibility, which in his estimation made the God of light entirely devoid of the material realm (the latter being products of passible, lesser emanations), and yet he could affirm an impassible God who also relates to the world through his "hands", namely the Son and the Spirit.

As with the case of Ignatius, Irenaeus can speak of God and (im)passibility through a rigorous christological application. In words reminiscent of the martyr, Irenaeus states: "Thus [the Word of God] took up man into Himself, the invisible becoming visible, the incomprehensible being made comprehensible, the impassible becoming capable of suffering, and the Word being made man, thus summing up all things in Himself."[35] For those Gnostics who drew a sharp distinction between Jesus and the Christ – the one suffering; the other not – Irenaeus counters with a unified account of the person of Christ, claiming that salvation could be granted only by one who originally was incorruptible and immortal and who became corruptible and mortal for our sakes: "For by no other means could we have attained to incorruptibility and immortality, unless we had been united to incorruptibility and immortality."[36] Such a "high" view is complemented by the revelatory suggestion that "He was a man without comeliness, and liable to suffering".[37] At least in its Valentinian version, Gnosticism could not account for Irenaeus' christological negotiation of divine

---

[34] Weinandy accurately states: "The act of creation became, for Irenaeus, the fundamental hermeneutical principle which governed his conception of God and of God's relation to the created order . . . . Placing the notion of creation at the centre of his theology allowed Irenaeus to do two absolutely essential things. First, as in the Hebrew scriptures, it establishes the wholly otherness of God in a manner that is far more radical than that of the Gnostics . . . . Second and simultaneously, it establishes, as also found in the Bible, God's immediate relationship to the created order" (*Does God Suffer?*, p. 91).

[35] Irenaeus, *Against the Heresies*, III, 16, 6.

[36] Irenaeus, *Against the Heresies*, III, 19, 1.

[37] Irenaeus, *Against the Heresies*, III, 19, 2.

impassibility.[38] What we encounter in Irenaeus is a christology that attempts to attend to the unity and logic implied by the incarnation. The tension of divine (im)passibility is maintained so as to account for transcendent and economic implications of the Christ-event. Such views prefigure what would be further nuanced at Chalcedon.

B.4. From Anthropopathy to Theopathy: Tertullian

Moving to the Western tradition, one finds Tertullian, the father of Latin Christianity, opposing the early threat of Patripassianism. In his treatise *Against Praxeas*, Tertullian accuses the devil of taking the doctrine of the unity of the godhead (a notion that tends to divine immutability and impassibility) in order to "fabricate a heresy", namely that "the Father Himself came down into the Virgin, was Himself born of her, Himself suffered, indeed was Himself Jesus Christ".[39] A certain Praxeas imported these views into Rome, thereby committing a double error: "He drove away prophecy, and he brought in heresy; he put to flight the Paraclete, and he crucified the Father."[40] Although this phrasing certainly appears to be hyperbole on the part of Tertullian, a more modest interpretation of the heretics would include a distinction between "passion" and "com-passion". In a very telling passage, Tertullian states:

> The heretics, indeed fearing to incur direct blasphemy against the Father, hope to diminish it by this expedient: they grant us so far that the Father and the Son are Two; adding that, since it is the Son indeed who suffers, the Father is only His fellow-sufferer. But how absurd are they even in this conceit! For what is the meaning of "fellow-suffering", but the endurance of suffering along with another? Now if the Father is incapable of suffering, He is incapable of suffering in company with another; otherwise, if He can suffer with another, He is of course capable of suffering.[41]

---

[38] According to Mozley's understanding of Valentinian christology, "In respect of two of the four elements of which Christ the Saviour was composed, He was incapable of suffering. Not only did the pre-existent Saviour, who descended at the baptism, remain impassible" but even the seed implanted in Christ's mother did not suffer (*The Impassibility of God*, p. 25, with an apparent allusion to Irenaeus, *Against the Heresies*, I, 7, 2).

[39] Tertullian, *Against Praxeas*, 1.

[40] Tertullian, *Against Praxeas*, 1.

[41] Tertullian, *Against Praxeas*, 29. A similar passage occurs in Hippolytus' account of Callistus' position: "Callistus alleges that the Logos Himself is Son, and that Himself is Father; and that though denominated by a different title, yet that in reality He is one indivisible spirit . . . . And in this way Callistus contends that the Father suffered along with the Son; for he does not wish to assert that the Father suffered, and is one Person, being careful to avoid blasphemy against the Father" (*The Refutation of All Heresies*,

In their efforts to avoid heresy and in honoring the unity of the godhead, these thinkers made the equally damaging move of making no distinction within the godhead; but for Tertullian, it was possible to maintain exactly this tension.[42]

In another work, *Against Marcion*, Tertullian demonstrates himself to be in line with the patristic interpretation of those passages which attribute passions to God, yet he also makes some important contributions to the debate. Tertullian grants that heretics use the Christian confession to espouse a view that would imply that God is corruptible and mortal because it is said in Scripture that he is roused, angry, and jealous. Tertullian admits that it is true that God is said to die within the Christian confession, "and yet . . . He is alive for evermore."[43] The way that Tertullian manages these pathic designations of God is through the following: "Discriminate between the natures, and assign to them their respective senses, which are as diverse as their natures require, although they seem to have a community of designations."[44] As an example, it appears that God has hands, feet, and other human traits because the same names are used for both God and humans, yet the difference of natures should qualify how the two sets of designations can and should be differentiated.

In a breath of theological creativity, Tertullian re-narrates what are considered "anthropomorphisms" in pathic speech of God as "theomorphisms"; he reverses the direction of pathic speech, stating that God ultimately qualifies this language and not humans or their experiences. Tertullian justifies this move because the human soul is from God, and within it are the emotions and sensations that he deems "the likeness of God in man"; therefore, "the human soul [has] the same emotions and sensations as God, although they are not of the same kind" since God is their ultimate exemplar.[45] By being moved in "His own way", God is never subverted by his own "affectional life"; rather, Tertullian believes God is moved in a peculiar manner all his own, and "it is owing to Him that man is also similarly affected in a way which is equally his own".[46]

What one finds in Tertullian's reflections is not so much a contradiction as a negotiation of tensions that are implicit within the biblical testimony of who God is. In the spirit of the scriptures of Israel, Tertullian thinks of God's perfection and his relationship to his people as dynamic and active, and this

---

IX, 7). One of the more stringent Patripassianists was Noetus, who was refuted by Hippolytus as well; Noetus apparently espoused that "Christ was the Father Himself, and that the Father Himself was born, and suffered, and died", a belief that stemmed from a strong conviction of the unity of God (*Against the Heresy of One Noetus*, 1 and 2).

[42] "On our side the Father and the Son are demonstrated to be distinct; I say distinct, but not separate" (Tertullian, *Against Praxeas*, 11).

[43] Tertullian, *Against Marcion*, II, 16.

[44] Tertullian, *Against Marcion*, II, 16.

[45] Tertullian, *Against Marcion*, II, 16.

[46] Tertullian, *Against Marcion*, II, 16.

admission is tempered by an understanding that God's passions are different from human passions since the overriding distinction of God-human or creator-creation always exists for him. On the one hand, Tertullian can admit in *Against Praxeas* that an element of impassibility is crucial for advancing a trinitarian account of the godhead, yet on the other he can still offer a complex model for pathic attribution in *Against Marcion*.

B.5. The Demonstration of Impassibility via Passibility: Gregory Thaumaturgus

Moving back to the East, one must consider the figures of Origen and Gregory Thaumaturgus, teacher and student, respectively. In the case of Origen, one finds a brilliant thinker who was capable of extensive literary output. With his many commentaries, homilies, and other writings, Origen was one of the most influential fathers of the East. With regard to the theme of divine impassibility, one finds a tension within his position. On the one hand, he is a staunch impassibilist, stating in such works as *De Principiis* and *Contra Celsum* the notion of divine impassibility; on the other hand, in his oft-quoted homilies on Ezekiel, he states not only that the Son suffered prior to the incarnation (therefore precipitating his descent) but even that the "Father Himself is not impassible" for "if He is besought, He is pitiful and compassionate, He suffers something of love, and in those things in which because of the greatness of His nature He cannot subsist He shares, and because of us He endures human sufferings".[47] This tension in Origen is not altogether resolved. Needless to say, some scholars have frequently used the latter passage to support the *pathos* of the Father,[48] even though it is the only significant passage of its kind within Origen's literary *corpus*.

In a more constructive direction, one of Origen's students, Gregory "the Wonderworker", attempted to press these issues in the text "To Theopompus, on the Impassibility and Passibility of God" in which the subject is broached in a Platonic, dialogical style. At the beginning of the work, divine impassibility is assumed as fitting to describe the divine nature, but shortly thereafter Theopompus, Gregory's dialogue partner in the piece, poses a key question as to whether God could suffer even if he wished to since suffering is opposed to the divine nature. Essentially, Theopompus operates from a nature-will dichotomy that Gregory dismisses from the outset in order to affirm the divine freedom. Although the nature-will dichotomy may hold for human beings, Gregory affirms that "God is one, and it is precisely this same God who is not prevented by any constraint from doing what he wills, since its own essence

---

[47] Origen, *Homilies on Ezekiel*, vi, 6, the translation being Mozley's (*The Impassibility of God*, p. 61).

[48] Most notably in this camp is Hallman (*The Descent of God*, pp. 40-41).

does not consist of different, mutually opposed, substances."[49] In a move that informs the tenor of the entire piece, Gregory states that God debased himself in order to heal humankind, and in doing so:

> His blessed and impassible nature manifested its impassibility precisely in its passion. For whatever suffers is subject to passion when destructive passion prevails over it against the will of the one who suffers. But when someone voluntarily – being by nature impassible – is involved in the passions so as to defeat them, we do not say that he has been subjected to passion, even though he shared in passions by his own will.[50]

For Gregory, the passions are conquered in Christ because they were taken up by one who was by nature impassible. Interestingly, Gregory puts a unique spin on the interplay at this very point: In a similar way that passible beings "suffer" the passions, so God, who by nature is impassible, *made the passions suffer by his passion.* By engaging the passions, God made them suffer due to his impassible self, and in this process, he chastened and removed their sting. Quite logically, Gregory ties into the discussion Christ's resurrection as an act of overcoming death, thereby suggesting that God has made it possible to overcome the crippling effects of the passions by taking them upon himself incarnationally. In sum, Gregory can state, "Impassibility is not exalted over the passions unless it first shows its power through suffering."[51]

---

[49] Gregory Thaumaturgus, *To Theopompus*, 4; quotes are from *St. Gregory Thaumaturgus, Life and Works* (trans. M. Slusser; *The Fathers of the Church*, vol. 98; Washington, D.C.: Catholic University of America Press, 1998).

[50] Gregory Thaumaturgus, *To Theopompus*, 6.

[51] Gregory Thaumaturgus, *To Theopompus*, 7. Although Gregory's model is suggestive on a number of fronts, one has to admit that he remained sympathethic to some of the philosophical conventions of his day regarding the passions. Particularly, he does not offer a positive account of the passions but rather associates them with death and the need to conquer them. Such a view complicates a priori how he would move to relate the passions to God. Whereas the constructive quality of his work suggests that God overcame the passions through his impassibility/passion, he can also make such statements as, "Therefore, God enters the gates of death without knowing death" (8) and "by his powerful will [he] accomplished what he set out to do, maintaining his divine power, *remaining what he was, and suffering nothing in his suffering, because in his sufferings his impassible nature continued as it is*" (9, emphases added). Evidently, Gregory portrays a bias against any positive account of God's passions, an aversion to a *eutheopatheia* so to speak. At this point, Gregory's acount may not be sufficiently nuanced for contemporary sensibilities (including those of the present work), but his dialectical fashioning of (im)passibility suggests a conceptual breakthrough in the midst of this polarized debate even though he apparently did not develop it consistently throughout *To Theopompus*.

B.6. Conclusion

Although this survey of the patristic understanding of divine impassibility has not been comprehensive,[52] it demonstrates that despite the passing of centuries and despite differences in philosophical orientations (whether East or West, Platonic or Stoic), the fathers maintained a fairly consistent argument: Divine impassibility served to differentiate God from his creation in important ways. That this tenet was axiomatic for many of the fathers is without question, but equally so many did not allow what was for them a "self-evident truth" to stand alone without consistent and detailed support and nuancing. Many of these thinkers were aware of the positive contribution Hellenistic metaphysics could make in substantiating and elaborating theological reflection about the divine being; nevertheless, they stood before Scripture, allowing the testimony of the prophets and of the gospels to curb their theological constructs. Exceptions to this kind of interpretation certainly existed, but the community of those who espoused a chastened view of God's impassibility includes some of the more prominent figures in pre-Nicene theology.

From these thinkers, one can detect two passibilist strands in their work. One is the Old Testament accounts that use pathic language to speak of God, and the second is the gospel that proclaims the Son as having become incarnate, dying, and rising once again. With regard to the Old Testament, the authors surveyed generally did not go to Philo's extreme in which the language was interpreted as existing for the sole purpose of instruction; like Tertullian, Christians distinguished natures in an attempt to acknowledge the differences involved when applying affectional language to God and humans. The second strand, namely the gospel accounts relating the Son's incarnation, was acknowledged in pre-Chalcedonian simplicity; Jesus Christ's suffering was considered true suffering (*contra* the Docetists, among others), and yet within the plan of salvation a natural progress was detectable: impassibility (pre-incarnation), passibility (incarnation through crucifixion), and impassibility once again (resurrection).

In addition to its christological application, the term "impassibility" was used apophatically by early Christian theologians. Rather than stating what God was, the term differentiated God from the religious pantheon of gods and human beings in general. In this way, the term served a greater purpose of distinguishing God from other conceptions that would taint God's perfection, goodness, and sovereignty. Within this trajectory of Christian reflection, the attributes of "classical theism" were interrelated in a complex way with other ones, including God's love, mercy, and justice. Unfortunately, as Christian

---

[52] Other figures who contributed to the discussion but who were not considered in detail include Melito of Sardis, Aristides, Clement of Alexandria, Novatian, and Lactantius (among others). In addition to Mozley, Hallman, and Weinandy, a very detailed exposition of the fathers regarding divine impassibility is H. Frohnhofen, *Apatheia tou Theou* (New York: Peter Lang, 1987).

theology became more complex and developed on a number of different fronts within changing contexts, there was a loss of the intricate negotiations necessary to keep the language of divine (im)passibility useful and suggestive. The language came to be assumed within theological discourse, and without careful nuancing, its unique role within theology went unnoticed.

C. The Misunderstanding and Unquestioned Promulgation of a Chastened Concept

C.1. Pre-Modern Voices

The above survey was limited to pre-Nicene theologians, for if Christianity had been "Hellenized", it would have been during this time period. Although the Nicene and Chalcedonian time frames, with their respective conciliar achievements, will be treated in subsequent sections of this study, suffice it to say here that divine impassibility continued to be traditionalized as a supposed tenet of speaking about the godhead. Certainly, one does not find in later iterations of divine impassibility the kind of laborious qualification and nuancing that the fathers of the first few centuries of Christian theological reflection engaged in, one possible reason being that the issues under dispute in subsequent periods were located on other fronts. Divine impassibility, nevertheless, was retained, if for no other reason than convention. As movements and issues changed, however, this axiom appeared to be an increasingly awkward remnant of a surpassed theological era.

Augustine of Hippo, the towering figure of Western Christianity, apparently found divine impassibility to be agreeable to his view of God, but references to the axiom within his work are sparse. One important example can be found in the *Civitatis Dei*; in speaking of demons, Augustine makes a general statement about emotions that is quite commonplace for the philosophical climate of his day: "for the Greek word *pathos* means perturbation, whence [Apuleius] chose to call the demons 'passive in soul,' because the word passion, which is derived from *pathos*, signified a commotion 'of the mind contrary to reason."[53] Augustine is merely continuing the philosophical tradition of Platonic and Stoic sensibilities when he believes passions are irrational. Since they are irrational, the passions do not fit the general understanding of God, even in those passages

---

[53] Augustine, *City of God*, VIII, 17. Further considerations of the term can be found in XIV, 9, where Augustine states, "And therefore that which the Greeks call *apatheia*, and what the Latins would call, if their language would allow them, 'impassibilitas,' if it be taken to mean an impassibility of spirit and not of body, or, in other words, a freedom from those emotions which are contrary to reason and disturb the mind, then it is obviously a good and most desirable quality, but it is not one which is attainable in this life." In this passage, Augustine clarifies that this state is for the afterlife because it requires sinlessness; nevertheless, he believes the afterlife will be characterized by love and gladness, these being improperly attributed to *apatheia*.

that refer to such "states" of God as his anger and repentance. In such cases, Augustine again follows a conventional hermeneutical procedure in which he believes that these terms are limited in their own right when applied to God and affirm something different of him than they do for human beings. In summary of his position, Augustine can state: "For if we conceive of [jealousy, wrath, etc.] as they be in us, in Him are none. We, namely, can feel none of these without molestation: but be it far from us to surmise that the impassible nature of God is liable to any molestation. But like as He is jealous without any darkening of spirit, wroth without any perturbation, pitiful without any pain . . . so is He patient without aught of passion."[54]

Even when the philosophical mood shifted from Platonism and Stoicism to Aristotelianism, as was the case with the scholastic movement of the Middle Ages, divine impassibility continued to be retained and assumed, partly because Aristotle referred to the concept in his metaphysical thought. Anselm of Canterbury affirms the notion in similar ways to the fathers,[55] and the great Angelic Doctor himself points to the notion of divine impassibility by elaborating the being of God and qualifying the term *passio* as follows: By being "pure actuality",[56] God cannot be said to have *passio*, since the term denotes external influence that leads to change.[57]

C.2. The Rise of Modernity

The landscape shifted significantly with the advent of the Reformation, which in many ways contributed to what is generally thought to be modernity. Protestants, in claiming a renewed interest in biblical scholarship and the faith of the believer, altered the course of theology. Lost were the minutiae of scholastic speculative endeavors in light of more "practical" matters: they occupied their time in justifying their movement over and against both Roman Catholicism and the subsequent rise of "new heretics" such as the Anabaptists. Additionally, biblical commentaries were very important to the movement,

---

[54] Augustine, *On Patience*, I. Another place where Augustine speaks of passions is the *Confessions*, yet the elaborations here are interesting, for "it is a rough jolt, to discover that at those very points in his life where we find Augustine most appealing, he, from the time of his conversion onward, found himself thoroughly disgusting" (N. Wolterstorff, "Suffering Love" in T. V. Morris (ed), *Philosophy and the Christian Faith* [Notre Dame: University of Notre Dame Press, 1988], p. 196).

[55] "But how are You at once both merciful and impassible? . . . How, then, are You merciful and not merciful, O Lord, unless it be that You are merciful in relation to us and not in relation to Yourself?" (Anselm, *Proslogion*, 8; version is from *Anselm of Canterbury: The Major Works* [eds. B. Davies and G. Evans; Oxford: Oxford University Press, 1998]).

[56] A good section to consider Aquinas' position is his treatment of the question on the immutability of God (*Summa theologica*, I, 9, 1; hereafter *ST*).

[57] Aquinas, *ST*, I-II, 22, 1.

thereby underscoring the stress placed upon the faithful interpretation of Scripture. These activities show that the Reformers did not aspire to be great speculative theologians, and their agendas did not include detailed and expansive metaphysical systems. Divine impassibility was, if ever mentioned, a short and passing gesture within the context of a larger and more pressing set of issues.[58]

Protestants nevertheless influenced the fate of divine impassibility for subsequent theological discourse, for their methods challenged the conventional uses of certain terms within the parameters normally associated with divine impassibility. Since the issues of the day largely revolved around soteriology and the sacraments, the Reformers teased out important christological statements. Although their theological reflection was not very considerable regarding the Father or the Holy Spirit, they did work out strong christologies.

Perhaps the most important christological motif during this time period for altering the course of divine impassibility was Luther's understanding of the *communicatio idiomatum.* In line with the dialectical reasoning characteristic of Luther's other works, this theme can be summarized through the following consideration: "The two natures, the human and the divine, are inseparable. They are so united in one Person that the properties of the one nature are also attributed to the other . . . . Now we can say: 'God became man, God suffered, and God died.'"[59] This application of the two-natures doctrine only contributed to an even more significant christological move by Luther, one that P. Althaus labels the "new meaning and importance of the deity of Jesus Christ for Luther".[60] In summary of this "new" meaning, Althaus states: "We can say that before Luther, the church and its theologians were primarily concerned with the divine in Christ. They looked for his divine nature, his divine life, and for the significance of his satisfaction. Luther, however, looks and finds *God the Father himself* in person in Jesus Christ."[61] Although the notion has some basis

---

[58] Two of the more popular examples that simply repeat customary overtures to divine impassibility can be found in the 39 Articles of Religion of the Anglican Church (1562) and the Westminster Confession (1647). The former includes in its first article the notion that God is "without passions"; the latter in its second chapter mentions a similar notion. Neither instance includes extensive engagement or discussion of the theme, proving that the issue was more conventional than controversial. For complete texts of these documents, see P. Schaff (ed), *The Creeds of Christendom* (3 vols; Grand Rapids: Baker, 1993).

[59] M. Luther, *Luther's Works* (55 vols; eds. J. Pelikan and H. T. Lehmann; Saint Louis: Concordia; Philadelphia: Fortress, 1958-1986), XXII, p. 492; volumes within this American version of Luther's works will be subsequently referenced as *LW.*

[60] P. Althaus, *The Theology of Martin Luther* (trans. R. C. Schultz; Philadelphia: Fortress, 1966), p. 182.

[61] Althaus, *Theology of Martin Luther*, p. 182 (emphases mine). One of the strongest expressions of this belief can be found in Luther's works on the sacraments, especially in "That These Words of Christ, 'This is My Body', etc. Still Stand Firm against the Fanatics" (1527): "For in [Christ] God not only is present in his essence as in all others,

in Scripture[62] and has been considered in earlier iterations,[63] the fresh impact that this speech practice had upon the modern theological mindset cannot be overestimated. Gone is the centrality of the godhead that is partly conformable to Hellenistic metaphysics, especially in light of affirming immutability and impassibility for purposes of distinguishing God from the world. In its place is the incarnate Son and his representation of the Father. This testimony becomes the key moment for understanding the godhead, and since Christ suffered and died on the cross, the logic suggests that one can say God experienced these moments as well.

Following the lead of Luther, whether directly or indirectly, the modern theological milieu has continued this practice of God-talk. With modernity's "turn to the subject" and its implied epistemological concerns, metaphysics came to wither in its importance within philosophical speculation, especially after Kant. One such example of these changes is the work of F. Schleiermacher, the father of liberal theology. Schleiermacher emphasized Jesus' "God-consciousness" and his feeling of absolute dependence on God, but alongside these "subject-oriented" claims is a section in *The Christian Faith* devoted to divine attributes. Interestingly, divine impassibility and divine immutability are not even included at this juncture.[64] With Kant and Schleiermacher as some of the pivotal influences upon Protestant theology in the modern period, theologians simply followed their example and avoided the kind of metaphysical speculation in which divine impassibility would be systematically considered. Given the way speech about the godhead has generally been undertaken within modernity, namely with primacy given to Christ, passibility was acknowledged and accepted as the norm, and impassibility came to be increasingly viewed as a Hellenistic metaphysical importation into Christian God-talk. In coming to this point, one sees that the turning of the tide occurred, and little fanfare took place when it did: While another way of speaking about the godhead became conventionalized, divine impassibility was excluded from formal theological discussions, and no one paid much attention to its absence. Certainly, divine impassibility continued to

---

but also dwells bodily in him in such a way that one person is man and God . . . of Christ faith asserts not only that God is in him but that Christ is God himself" (Luther, *LW*, XXXVII, p. 62).

[62] Althaus states that this view is Johannine, as evidenced in John 14:9 and other passages.

[63] According to Althaus, Augustine is Luther's closest forerunner in this regard (*Theology of Martin Luther*, p. 183).

[64] Eternality, omnipresence, omnipotence, and omniscience are held in high esteem by Schleiermacher, and to a lesser extent he mentions the attributes of unity, infinity, and simplicity; the latter category of attributes, however, lack dogmatic content in that "unlike the other four, they do not issue from the relationship between the feeling of absolute dependence and the sensibly stimulated self-consciousness, nor are they statements about it" (*The Christian Faith* [eds. H. R. Mackintosh and J. S. Steward; Edinburgh: T & T Clark, 1999], p. 229).

be maintained in some quarters of the tradition because of the requirements of particular systems, but at least in modern Protestant theological circles, divine impassibility quickly became a non-issue, requiring neither consideration nor refutation.[65]

D. Divine Impassibility as a Divine Attribute

What kind of conclusions can be generated about the fate of divine impassibility from this all-too-brief survey? Apparently, one of the most difficult aspects surrounding divine impassibility is that it means different things to different people. The term is unwieldy in that it can operate within different connotative domains in large part because those who use the term negotiate its meaning and use on the basis of different operational premises. Early on, divine impassibility made sense to Christians because it fit within conventional metaphysical thought forms. With the passing of time, it moved to the periphery of the controversies that came to dominate the theological scene so that at the Reformation, when much of the fervor surrounded issues of christology, it came to be significantly out of place in light of the crucified Son of God.

Behind such historical minutiae is a broader question, one relating to the shape of divine predication or, put differently, the logic of the divine attributes. The divine (im)passibility debates rest on an account of divine attribution, thereby begging the question: If divine impassibility is going to be a fruitful element of God-talk on the contemporary scene, how would one go about locating it within a theology of the divine attributes? Now that Greek metaphysics has been challenged by more dynamic models of thought, how could one conceive of divine impassibility within today's context?

D.1. Propriety in God-talk

In order to answer such questions, one must first ask about the general notion of propriety in God-talk. Propriety rests largely on convention, and convention stems from assumed authority; therefore, the question of propriety is significantly related to what is perceived to be authoritative, and in issues of theology, different norms have been used within different contexts in order to negotiate the validity and shape of varying claims.

Christians have perpetually discussed what ultimately should be authoritative within the theological task, and a number of proposals have been offered throughout history. In what has been surveyed so far in this study, two

---

[65] This survey falls short of considering what are normally referred to as the "Anglican Debates", which will be considered in Chapter 5.

major strands of thought have emerged: the biblical witness (which has largely taken the form of the Old Testament in this study) and the broader philosophical culture in which Christianity gained prominence during its first few centuries – namely, its Hellenistic environs. It would be too facile to suggest that the difference between the two rests on the obvious discrepancies between the Hebrew and Greek mindset, largely because the two were wedded in first-century Palestine. Nevertheless, one does sense a difference between the way God is portrayed in Genesis and the manner in which Philo seems to consider God as he comments on the first book of the Pentateuch. It was only natural that the early Christians would employ the linguistic and conceptual conventions they knew in order to articulate and explain the truth they apprehended in Christianity. As many within the postcolonial camp would suggest today, "theology always takes place somewhere," and so the early Christians drew from their pagan neighbors in significant ways. Had Christianity not emerged within the Greco-Roman world, it could very well be the case that the terminology of divine impassibility would not have been prominent within the tradition and so not an issue for systematics today. The present study does not pretend otherwise: the language of *apatheia tou theou* is inherently Hellenistic, leading some to say polemically that it has pagan origins. On a strictly historical view, this judgment is irrefutable; divine impassibility is no different from other terms (even conciliar ones) that have been used throughout Christian antiquity. Such pagan backgrounds, however, do not necessarily imply that such terms retained the full scope of their pagan connotations throughout their appropriation within Christian history.

Because divine attribution is contextual, one finds that this feature of God-talk is both promising and perilous; it is the former because contextuality suggests accessibility; it is the latter because the danger of projection is always possible. In a very basic sense, attribution in and of itself is idolatry because it suggests that we determine who God is and what he is like. In this regard, K. Barth was right to reconfigure the discourse of the divine attributes and suggest the specific term of the divine "perfections". Such language shifts the direction of divine attribution so that God becomes the ultimate determiner of what the "perfections" consist of. As he begins his section in *Church Dogmatics* on the topic, Barth notes, "we choose the last [i.e., *perfectiones*] because it points at once to the thing itself instead of merely to its formal aspect, and because instead of something general it expresses at once that which is clearly distinctive".[66] In using the term "perfections", Barth is suggesting that which can apply only to God, thereby marking from the beginning the process of divine attribution as a *theological* activity as secured by the prioritization of divine self-disclosure.

Such proposals fall in line with the general contours of this study. It is no

---

[66] K. Barth, *Church Dogmatics* (14 vols; eds. G. W. Bromiley and T. F. Torrance; Edinburgh: T & T Clark, 1936-1975), II/1, p. 322; hereafter *CD*.

accident that the present work began with the testimony of Scripture before moving to the reflection of the church. In line with a faith-tenored reading of Christian history, the present work submits as a nonnegotiable the authority of the biblical witness as not being "one among many" norms but rather "one before all others". For this reason, a certain sympathy is on display for the move to retrieve or recapture the biblical text's importance for the theological task. Such a move is welcomed and actually gaining momentum not only in the guild of systematics but in biblical studies as well.[67] God's self-revelation-in-act, as it is on display in the biblical narratives, suggests a modality of action as determinative for the subsequent consideration of being.

Key in the present discussion of divine attributes is the distinction between relational/act and metaphysical/abstract attributes. C. Schwöbel rightly remarks that these two alternatives represent discourses that have been present in any discussion of the divine attributes. The first is inflected heavily by the narrative display of Scripture; the latter rests on an "understanding of the world according to which the world is seen as a rationally structured and purposefully ordered whole".[68] Schwöbel urges for a model of complementarity, arguing that extremes of emphasizing one discourse over another are unhelpful. Given the general shape of divine impassibility, in which the assumption is that it belongs to the metaphysical/abstract camp, there is a sense in which a complementary approach has to be nuanced, but the fact that Schwöbel is even moving in this direction by granting a certain legitimacy to relational/act attributes seems to be a step in the right direction.

That this commitment to complementarity was lost on many within the history of Christian reflection is undeniable. C. Gunton is quite right to suggest that the philosophical conventions of Hellenism emphasized negation, causation, and opposition between the realms of the material and the ideal, and that as a result the negative has often outweighed the positive in divine attribution: "The negative theology has in effect driven out the positive, so that the God who makes himself known in scripture has been turned into one who cannot be known as he is."[69] Gunton's principal example, perhaps the likely suspect in these matters, is Denys the Areopagite. According to Gunton's reading, Denys is a much more capable Neoplatonist than interpreter of Scripture so that when pivotal moments present themselves for the naming of God in *The Divine Names*, he opts not for the moment of the burning bush in Exodus but rather the abstract notions of being, beauty, goodness, and the like.[70]

---

[67] The many contemporary gestures supporting the "theological interpretation of Scripture" are but one prominent indication of this development.

[68] C. Schwöbel, *God: Action and Revelation* (Kampen: Kok Pharos, 1992), p. 50.

[69] Gunton, *Act and Being*, p. 17.

[70] Gunton, *Act and Being*, p. 15. Gunton's reading of Denys has been recently challenged by D. Hou, "The Infinity of God in the Biblical Theology of Denys the

Given the evidence that Gunton mounts, it would seem that the easiest, and quite popular, alternative would be to abandon divine impassibility. Interestingly enough, however, Gunton's staunch polemic against Neoplatonic apophaticists like Denys does not call for an outright dismissal of divine impassibility. Why not? Because according to Gunton, divine attributes of action require something akin to divine attributes of being in order to be fully intelligible. The act-being dyad he uses as a model for his reflection implies integrality rather than opposition; both aspects of divine attribution are mutually conditioning.[71] Gunton, therefore, is espousing the general arguments made by Schwöbel referenced above. It would seem that divine impassibility could inhabit such an environment of mutuality.

D.2. Moving Forward

What constitutes, then, a helpful and faithful appropriation of (im)passibilist language? When does divine impassibility shift from being an orthodox divine attribute to a heretical one?

First, any account of divine impassibility that compromises the personal nature of God is ill-devised and contrary to the revelation of God's self in the biblical witness. By "personal nature", I am suggesting the manner in which God reveals himself in covenant relationship to his people within a historical/narrative display of fellowship. In this regard, the "metanarrative" of God's salvific, renewing, and redeeming work maintains an epistemological priority that subsequently informs any ontological claims. An operational *regula fidei* suggests itself for precisely the possibility of distinguishing when the gospel has been compromised. That past voices made this move in previous constructive endeavors makes the generalizing claims surrounding the shibboleth of "classical theism" a false notion; that enough individuals did not heed this primary orienting concern perpetuates the momentum of the "Theory

---

Areopagite", *International Journal of Systematic Theology* 10.3 (July 2008), pp. 249-66. One can agree with Hou that Gunton's claims are very general and perhaps misleading as to the general shape of Dionysian theology. At the same time, with such nuancing, one can still appreciate the point that Gunton is making, as his was not simply based on a reading of Denys but also descriptive of what has happened in the course of Christian theological reflection.

[71] At this point, Gunton cites the work of Schwöbel noted above. Complementarity for Gunton, however, only works if the privileging of "act attributes" is granted over "being-attributes" so that the basic claims surrounding the "good news" of Christianity are not compromised. As Gunton eloquently states regarding the succumbed danger of the past, "Sometimes a metaphysic of being seems to have so predetermined the shape of the theology of the attributes so that it becomes difficult, if not impossible, to attribute to God forms of action without which the gospel ceases to be the gospel" (*Act and Being*, p. 23).

of Theology's Fall into Hellenistic Philosophy".

Following this orienting concern, one must continue to suggest that divine impassibility makes theological sense only if it participates within its connotative spectrum in the realm of the "act attributes". In other words, divine impassibility, if it is going to retain a valid place in contemporary God-talk, has to be "divine impassibility in action" and not simply an abstract notion. Here, we are pushing a bit further than Gavrilyuk's suggestion that the *apatheia tou theou* served as an apophatic qualifier in the early church; it certainly did that, but it provided much more than simply a "check" on theological speech. In many of the accounts in which divine impassibility was a helpful consideration within God-talk, it was so because it was integral to the logic of salvation history.

Ultimately, what I am suggesting is that divine impassibility must make its way into the narration of who God is *and* what God is like for it to be relevant in any way within contemporary God-talk. Therefore, one can contend that at those key doctrinal moments when theological work is undertaken to understand the nature and character of the godhead, the use of divine impassibility cannot simply be jettisoned to the abstract; it has to retain a status within the active element as well; it has to be transfigured from what appears to be an irredeemably ontological/metaphysical attribute to a workable relational/act one.

Such an endeavor is not out of line with the activity of divine attribution because examples exist in which the categories of act-being are challenged. In Gunton's own work, he cites holiness and omnipotence as attributes that defy the act-being template.[72] In many ways, the divine (im)passibility dynamic challenges this bifurcation as well. As the different examples surveyed above show, it is not enough to suggest simply that God is passible *or* impassible. Too many tangential factors contribute to the discussion to make any adjudication of the matter a simple one.

D.3. Conclusion

This historical survey has attempted to show the diverse ways divine impassibility was used throughout the history of theological reflection and how this history took a turn in modernity that sealed divine impassibility's contemporary fate. These usages varied in ways, but as an element that coincided quite well with the cultural-philosophical conventions of previous ages, divine impassibility made sense within certain expressions of theological

---

[72] Gunton mentions that holiness seems to imply both act and being in that it is part and parcel to the logic of a holy God that he would act holy because he is; as for omnipotence, Gunton narrates the attribute as being a natural consequence of Irenaeus' formulation of the *creatio ex nihilo*; see *Act and Being*, pp. 24-26.

discourse. Naturally, times change and sensibilities do, too. It could very well be the case that the language of divine (im)passibility has run its course and that new terms need to replace it. Nevertheless, when thinkers continue to say that God "suffers" and do so in ways that are insufficiently self-aware and self-critical, the issue of divine (im)passibility is recalled implicitly. In that regard, the divine (im)passibility debates prove to be moments in which the language of God's suffering can be chastened, qualified, and substantiated in order that it may be consonant with the claims of the gospel.

To speak of divine impassibility and the gospel suggests that constructive work ought to move into the realm of the doctrinal. In what follows in this work, divine impassibility will be used as a hermeneutical angle for considering church dogma relating to the triune doctrine of God, christology, and pneumatology. In attempting this shift of making divine impassibility more of a relational/act attribute, it is fitting to locate it in the different ways that Christians suggest how God is *pro nobis* and how in fact the gospel is "good news".

CHAPTER 4

Moltmann and the Limits of Trinitarian Passibility

Now that some broad issues in biblical and historical studies have been considered in this work, it would be fitting to delve into specifically theological topics. In the remaining chapters of this study, the loci of the Trinity (with special emphasis on the person of the Father), christology, and pneumatology will be considered. And when one considers the doctrine of the Trinity and the axiom of divine (im)passibility, perhaps no figure is more relevant to the discussion than Jürgen Moltmann.

A. The Context of Moltmann's Theology

Whenever a discussion arises concerning God and suffering, the name of Jürgen Moltmann usually appears. This German theologian, who taught for many years at Tübingen, has made many lasting contributions to theology, and one of them has consistently been the notion of a "suffering God". So extensive has been his influence along these lines that even those outside the realm of systematic theology have found it helpful. Brueggemann remarks that Moltmann is in theological succession to the work of the prominent Old Testament scholar Eichrodt: "It remained for others long after Eichrodt, and perhaps culminating in Jürgen Moltmann's 'The Crucified God', to see that God's relatedness entails God's risk and vulnerability."[1] One even sees Moltmann's influence on the field of pastoral care: L. H. Henning claims that Moltmann's work, specifically in *The Crucified God*, offers the field of pastoral care its long-lost theological center of the crucified Christ.[2]

---

[1] Brueggemann, *Theology of the Old Testament*, p. 29. It has already been noted in Chapter 2 how many Old Testament scholars have gravitated to the notion of a "suffering God". One can say that Moltmann helped this process along by offering OT scholars a theological resource for such a move.

[2] L. H. Henning, "The Cross and Pastoral Care", *Currents in Theology and Mission* 13.1 (1986), pp. 22-29. The principles suggested are "the cross and resurrection form the central content of Christian pastoral care", "the cross as trinitarian event is the central guide that informs the process of pastoral care", and "the cross as trinitarian event informs [people's] identity as pastors or pastoral counselors". R. J. Hunter also finds Moltmann helpful in this field; see "Moltmann's Theology of the Cross and the Dilemma of Contemporary Pastoral Care" in T. Runyon (ed), *Hope for the Church* (Nashville: Abingdon, 1979), pp. 75-92.

If Moltmann's efforts have had such interdisciplinary ramifications, it is safe to say that in the area of theology proper Moltmann has enjoyed a similar reputation. Any modern treatment of divine (im)passibility has to consider Moltmann, specifically in *The Crucified God* and *The Trinity and the Kingdom*. That many today speak of God's suffering without any conceptual or linguistic difficulty is due in large part to Moltmann and the favorable way he has been read by the academy along these lines. For these reasons, this chapter will deal exclusively with Moltmann's legacy regarding the issue of (im)passibility, for no single theological voice has done more to shape the current debate.

Key to Moltmann's argument is that God's passibility is integral to the doctrine of God, specifically the doctrine of the triune God. When one considers the doctrine of God in light of the death of Jesus, there is no question for Moltmann: Suffering is part of the very nature of God. He sees Calvary as a trinitarian moment in which God shows his very love for the world by the way he suffers for it. Suffering and trinitarianism thus become inextricably linked.

Obviously, Moltmann's depiction presents a number of difficulties for the task of retrieving the notion of divine impassibility. Certainly, Moltmann's theological vision has offered a number of possibilities that have too long been ignored or deemed impossible for the theological task, but in the case of Moltmann one sees also the most prominent example of how far the pendulum has swung in favor of divine passibility within the contemporary theological scene. Therefore, the task at hand is to show how trinitarianism does not singularly imply divine passibility but rather requires something akin to an impassibilist account in order to make the articulation vibrantly theological.

A.1. Theology as Biography

Before proceeding to conceptual matters, it is important to realize that for Moltmann the theme of a "suffering God" is not simply an intellectual option; rather, it is a matter of spiritual life or death. Moltmann came to faith as a POW during the Second World War, and it was during his imprisonment in Scotland that he began a spiritual journey that took him to unanticipated places, especially given his secular upbringing. Shortly before his imprisonment, the "God-question" first struck him after he witnessed a friend die from a bomb explosion. In captivity, the question continued to loom, and in those moments as a POW, he came to find "that comfort in the Christ who in his passion became [his] brother in need, and through his resurrection from the dead awakened [him] too to a living hope".[3] What Moltmann found was key to his

---

[3] Moltmann, *Experiences in Theology* (trans. M. Kohl; Minneapolis: Fortress, 2000), p. 4. For a more extensive account of Moltmann's spiritual journey, see his recently released autobiography *A Broad Place: An Autobiography* (trans. M. Kohl; Minneapolis: Fortress, 2008).

survival in the aftermath of the war: "And in this collapse [I] found a new hope in the Christian faith, which brought me not only spiritual but also (I think) physical survival, because it rescued me from despair and from giving up. I returned to Germany a Christian and with the new 'individual approach' to study theology, in order to understand that power of hope to which I owed my life."[4]

From such a testimony, it is easy to see why the theme of a "suffering God" and its implications for divine impassibility retain such a vital place in Moltmann's thought: He came to faith largely because of the hope that he found in Jesus' solidarity with him in his despair as a POW. One cannot argue with the power of such an account and its resulting convictions. As Moltmann continued to develop his theological program, time and time again he would return to the importance of such imagery, and after making a name for himself with *Theology of Hope*,[5] it is no wonder he began his formal reflections upon the doctrine of God via a text titled *The Crucified God*. God crucified is for Moltmann the heart of the gospel.[6]

A.2. Moving from the "Whole of Theology" to a "Contribution"

Moltmann's first three works are oftentimes considered his "trilogy", and apparently Moltmann does not seem to disagree. Although they succeeded one another, many find it difficult to see a general continuity among *Theology of Hope*, *The Crucified God*, and *The Church in the Power of the Spirit*.[7] Part of the difficulty seems to be that Moltmann considered them a trilogy of sorts only

---

[4] Moltmann, *History and the Triune God* (trans. J. Bowden; New York: Crossroad, 1992), p. 166; hereafter *HTG*. Interestingly, Moltmann uses the same imagery to describe his predicament in his autobiography that he uses to describe the crucified Jesus in *CG*. Moltmann remarks that the lament psalms, especially Psalm 39, were important to him, and when he began to read the gospel of Mark, especially the passion of Christ, the cry of dereliction was quite moving: "When I heard Jesus' death cry, 'My God, why have you forsaken me?' I felt growing within me the conviction: this is someone who understands you completely, who is with you in your cry to God and has felt the same forsakenness you are living in now. I began to understand the assailed, forsaken Christ because I knew that he understood me" (Moltmann, *A Broad Place*, p. 30).

[5] Moltmann, *Theology of Hope* (trans. J. W. Leitch; New York: Harper and Row, 1967); hereafter *TH*.

[6] For accounts of the events that led to the publication of *CG*, see Moltmann, *HTG*, pp. 176-78 and J. L. Wakefield, "Introduction" in *Jürgen Moltmann: A Research Bibliography* (Langham, MD: Scarecrow, 2002), pp. 14-17.

[7] Moltmann, *The Church in the Power of the Spirit* (trans. M. Kohl; Minneapolis: Fortress, 1993).

post factum.[8] Rather than a thematic continuity,[9] however, these texts do have an affinity with one another largely on the grounds of method. Moltmann remarks at one point: "The theological method which I used in the three books can be described as: *the whole of theology in one focal point*."[10] In other words, given Moltmann's selected theme, his goal was to narrate "the whole of theology" under an overarching motif. This elected method for theological reflection largely explains the perceived disparity among the three works. Such a way of proceeding obviously creates a certain imbalance, largely because each theme highlights different theological strata. The burden of making "the whole of theology" fit within a single "focal point" resulted in difficulties for readers of Moltmann.

Having concluded the "trilogy", Moltmann proceeded in his next major division of works with a different theological methodology. The less ambitious way of describing this second way is through the term "contributions", which Moltmann describes in the following way:

> In calling them contributions I want to indicate that I do not plan a total system or a dogmatics of pure and universal doctrine. This is not a renunciation on my part, but an expression of my involvement in the wider dialogue complexes of Christian theology. It is also meant to express a realistic estimation of the limitations of my own standpoint and personal context and the way in which it is conditioned. I am not claiming to say everything or depict the whole of Christian theology. Rather, with these books, as a whole, I seek to be part of the wider community of theology to which I want to make a contribution.[11]

The theme of a "suffering God" spans both sections of Moltmann's major works: *CG*, his first major work to treat of the doctrine of God, and *TK*, the first of his many "contributions", span the divide between his early and late periods. Along with *HTG*, these texts represent Moltmann's early and most sustained effort for advocating divine passibility and its corollary dismissal of divine

---

[8] Moltmann remarks, "Though I had not planned it from the start, in retrospect I found that these three books belonged together. They have therefore been called a 'trilogy', and I have nothing against that" (*HTG*, p. 176).

[9] Moltmann does on occasion wish to stress the interrelationship between *TH* and *CG*, as when he states, "After the grounding of Christian eschatology in the resurrection of the crucified Christ, the other side also had to be emphasized: the cross of the Risen Christ" (J. Moltmann [ed], *How I Have Changed* [Harrisburg, PA: Trinity Press International, 1997], p. 18). Broadly speaking, however, the continuities within the "trilogy" are difficult to detect, especially when one includes *The Church in the Power of the Spirit*.

[10] Foreword to R. Bauckham, *Moltmann: Messianic Theology in the Making* (Basingstoke: Marshall Pickering, 1987), p. ix. For the most complete introduction to Moltmann, see Bauckham's, *The Theology of Jürgen Moltmann* (Edinburgh: T & T Clark, 1995).

[11] Moltmann, *HTG*, pp. 180-81.

impassibility. For this reason, these works will form the basis for the rest of the chapter's engagement with Moltmann.

B. Moltmann's Vision of the Crucified God

B.1. The Instantiating Dilemma in CG

Moltmann attempts something slightly more nuanced in *CG* than he does in the other two works of the "trilogy", for in *CG* Moltmann dares to say that he is dealing with the criterion of all Christian theology: the crucified Christ.[12] This norm is pivotal in that the church perpetually faces crises of its own identity and relevance, crises that push the church to be either resigned or irrelevant.[13] In Moltmann's estimation, the church embodies these extremes when it fails to be challenged and criticized by its foundation and center, the Son of God crucified; therefore, the significance of a crucified God, as stated in a theology of the cross, is not for Moltmann simply another model or metaphor for engaging in theological reflection; instead, it is the *principal means* by which the church can be a vital and effective presence in the midst of a fallen, antagonistic, and pluralistic world.[14]

Interestingly, Moltmann begins with the crisis of relevance before engaging the crisis of identity, a sign perhaps of Moltmann's broader methodological concerns and an indicator of where he will arrive regarding the fate of impassibility. He paints a picture of a church in modern society that has lost its relevance with regard to the vast changes that have occurred in post-World War II society. The church has come to have a "lack of contact and blindness to reality", thereby forcing many to leave the church to pursue other endeavors in which "they feel . . . they can contribute more to solving the conflicts of [European] fragmented society."[15] In portraying the matter in this way, Moltmann implies that this loss of "credibility" applies to the European

---

[12] "There is an inner criterion of all theology, and of every church which claims to be Christian, and this criterion goes far beyond all political, ideological and psychological criticism from outside. It is the crucified Christ himself" (Moltmann, *CG*, p. 2). Given such general claims, Moltmann's perspective in *CG* will occasionally be termed "staurocentric" in this chapter.

[13] Moltmann labels this situation the "identity-involvement dilemma" (*CG*, p. 7). The crises are complementary: "The more theology and the church attempt to become relevant to the problems of the present day, the more deeply they are drawn into the crisis of their own Christian identity. The more they attempt to assert their identity in traditional dogmas, rights and moral notions, the more irrelevant and unbelievable they become" (*CG*, p. 7).

[14] Given the status of theology in a post-Christian Europe, Moltmann asserts: "It is clear that theology can no longer find a permanent basis in the general thinking, feeling and action of contemporary society" (*CG*, p. 10).

[15] Moltmann, *CG*, p. 8.

context, as seen in the examples he offers in defense of his analysis. Such provinciality, although necessary in contextualizing Moltmann, need not detract from his larger concern, namely that the church must maintain a vital witness that is contemporaneous with the *Sitz im Leben* in which it finds itself.

The crisis of identity is intimately tied with the crisis of relevance, for "the question of relevance arises only where identity is a matter of experience and belief".[16] Far too often, Christians have failed to realize the extent of the implications of serving a God who bore the death of a criminal; instead, Christians have associated their faith with creeds, traditional loyalties, and other elements. Such conditions have naturally led to a precarious understanding of what it means to be Christian.

Moltmann's alternative to this situation is one that requires Christians to reconsider one of their more prominent symbols: "Christian identity can be understood only as an act of identification with the crucified, to the extent to which one has accepted the proclamation that in him God has identified himself with the godless and those abandoned by God, to whom one belongs oneself."[17] With this programmatic statement, Moltmann attempts to address these dual crises of identity and relevance: Christian identity revolves around God's solidarity with the lost, and its relevance stems from that solidarity being available to the rest of suffering and dying humanity.[18]

Moltmann's understanding of a theology of the cross questions the corruption of the gospel, the complicity of the church with the oppressive structures of society, and the domestication of the fact that Christians worship a crucified God. The latter concern in particular leads Moltmann to reverse the question normally associated with the cross; in Moltmann's own words, "Instead of asking just *what God means for us human beings* in the cross of Christ, I asked too *what this human cross of Christ means for God*."[19] Such a reversal creates many possibilities for Moltmann, ones that he believes have been neglected in Christian theology for too long. With a sense of self-conscious grandeur, Moltmann states that this view represents a "revolution in

---

[16] Moltmann, *CG*, p. 18.

[17] Moltmann, *CG*, p. 19.

[18] The term "solidarity" (*Solidarität*) is one that Moltmann uses quite extensively without acknowledging its origin, the extent of its value, or the limits of its applicability. It is a term used to relate how God interacts with humanity in light of the cross as well as one that applies to the way Christians can engage in "orthopraxy" in light of the crucified Christ; as Moltmann states, "Christian identification with the crucified Christ means solidarity with the sufferings of the poor and the misery both of the oppressed and the oppressors" (*CG*, p. 25). The term implies a sense of active participation with those undergoing suffering: "To the extent that men in misery feel [Jesus'] solidarity with them, their solidarity with his sufferings brings them out of their situation" (*CG*, p. 51). These statements and a few others are all that the reader has available for substantiating the term.

[19] Moltmann, *CG*, p. x.

the concept of God".[20] In brief, Moltmann sees the drama between the Father and the Son, exemplified in particular through the cry of dereliction, as a moment in which God incorporates godforsakenness (and therefore "suffering"[21]) into his very being. The significance of this moment is pivotal for Moltmann, for he states that "all Christian theology and all Christian life is basically an answer to the question which Jesus asked as he died".[22] In conceiving of the cross in this manner, as an event "in God", Moltmann believes he provides a response to those who would seek for an account of human suffering in light of the Christian belief in a merciful and loving God.

Not surprisingly, of all the themes that *CG* encompasses, perhaps the most commonly referenced is the notion of a "suffering God". Moltmann's account is often cited and used as a Christian response to those who have become dissatisfied with traditional Christian answers to questions relating to theodicy and protest atheism. As outlined briefly above, *The Crucified God* has garnered significant attention in large part because of Moltmann's portrayal of a God who is relational, in solidarity with the suffering and the oppressed, and capable of sharing in the sufferings of his creatures. Other alternatives, including the portrayal of God in "classical theism" as impassible, immutable, and so forth, are generally considered to falter in light of Moltmann's more appealing alternative.

Given Moltmann's commitment to speaking of a God who suffers because of the way he interprets Christ's cross, it comes as no surprise that Moltmann conceives of divine impassibility as being an unhelpful and unnecessary tenet of God-talk. For Moltmann, divine impassibility is an axiom of philosophical theology that merits abandonment. In fact, he believes that the two portrayals – his and the one normally associated with "classical theism" – are mutually exclusive: "If this concept of God [in classical theism] is applied to Christ's death on the cross, the cross *must* be 'evacuated' of deity, for by definition God cannot suffer and die."[23] Interestingly, Moltmann finds that the theology of the cross and the doctrine of the Trinity were developments in the early church that attempted to "break the spell of the old philosophical concept of God".[24]

Moltmann leaves no room for negotiation along these lines. Finding the tradition excessively wedded to the Hellenistic notion of *apatheia*, he argues that such a view is unfaithful to other important beliefs about the godhead, including the capacity to love. Moltmann has continued to narrate the tradition

---

[20] Moltmann, *CG*, p. 201.

[21] As with many terms in Moltmann's text in particular and in discussions regarding the "rise of a new theism" in general, the term "suffering" is used repeatedly and yet remains elusive and unclear. These difficulties have already been considered in this study, and unfortunately, Moltmann does not engage in the kind of clarification necessary for such a vital term.

[22] Moltmann, *CG*, p. 4.

[23] Moltmann, *CG*, p. 214.

[24] Moltmann, *CG*, p. 215.

in this way and to speak about the untenable nature of God's impassibility,[25] all the while receiving critical support for doing so.

B.2. The Broad Features of CG

Given that Moltmann begins to engage the "God question" from *CG* on, one must take into account what Moltmann says about the divine nature during this early period of his career. One can detect a number of themes in *CG* – the cross as the center of Christian theology, the communal/relational aspects of the Trinity, and the undeterred passion of God – that have become significant for his theological project over the years.

Although Chapter 6 of *CG* garners most of the scholarly attention, one cannot simply look at this chapter and divorce it from the rest of the book. Looking at the text as a whole, one can see that Chapters 1 and 2 stand in closer connection to general themes concerning the doctrine of God than do Chapters 3 through 5 since the latter are specifically christological in nature. In Chapter 1, "The Identity and Relevance of Faith", Moltmann sets out the two crises of the church alluded to above. Moltmann's staurocentrism is crucial within his proposed alternatives for ameliorating the condition of the church: "Christian identity can be understood only as an act of identification with the crucified Christ, to the extent to which one has accepted the proclamation that in him God has identified himself with the godless and those abandoned by God, to whom one belongs oneself."[26] If the church has lost its identity, it is because it has lost sight of the significance of Christ's cross, a development in large part due to how unsettling and horrendous the cross really is.

Moltmann notes that the cross "resists interpretation" (a phrase that forms the title of the second chapter) in that it affirms many things that we least associate with the godhead, including suffering, marginalization, and vulnerability. This function proves to be the contemporary relevance of the cross, for its role within theology is not only as its foundation or center but also as its criterion and criticism.[27] In light of the cross's function in unsettling believers from their godlessness, Moltmann remarks that "it is necessary for Christian faith first of all to abandon the traditional theories of salvation which have made the way the cross is spoken of in Christianity a mere habit".[28] The point here is that people have tried to sidestep or avoid the implications of the

---

[25] Moltmann speaks at greater length about these issues in *TK*, Chapter 2.

[26] Moltmann, *CG*, p. 19.

[27] As a running argument throughout the text, this theme was appropriately chosen for the subtitle of *CG*, which is "the cross of Christ as the foundation and criticism of Christian theology".

[28] Moltmann, *CG*, p. 33. Similarly, "But the more the church of the crucified Christ became the prevailing religion of society, and set about satisfying the personal and public needs of this society, the more it left the cross behind it, and gilded the cross with the expectations and ideas of salvation" (*CG*, p. 41).

cross for daily life by "adding roses to it" in the hopes that it would be more acceptable to human accounts of respectability and propriety[29] – tendencies that the cross itself, when observed on its own terms, challenges and questions.

The role of the cross in Moltmann's work is crucial for what he believes to be the "conceptual revolution" he is introducing to the doctrine of God. Rather than focusing on the soteriological benefits of the cross and resurrection, he comes to ask what the cross means for God himself. Essentially, Moltmann is introducing conflict or negativity within the godhead via the "God against God" motif he detects in the drama of the crucifixion.[30] One sees in primitive form how Moltmann answers this problematic and how a quasi-Hegelian influence can be detected through his use of 1) certain biblical passages, especially from the Pauline *corpus* (especially 2 Corinthians 5:19-21, in which God is depicted to be "in Christ") and 2) the cry of dereliction as found in Mark and Matthew. "God not only acted in the crucifixion of Jesus or sorrowfully allowed it to happen", Moltmann writes, "but was himself active *with his own being* in the dying Jesus and suffered with him."[31] Beyond such broad claims, however, the matter does not receive any more attention until Chapter 6, a section that must now be considered because it is here that Moltmann attempts to defend these prior claims in light of how he narrates the contemporary experience of God.

B.3. The Crucified God, Chapter 6: Contributing Frameworks

Chapter 6 of *CG* stands in significant tension with the rest of the work because of its swift and multifaceted structure, a feature that complicates the hermeneutical task. Certainly, the general theme of the interrelationship between the cross and the Trinity is detectable, but Moltmann moves from one issue to another, whether it be Luther's *theologia crucis* or Calvinist christology, the ancient tradition of *apatheia* or protest atheism. Given this set

---

[29] The reference here is to Luther's coat of arms, which received quite a bit of attention during modern, humanist Germany when the cross was considered as a specific topic. Moltmann quotes a relevant passage from Goethe: "'There the cross stands, thickly wreathed in roses. Who put the roses on the cross? The wreath grows bigger, so that on every side the harsh cross is surrounded by gentleness'" (*CG*, p. 35).

[30] Moltmann makes a number of statements with these overtones, such as: "If, abandoned by his God and Father, he was raised through the 'glory of the Father', then eschatological faith in the cross of Jesus Christ must acknowledge the theological trial (*Prozeß*) between God and God. The cross of the Son divides God from God to the utmost degree of enmity and distinction" (*CG*, p. 152).

[31] Moltmann, *CG*, p. 190 (emphases mine). The result of God's involvement with his very being strikes a note that is at odds with other themes in *CG*: "[God] is acting in himself in this manner of suffering and dying in order to open up in himself life and freedom for sinners" (*CG*, p. 192). Interestingly, despite Moltmann's explicit statements to the contrary, soteriology occasionally makes its way into his reflections when he has to speak of the rationale or *telos* of the crucifixion.

of circumstances, one must approach Chapter 6 with a bit of caution in that final conclusions cannot be reached until one considers its entirety (and even doing so undoubtedly will leave the reader perplexed on a number of points).

B.3.a. MOLTMANN'S STAUROCENTRISM

One of the prominent themes of *CG*'s Chapter 6 is Moltmann's staurocentrism. "The death of Jesus on the cross is the *centre* of all Christian theology."[32] General statements such as this one require justification, and because Luther is generally considered the first to advance a "theology of the cross", Moltmann does not hesitate to employ the backing of the Reformer in making such claims regarding the nature of Christian theology. Moltmann's staurocentrism makes considerable use of both Luther's *theologia crucis* as well as currents within modern theology in general (across both Protestant and Catholic lines) in order to offer suggestions for negotiating the precarious state of modern God-talk.

Luther never advanced a self-sustaining program entitled "the theology of the cross"; rather, the phrase emerged for the Reformer as he was attempting to make general theological claims in a presentation he had prepared for the triennial convention of the Augustinian order in Germany that was being held in Heidelberg in the year 1518.[33] Luther's presentation at the convention, usually titled the "Heidelberg Disputation of 1518", hints at a theological methodology[34] based upon a particular reading of the Apostle Paul. The central tenet of this method is that God reveals and declares himself *absconditus sub contrario*, i.e., "hidden under its contrary". For example, God's power would be shown in his weakness, his exaltation in his humiliation, and so on. Such dialectical claims require faith as a guide of discernment because Luther believed that we tend to pride ourselves with our intellectual capacities, especially when attempting to detect and understand the presence and work of God.

One finds this dialectical method in a number of theses within the Disputation, especially when Luther contrasts the "theologian of glory" with

---

[32] Moltmann, *CG*, p. 204. Moltmann is going one step further than M. Kähler's christological statement that he makes use of from time to time. The quotation is: "Without the cross there is no christology, nor is there any feature of christology which can escape justifying itself by the cross" (as quoted in *CG*, p. 114).

[33] The theme is used by Luther prior to the Heidelberg Disputation, but usually the matter is most often associated with it. For an extensive study of these other sources, see J. E. Vercruysse, "Luther's Theology of the Cross at the Time of the Heidelberg Disputation", *Gregorianum* 57.3 (1976), pp. 523-48.

[34] In contradistinction from earlier interpreters, W. von Loewenich defends in his classic study the notion that the implications of Luther's "theology of the cross" were not simply limited to a pre-Reformation period but rather constituted "a principle of Luther's entire theology" (*Luther's Theology of the Cross* [trans. H. J. A. Bouman; Minneapolis: Augsburg Publishing House, 1976], p. 13).

the "theologian of the cross". The first kind of theologian attempts to find God in works and in nature, all the while building systems and concepts, but such a person for Luther is not truly a theologian: "That person does not deserve to be called a theologian who looks upon the invisible things of God as though they were clearly perceptible in those things which have actually happened."[35] Luther is referring to the Scholastics among others who speculate about the existence of God on the basis of natural theologies that lend themselves to be considered human works or achievements. Contrary to these endeavors and to this kind of theologian, Luther cites the Pauline notion that "since, in the wisdom of God, the world did not know God through wisdom, God decided, through the foolishness of our proclamation, to save those who believe".[36] This perceived state of affairs as shared by the Apostle makes it quite clear to Luther that a true theologian, a theologian of the cross, finds God's revelation hidden in its opposite, searches and finds the "backside of God" in faith and can call something "what it actually is".[37]

Some have taken exception to the dialectical thinking of Luther in that it distinguishes a *Deus absconditus* and a *Deus revelatus*, leaving one wondering whether the revelation in question is truthful.[38] Luther scholars have noted that at times he pushes the dialectic to its limits, but all appear to agree that Luther maintained the veracity of revelation in spite of its indirect manifestation.[39] Since humans are infinite and sinful and therefore incapable of beholding the revelation of God in its glory,[40] the rationale for Luther's tendencies at this point is quite simple. Given these limits, Luther's dialectical reasoning helps put a check to human concepts about God, especially with regard to analogical language.[41] The principle applies to Luther himself in that his theopaschitism can be qualified by a transcendence that is preserved by the notion of God's

---

[35] Luther, Thesis 19, "Heidelberg Disputation", *LW*, XXXI, p. 40.

[36] 1 Cor. 1:21.

[37] Luther, Thesis 21, "Heidelberg Disputation", *LW*, XXXI, p. 40.

[38] Moltmann cites Barth as a case in point. Most likely the reference is to such statements as found in § 27 of *CD*, II/1.

[39] A. E. McGrath notes: "The cross does indeed reveal God – but that revelation is of the *posteriora Dei*. In that it is the *posteriora Dei* which are made visible, this revelation of God must be regarded as an indirect revelation – but a genuine revelation nonetheless" (*Luther's Theology of the Cross* [Grand Rapids: Baker, 1990], p. 149). McGrath also considers the extreme tendencies of Luther in pushing the dialectic (pp. 165-67).

[40] D. C. Steinmetz, *Luther in Context* (2nd ed; Grand Rapids: Baker, 2002), p. 25.

[41] "Underlying the *theologia crucis* and the discovery of the 'righteousness of God' is a radical critique of the analogical nature of theological language" (McGrath, *Luther's Theology of the Cross*, p. 158). In an admittedly anachronistic move, McGrath believes Luther predates the dialectical theologians of the twentieth century on this score, but the point is taken in that one can find such statements as *Crux probat omnia* within the Lutheran *corpus* (p. 159).

hiddenness.[42] These claims form an inner logic in that it is important for Luther to maintain God's transcendence since the soteriological implications of Christ's cross are crucial for all that Luther wants to claim about it.[43]

These general points of Luther's *theologia crucis* have been used by theologians in the modern period in order to espouse various "theologies of the cross" that are in many cases only nominally related to Luther. These efforts have been sufficiently intertwined to merit the nomenclature of the *Kreuzestheologie* movement within German theology.[44] This movement defies ecumenical boundaries in that both Protestants and Catholics have come to reconsider the implications of the cross for theology.[45] Moltmann places himself within this trajectory as he finds the cross to be the critical tool for negotiating the two instantiating crises of *CG*. Moltmann's "theology of the cross", however, is considerably different from Luther's program as well as from past proposals within the *Kreuzestheologie* movement. Moltmann's dependence upon these figures is significant, but such indebtedness does not prohibit him from granting a certain nuance to his own project.

Rather than delineating how Moltmann distinguishes himself from other figures who espouse modern "theologies of the cross", one should note the differences between Luther and Moltmann since the assumption by many has been that Moltmann has extended Luther's claims within the modern context. Although such a general claim is not warranted, it is true that both theologians share a number of apparent similarities, including a focus on revelation and the primacy of Christ's cross for Christian reflection and for theological statements. As proof of these similarities, the following quotation from Moltmann could easily be applied to Luther: "To know God in the cross of Christ is a crucifying form of knowledge, because it shatters everything to which a man can hold and on which he can build, both his works and his knowledge of reality, and precisely in so doing sets him free".[46] One detects in this statement a significant influence from the theses of the Heidelberg Disputation.

---

[42] Steinmetz makes the move of relating the principle of God's transcendence with the *Deus absconditus* (see *Luther in Context*, p. 24).

[43] For an extended survey of Luther's theology of the cross in relation to soteriology, see D. Ngien, *The Suffering of God according to Martin Luther's "Theologia Crucis"* (Eugene, OR: Wipf and Stock, 2001), Chapter Four. Although Ngien's work helpfully engages the primary resources, on certain issues he makes Luther's account more amenable to the spirit of Moltmann's work in *CG* than is warranted, as can be seen by his principal thesis that "the suffering of God has an 'ontological status' in Luther's *theologia crucis*" (p. 175).

[44] P. Fiddes believes that an ecumenical conference in Grafrath in October of 1972 represents a crucial moment when the movement took off as a recurrent theme within modern theology (*The Creative Suffering of God* [Oxford: Clarendon, 1988], p. 12, n. 36).

[45] Among the many figures Moltmann mentions in this regard, some of the more significant are Schlatter, Althaus, Jüngel, Küng, Mühlen, Rahner, and von Balthasar.

[46] Moltmann, *CG*, p. 212.

Despite these and other similarities, important differences exist between the two theologians, differences that are both explicit and implicit within Moltmann's appropriation of the Reformer's thought. Although Luther is important for Moltmann on a number of points, the Tübingen scholar makes a general critique regarding the German Reformer that he extends to other theologians as well, namely that Luther was insufficiently trinitarian in his theopaschitism: "[Luther's] christology was formed in terms of incarnation and the theology of the cross, but not always in trinitarian terms."[47] In other words, Luther falls under Moltmann's critique, much as Barth does, for not being "consistent" with his use of the term "God".[48] Rather than finding clear demarcations for the roles of the Father and the Son, one finds in Luther "paradoxical distinctions between God and God: between the God who crucifies and the crucified God; the God who is dead and yet is not dead; between the manifest God in Christ and the hidden God above and beyond Christ".[49] Not only does this practice of Luther point to a deficiency of a christologically devised trinitarianism, but it also implicates the Reformer in a certain unitary account of the godhead, a kind of monotheism that Moltmann attempts to discount at a number of places.

Moltmann also finds problematic a couple of other themes within Luther. The *Deus absconditus/Deus revelatus* terminology falls in line with the critiques he levels at the economic/immanent Trinity: both sets of distinctions create a barrier between what has been revealed in Christ and what is thought to be the unapproachable "heavenly mysteries". Moltmann explicitly states he wants to obliterate those categories that capture the mind in metaphysical riddles in favor of the trinitarian event of the cross. He also chooses not to emphasize sufficiently the case that for Luther "the theology of the cross presupposes the doctrine of universal sinfulness".[50] With the category of sin, naturally one is also faced with soteriology, and the Tübingen scholar wishes to sidestep this part of the crucifixion as much as he can in order to offer a more compelling account of the significance of the cross for the doctrine of God.

Other issues could be raised to show how Moltmann differs from Luther and employs him for specific purposes,[51] but the point is clear: Moltmann appropriates the Reformer when the latter is helpful in making a claim or judgment about the theological task. What Moltmann fails to appreciate is that Luther's *theologia crucis*, which emphasizes a "knowledge of God in the suffering and death of Christ [that] takes this perverse situation of man

---

[47] Moltmann, *CG*, p. 235.

[48] Interestingly, Moltmann does not seem to mind the "inconsistency" of language when choosing the title of his own book, for Luther used the phrase "the crucified God" in his own writings, most notably in his lectures on Psalms. See Luther, *LW*, XIV, p. 105.

[49] Moltmann, *CG*, p. 235.

[50] J. G. Strelan, "Theologia Crucis, Theologia Gloriae: A Study in Opposing Theologies", *Lutheran Theological Journal* 23.3 (1989), p. 103.

[51] For a more in-depth comparison, see B. F. Eckardt, Jr., "Luther and Moltmann: The Theology of the Cross", *Concordia Theological Quarterly* 49.1 (1985), pp. 19-28.

seriously", *can do so only because* it actively includes the categories of sin and redemption.[52] In other words the "condition and the cure" are very much at the forefront of Luther's mind when elaborating these theses for theological epistemology, but such a soteriological context lacks a similar counterpart within Moltmann's *CG*.[53]

B.3.b. THE HEGEL FACTOR

As other proponents of the *Kreuzestheologie* movement have done, Moltmann not only makes use of Luther's theology of the cross but also of quasi-Hegelian ontological claims.[54] Many have remarked that the "Hegelian" character of Moltmann's work is quite pronounced,[55] but these observations vary in their judgments and estimations of this factor. Some speak of the indebtedness in deriding terms, as when Fiddes states that Moltmann's Hegelianism is perhaps one of the more problematic characteristics of *CG*.[56]

Of course, quasi-Hegelian themes can be found not only in Moltmann but also among other prominent theologians as well since the tendency within the modern theological academy is toward "dynamic ontological schemes" rather than the classical or "static" models of past tendencies. Although most of these figures would not characterize themselves as "Hegelians", critics of their work often revert to this label because it is a convenient way of stating that these theologians are moving beyond the traditional, self-contained notions of "being" within Hellenistic metaphysics to more "open" systems that include change, dialectical reasoning, sublation, and movement.

Such is the case with Moltmann because in a strict sense he is not a

---

[52] G. O. Forde stresses the point when in his book he begins by stating, "The cross is in the first instance God's attack on human sin" (*On Being a Theologian of the Cross* [Grand Rapids: Eerdmans, 1997], p. 1).

[53] Of Moltmann's many articles that predated in substance and form the arguments of *CG*, one in particular, namely the essay, "The Theology of the Cross Today" in Moltmann's *The Future of Creation* (trans. M. Kohl; Philadelphia: Fortress, 1979), does make some use of the category of sin; nevertheless, one is hard-pressed to find a similar gesture in the text of *CG*. Given the greater impact *CG* has had in comparison to a collection of essays like *The Future of Creation*, such an omission is lamentable.

[54] Fiddes documents this interrelationship between Luther and Hegel, stating that Hegel is both criticized and appropriated within this theological movement along the lines of "God's encounter with nothingness and death in the midst of the worldly sphere" (*The Creative Suffering of God*, p. 13).

[55] W. McWilliams characterizes Hegel's influence as having a "powerful impact on Moltmann" (*The Passion of God* [Macon, GA: Mercer University Press, 1985], p. 41).

[56] Fiddes, *The Creative Suffering of God*, p. 13. Less generous are the remarks of Hart when he states that "a far more incautious and vulgar 'Hegelianism' [is] prodigally displayed in the loose, rhapsodic, paraenetic discourse of Jürgen Moltmann, with all its chaotic sentimentalism" (Hart, "No Shadow of Turning", p. 189).

Hegelian,[57] yet themes that are popularly associated with the 19th-century philosopher are detectable within *CG* and beyond. One of the more recurrent themes can be termed the "Hegelian dialectical method of determinate negation",[58] the "process whereby a new form not only negates the old but also preserves and elevates the old form in itself", thereby resulting in a unity between itself and its opposite.[59] One detects this understanding within Moltmann's concept of God, for he can speak of the crucifixion as an absorption of negativity or "godforsakenness"[60] into the life of God; Jesus' death is a death "in" God where God can be said to be constituted by this event in such a way that he now exhibits a history with the world because he has absorbed the world's godlessness and negativity as well as death itself.[61]

Given this dynamism, Moltmann can speak of God as a "process"[62] or an "event"[63] from time to time. Such language is available to Moltmann because of prior ontological moves he has offered in *Theology of Hope*. Although it is difficult to say that Moltmann has an ontology *per se*, he does offer suggestions that point to what a "Moltmannian ontology" could be,[64] and those can be found in the eschatological musings of his first major work. Moltmann speaks of God as coming from the future and argues that his "potentiality" in the future is the foundation for his "actuality" in the present. Naturally, this move

---

[57] This assessment is found in J. A. Miller, *The Eschatological Ontology of Jürgen Moltmann* (PhD thesis, Emory University, 1972). Given the date of writing, Miller only treats of *Theology of Hope* when making his assessment, but given the way he argues for Moltmann not being a Hegelian, it is hard to imagine anybody who would fit the designation, for he believes that, because Moltmann disagrees on only a few points with Hegel, he is not a "Hegelian" in a strict sense. Given both *TH* and *CG*, it is hard not to think of Moltmann as at least quasi-Hegelian.

[58] I am here using the phrasing of M. R. Ott, *Max Horkheimer's Critical Theory of Religion* (Lanham, MD: University Press of America, 2001), p. 11. Given that Moltmann and Horkheimer appear to use Hegelian themes in similar ways, it seems fitting to borrow the phrase from this source.

[59] Ott, *Max Horkheimer*, p. 12.

[60] The repeated use of the term "godforsakenness" rather than "sin" is duly noted given that the former was preferred by Hegel.

[61] In elaborating this current in light of the relation of the Father and the Son, Moltmann chooses to highlight the term *paradidonai* of the New Testament. This moment is one of the few places he employs Scripture in Chapter 6 (unlike *CG*'s other chapters); however, in this example one sees Moltmann's pattern of appropriating a resource for his strategic advantage: in this case, using a biblical term to fortify his speculative suggestions.

[62] Although Moltmann is prone to quote Whitehead from time to time (e.g., *CG*, pp. 250 and 255), the use of the word "process" should not lead readers to assume more than a superficial relationship between Moltmann and process thought. An extended comparison between the two can be found in O'Donnell's *Trinity and Temporality*.

[63] Moltmann, *CG*, p. 247.

[64] Miller is inclined to say that Moltmann has offered a "foundation" for an ontology but that it is "underdeveloped" in *TH* (*Eschatological Ontology of Jürgen Moltman*, p. 299).

contradicts past metaphysical tendencies that operated with the assumption that if something were to have potentiality it would first have to be actual.

Moltmann believes that he can look past these traditional ontological frameworks because of Hegel's "speculative Good Friday", a theme that Moltmann mentions both in *TH* and *CG*. The reference, traceable to the "Conclusion" of Hegel's *Faith and Knowledge*,[65] is opposed to the historic Good Friday and is used metaphorically by Hegel to denote the loss of meaning associated with Enlightenment and Romantic approaches to alienation and the search for human freedom. He spoke of the failure of these projects as "the experience of the absence of God", which led him to parallel his experience and Jesus' experience of godforsakenness during the crucifixion.[66] M. D. Meeks summarizes the matter when he states: "Hegel attempted to interpret the modern experience of the absence of God in terms of the historical Good Friday of the godforsakenness of Jesus",[67] thereby leading to the phrase "speculative Good Friday".

When Moltmann employs the phrase in *CG*, he is pointing to the need to move past one's individual appropriation of the cross in order that one may consider "the significance of the death of God on Christ's cross for the universal death of God today".[68] In other words, Moltmann is trying to move beyond existentialist interpretations of the cross to locate the cross's significance within universal history, a history which is interpenetrated with God's intervention from the future.

This last consideration brings to the forefront the notion that God is the subject of history rather than the object humans aspire to. This link is the way in which Moltmann can proceed to speak of how each person who suffers or dies is caught up within the "history" between the Father and the Son:

> The concrete "history of God" in the death of Jesus on the cross on Golgotha therefore contains within itself all the depths and abysses of human history and therefore can be understood as the history of history. All human history, however much it may be determined by guilt and death, is taken up into this "history of God", i.e. into the Trinity, and integrated into the future of the "history of God". There is no suffering which in this history of God is not God's suffering; no death which has not been God's death in the history of Golgotha.[69]

Passages such as this one amplify what Moltmann means when he uses the term "solidarity" as stemming forth from what Jesus did on the cross. Simply

---

[65] G. W. F. Hegel, *Faith and Knowledge* (trans. W. Cerf and H. S. Harris; Albany, NY: State University of New York Press, 1977), p. 191.

[66] M. D. Meeks, *Origins of the Theology of Hope* (Philadelphia: Fortress, 1974), pp. 35-36.

[67] Meeks, *Origins of the Theology of Hope*, p. 36.

[68] Moltmann, *CG*, p. 217.

[69] Moltmann, *CG*, p. 246.

put, love killed death through the "death of God", and the "negation of negation" occurred: "As the God-man, in his passion, Jesus sustained the contradiction between life and death, identity and difference, and thus achieved reconciliation . . . . God has made this death part of his life, which is called love and reconciliation."[70] Because of this act, Moltmann believes that "we participate in the trinitarian process of God's history".[71] The warrant for these claims stems from parallel moves in Hegel's own project; as Meeks points out: "Only if all of reality is negated can the self-contradiction of God in the dialectic of God's self-revelation in cross and resurrection be related to present reality. God is related to reality by his contradiction of the *nihil*, the power of death, to which all reality is subjected."[72]

In sum, Hegel provides the conceptual impetus for Moltmann's description of how God incorporates the world (and in this particular setting, the world's suffering) through the crucifixion and of how in doing so he suffers himself as well. Although not a strict "Hegelian" by any means, Moltmann certainly narrates what is at stake at the crucifixion in distinctive ways, which betrays some of the guiding ontological steps he finds promising. Before moving to consider other consequences of Moltmann's conceptual apparatus, at least one more realm of contention is worth surveying, namely, the agonistic and yet "familial" relationship between what Moltmann terms "classical theism" and "protest atheism".

B.3.c. CLASSICAL THEISM VS. PROTEST ATHEISM

Although the cross points the way forward for Christian identity, it is important to remember that in his duality Moltmann treats first the crisis of relevance, perhaps indicating the priority he places on the need for modern theology to say something of value to "contemporary man". In order for this goal to be successful, one must include in one's deliberations a reading of the contemporary situation. For Moltmann, this environment can be characterized by the interplay between "classical theism" and "protest atheism".

As noted earlier in this study, "classical theism" is a questionable phrase, partly because its perceived referent can be a number of different entities – natural theology, philosophical theism, or Hellenistic metaphysics – the linchpin being that they are inductive, speculative, metaphysical constructs, or

---

[70] Moltmann, *CG*, p. 254.

[71] Moltmann, *CG*, p. 255. Exactly who "we" refers to is a bit problematic. Given the universalist claims he is making, it is plausible to think that the plural pronoun applies to those who would be willing to claim this notion, but such a move questions the boundaries between church and society that Moltmann sometimes blurs when speaking of the church's openness to the future.

[72] Meeks, *Origins of the Theology of Hope*, p. 36.

"*theologia gloriae* from below".[73] Moltmann further adds to the ambiguity by adding connotative layers of "monarchy", "monotheism", and "simple concept of God" to these intertwined referents. While employing the "monarchical" designation, Moltmann has added political ramifications to his doctrine of God, some of which are directly related to his trinitarianism of "free and equal persons" within the godhead. His arguments against "monotheism", although more fully developed in later writings,[74] also rely upon a trinitarian self-differentiation that directly counters what he calls a "simple concept of God".

When speaking of a "simple concept of God", Moltmann does not mean the notion of divine simplicity; rather, he intends the undifferentiated employment of the term "God" to refer to a number of doctrinal matters when such usage can only lead to paradoxical statements such as: "What happened on the cross was an event between God and God" and "God died the death of the godless on the cross and yet did not die. God is dead and yet is not dead."[75] The issue has manifested itself already in this survey with Luther, but Moltmann also levels the criticism against Barth's project in *Church Dogmatics*. For all the praises Moltmann has for his fellow Reformed theologian, in *CG* he demonstrates that, in contrast to his prior opinion, theology could continue after Barth, and this example proves the case: Moltmann believes that Barth is too *theo*logical in his staurocentric and theopaschite claims, as when he states that "[Barth] uses a simple concept of God which is not sufficiently developed in a trinitarian direction."[76]

Moltmann's rejection of this kind of God-talk is not just on the grounds of consistency, for he seems to believe that because the language is paradoxical, the tendency among moderns who speak in such a way has been to revert to a conventional "monotheism", which has viewed God in terms dictated by "classical theism". In spite of the important and valid claims by Luther, Barth, and others who take the cross to be a central moment for understanding the nature of God, in Moltmann's opinion these views fall short if they do not denounce once and for all what he perceives to be the ancient speech patterns of conceiving God as a unitary, distant, unmoved mover.

In light of these linguistic conventions bequeathed to modernity from Greek metaphysics via the Christian tradition, Moltmann believes "protest atheism" is more than legitimate in rejecting this view of God because of its detrimental consequences for modern-day belief. Within this context one can understand

---

[73] Moltmann, *CG*, p. 216. "Classical theism" has already been extensively considered in this study, and given the general contours .of his work, Moltmann squarely places himself within the camp of scholars who advocate the "Theory of Theology's Fall into Hellenistic Philosophy".

[74] This theme receives significant attention in *TK*. One of the stronger objections to Moltmann's reading and depiction of the status of monotheism within Christianity is R. Otto, "Moltmann and the Anti-Monotheism Movement", *International Journal of Systematic Theology* 3.5 (2001), pp. 293-308.

[75] Moltmann, *CG*, p. 244.

[76] Moltmann, *CG*, p. 203.

better Bloch's statement that he is an "atheist for God's sake", for the general sentiment here is that Christianity falls short in its relevance to the *Zeitgeist* if its answer to the "Where is God?" question posed by millions of tortured and suffering victims is the God of the impassibilist tradition. Moltmann too sides with atheism if one is speaking of "the gods of the world and world history, the Caesars and the political demigods who follow them"[77] – in other words, the god of traditional theisms.

The critique of "classical theism" by "protest atheism" gives the latter a level of legitimacy unobtainable by the former in Moltmann's view, for "protest atheism" takes the suffering of lived experience seriously and does not try to diminish or explain away its impact or dignity through "eternal riddles" or "metaphysical theories".[78] Although Moltmann finds protest atheism to have dangers as well (especially when a discounted divinity is replaced by a divinised humanity), it is quite obvious which position has Moltmann's final approval in this "sibling rivalry". Because protest atheism will not "devalue" it (even though such a rigid grasp of experienced reality is precisely what leads to its atheistic and nihilistic features), human suffering claims a certain worth or level of "righteousness" by calling to account God's own righteousness in the midst of human tragedy.[79] Therefore, "the theodicy question remains unresolved", "the experience of atrocity defies explanation", and "atheists and Christians exist together in a solidarity of suffering".[80] At this point, we find the re-conceptualized theodicy question of the modern condition, and Moltmann does not fail to add to its legitimacy by making Jesus' cry of dereliction the instantiation *par excellence* of such a moment of "godforsakenness".

What can be made of this clash between these related alternatives to the God-question where given a robust staurocenrism, the outcome of each is unsatisfactory? Although Moltmann gives the upper hand to protest atheism, he still wants a way out of his imposed predicament, and the way forward rests on a theme he finds in the thought of Horkheimer. The main premise of this suggestion rests on an existentialist "longing": "that the murderer should not triumph over his innocent victim".[81] Moltmann admittedly reads into Horkheimer's comments in that he believes this longing – a "longing for a

---

[77] Moltmann, *CG*, p. 195.

[78] "This question of suffering and revolt is not answered by any cosmological argument for the existence of God or any theism, but is rather provoked by both of these. If one argues back from the state of the world and the fact of its existence to cause, ground and principle, one can just as well speak of 'God' as of the devil" (Moltmann, *CG*, p. 221).

[79] G. Hunsinger has called Moltmann's project a form of "Christian atheism" in that it leaves the problematic issues within protest atheism's arguments unresolved and the standard articulation of the modernized theodicy question in place. See "The Crucified God and the Political Theology of Violence: A Critical Survey of Jürgen Moltmann's Recent Thought: I", *Heythrop Journal* 14.3 (1973), pp. 273-74.

[80] Hunsinger, "The Crucified God and the Political Theology of Violence", pp. 273-74.

[81] Moltmann, *CG*, p. 223, quoting Horkheimer in *Die Sehnsucht nach dem ganz Anderen* (Hamburg: Furche Verlag, 1970), p. 62.

wholly other" – is a "longing for God". Moltmann goes so far as to say that in Horkheimer one finds a "protesting faith which takes us beyond the crude opposition of theism and atheism".[82] This longing can neither be dismissed nor given up. The only alternative would be nihilism. And faced with this predicament, Moltmann pushes the boundaries of what the framework of "protest atheism" can accommodate for the gospel. What one is left with in Moltmann's account is a progression of arguments that suddenly is halted from its logical conclusions by what appears to be a phenomenological and idiosyncratically experiential notion of "longing" that is based on a secularist-Marxist "religious" sentiment and safeguard.[83] For all practical purposes, this response is Moltmann's formal "resolution" to the modern debates between "classical theism" and "protest atheism". Such circumstances bode well for his introduction of the material fulfillment of this longing, namely the crucified God: "With a trinitarian theology of the cross faith escapes the dispute between and the alternative of theism and atheism."[84]

B.3.d. CONCLUSION

Do all of these influences and themes constitute an integrated whole? At least in Moltmann's mind they do. The *potpourri* of Reformation thought, post-Enlightenment ontological patterns, modern protest atheism, and Marxist critical theory sets the stage for Moltmann's constructive proposals. As with any compelling interlocutor, Moltmann appears to be convincing to a large degree because he has proposed a set of conditions and problems that are naturally resolved through his formal proposals. One of the underlying arguments of the present endeavor has been to discount how Moltmann creates the feasible conditions for his programmatic statements. Before engaging this task further, however, one must survey Moltmann's subsequent works for any development regarding the themes treated thus far.

B.4. The Trinity and the Kingdom

No work is more related to *CG* than Moltmann's *Trinity and the Kingdom*, the first of his "contributions to theology". Since the work is situated within the field of trinitarian theology, one can see that it would have to parallel its theological antecedent. Through this text, one is reminded yet again that for Moltmann trinitarianism is bound up with the suffering Christ: Without the

---

[82] Moltmann, *CG*, p. 224.

[83] Ironically, the project of Horkheimer and Adorno is to negate transcendence. Willis makes this point, while stating that this "longing" is more akin to traditional theism than the Frankfurt school would care to admit, thereby making it susceptible to the Feuerbachian critique (*Theism, Atheism, and the Doctrine of the Trinity*, pp. 85-86).

[84] Moltmann, *CG*, p. 252.

theme of divine passibility, Moltmann's trinitarian reflections would lose much of their theological and historical grounding. One sees such commitments in Chapter 2 of *TK*, where Moltmann self-consciously opts to begin from the notion of God's passion. Aware at this point of the need to differentiate divine from human suffering, Moltmann mentions the notion of "active suffering": "God does not suffer out of deficiency of being, like created being. To this extent he is 'apathetic'. But he suffers from the love which is the superabundance and overflowing of his being. In so far he is 'pathetic' (*pathisch*)."[85] The substance of this "active suffering" is "laying oneself open to another and allowing oneself to be intimately affected by him; that is to say, the suffering of passionate (*leidenschaftlichen*) love".[86]

In trying to develop a doctrine of "theopathy", Moltmann employs a wide range of sources, in part because he is aware that few thinkers have begun with God's passion. After a brief reference to Origen (a reference that takes into account only part of Origen's position on the matter), Moltmann moves to consider four other frameworks: Heschel's work on the prophets and the pathos of God, the British (im)passibilist debates, the work of M. de Unamuno and his notion of the "sorrow of God", and N. Berdyaev and the theme of "tragedy in God". Once again, Moltmann employs wide-ranging figures and movements in order to construct a tapestry of theological argumentation, but the artificiality of this construct appears greater than in *CG* because in *TK* Moltmann engages these figures quite extensively, leaving the reader to wonder how each figure/framework fits within Moltmann's broader claims. Moltmann makes the following four points: "The experience of the divine pathos inevitably leads to the perception of the self-differentiation of the one God"[87] (Jewish *Shekinah* theology); "the cross on Golgotha has revealed the eternal heart of the Trinity",[88] which naturally includes love and its perceived corollary of being able to suffer (British debates); "in this [redemptive] process God participates in the world's pain and suffers in all who suffer"[89] (M. de Unamuno); and "the secret of Christianity is the perception of *God's triune nature*, the perception of the movement in the divine nature which that implies, and the perception of the history of God's passion which springs from this"[90] (Berdyaev). These statements, written by Moltmann in relation to the figures he treats, have their counterparts in his arguments, usually in strikingly similar forms.

Outside of these references, which certainly amplify Moltmann's treatment of the issue of passibility itself,[91] other remarks regarding God's passion are important in this subsequent reiteration, for he has amplified certain themes that

---

[85] Moltmann, *TK*, p. 23.

[86] Moltmann, *TK*, p. 23.

[87] Moltmann, *TK*, p. 27.

[88] Moltmann, *TK*, p. 31.

[89] Moltmann, *TK*, p. 39.

[90] Moltmann, *TK*, p. 45.

[91] Moltmann admits that he did not know of the British (im)passibilist debates at the time of *CG*'s writing.

make *TK* more balanced and comprehensive at this stage in his career. First of all, he treats of theodicy more explicitly, at this point acknowledging that it must be maintained as an "open question" and even using imagery to state that it is the "*open wound of life* in this world".[92] Second, the hamartiological component of suffering and death is acknowledged with greater intensity by Moltmann, stating in fact that the relationship of sin to suffering is a Pauline view of the matter.[93] Finally, Moltmann takes greater care to differentiate God's passion from human passion by offering a section that includes six points on how one is to think of God's love.

Once again, however, Moltmann demonstrates certain limitations, some of which are present in *CG* and others that are logical consequences of previous arguments. One finds repeatedly the unquestioned connection between God and suffering: "It is in suffering that the whole human question about God arises."[94] Such assertiveness presses the issue of whether the God-question is limited to this context. Second, despite his gestures towards granting a more explicit role to the hamartiological component of suffering, Moltmann thinks its role is inconsequential: "In actual fact the experience of suffering goes far beyond the question of guilt and innocence, leaving it behind as totally superficial."[95] Understandably, Moltmann is trying to dispel the tendency to explain each instantiation of suffering from a framework of justice/punishment within a cosmic, divinely-initiated plan. But must one move to the other extreme of asserting that the notion of sin and its accompanying components "should be left behind" in the process of understanding suffering and death? At one point, Moltmann acknowledges the strong sense of the Fall within the biblical narrative only to dismiss its consequences at a later point. Finally, as in *CG*, Barth serves as an unfortunate case in which asserting the freedom of God compromises the integrity of God's love. In this regard, Moltmann characterizes Barth's proposals as "nominalist" in that they emphasize God's self-sufficiency to the point that it appears illogical to provide a rationale for why and how God relates to the world. In light of these claims, Moltmann challenges Barth's method in such broad strokes that the relevant issues do not make their way into Moltmann's criticisms and formal arguments; as a case in point, it is not clear how Moltmann steers clear of what Barth was trying to avoid through his formulation of God's freedom, namely stating that God requires or needs creation. In fact, Moltmann will push the issue himself through some of the questions he poses to Barth, especially when he asks, "Does God really not need those whom in the suffering of his love he loves unendingly?"[96]

---

[92] Moltmann, *TK*, p. 49.

[93] Moltmann, *TK*, p. 50.

[94] Moltmann, *TK*, p. 47.

[95] Moltmann, *TK*, p. 51.

[96] Moltmann, *TK*, p. 53.

B.5. History and the Triune God

A work of lesser significance (given that it is not part of the "trilogy" or "contributions") but one that is important for this discussion is Moltmann's *History and the Triune God*.[97] As the title suggests, this collection of essays deals with topics that are similar to the prominent themes of *CG* and *TK*. The work includes essays written in the ten years following *TK*'s publication and offers both programmatic statements regarding Moltmann's own work and engages prominent figures within the Christian tradition – Aquinas, Joachim of Fiore, Rahner, and others.

Although written many years after *CG*, *HTG* parallels a number of Moltmann's prior arguments, including the pain of the Father in addition to the pain of the Son,[98] the unquestionable interrelationship between suffering and the existence of God,[99] doing theology "after Auschwitz", and other relevant themes. Unabashedly, Moltmann states that he has "replaced the metaphysical axiom of the essential impassibility of the divine nature with the essential passion of the eternal love of God", a move that coincides with his observation that the notion of the essential impassibility of the divine nature is apparently disappearing from modern systematics.

A detail worth mentioning about this work is its inclusion of the posthumous exchange with the late Rahner. This interchange is quite important in that previously Rahner had influenced Moltmann on a number of points, including the tenability of trinitarian categories and certain issues for a contemporary theology of the cross. The letter quoted in *HTG* reflects Rahner's thoughts that are directed more to H. von Balthasar and his associate A. von Speyr than Moltmann *per se* (the latter only receiving a passing mention). The sum of Rahner's opinion can be seen through one of his remarks: "To put it crudely, it does not help me to escape from my mess and mix-up and despair if God is in the same predicament."[100] Rahner acknowledges that the interconnections between God and the world are to be emphasized, but he still attributes some value to the notion that "in a true and consoling sense" God does not suffer, is immutable, and so on.[101] To end the brief piece, Rahner raises the questions as to how one can know such precise information about God's being and just how much value God's suffering may have for the believer.

Given that Rahner is questioning Moltmann's project, the latter responds in a posthumous note, stating that Rahner "struck at the heart" of his theology. Moltmann can state that his faith is threatened by Rahner's claims since he recalls his experience of God in 1945 as a POW as one in which he felt both

---

[97] Other major works of Moltmann make the occasional reference to the themes treated here, but no major advances are made at these points; rather, the moments are just allusions and are not developments of the previously made claims.

[98] Moltmann, *HTG*, p. 24.

[99] Moltmann, *HTG*, p. 26.

[100] Moltmann, *HTG*, p. 122.

[101] Moltmann, *HTG*, p. 122.

tormented and godforsaken. Apparently, because Rahner's comments struck a chord with Moltmann's faith journey, the Tübingen theologian rapidly dismisses these remarks, stating that he finds "no connection between consolation and apathy".[102] At this point, Moltmann continues the trajectory begun in *CG* of speaking of "voluntary suffering" as a different form of suffering applicable to God, stating as well that "an impassible God is capable of neither love nor feeling".[103] Moltmann finishes the piece with some harsh words that are difficult to reconcile with his otherwise irenic spirit.[104]

C. A Critical Assessment of Moltmann's Doctrine of God

After considering some of the major influences on Moltmann's thought in *The Crucified God* and some developments in his later works on similar topics, one can proceed to engage his doctrine of God more broadly for its implications upon the axiom of divine impassibility.

It should be noted from the onset that Moltmann has offered a number of gifts to the wider theological discussion, ones that should not be slighted or overlooked. For instance, he has contributed to the "trinitarian revival" of the twentieth century, his emphasis on the cross of Christ has helped place the doctrine of God specifically within the realm of christology, and throughout his work he has demonstrated a pastoral sensitivity, one that takes seriously the particularity of the Christian message and its place within a hostile world.

Despite these and many other positive offerings, Moltmann's doctrine of God "suffers" in several critical ways. Much of what is controversial about Moltmann's suggestions, whether they be the notion of a "suffering God", that God is an "event", or that the Father suffers and does so differently from the Son, stems from prior theological commitments that make those suggestions necessary because other available options have become nonviable. In truth,

---

[102] Moltmann, *HTG*, p. 123.

[103] Moltmann, *HTG*, p. 123.

[104] Rahner comments that in living in the world he is "cemented into its horribleness", an expression that within its context lends itself to being interpreted as the horribleness and inescapability of human suffering. Moltmann, on the other hand, interprets the statement as being a skeptical expression of Rahner's views of life and proceeds to generalize: "That [expression] sounds like a life which is unloved and incapable of love. Indeed it sounds like a frozen, fossilized life, one which is already dead. Are these the pains of being cut off from natural relationships which celibacy imposes on a young man enthused by God? Is being 'cemented' in a special Jesuit experience of a complete lack of ties to the world so as to be available to God at any time? Or is it just the feeling of an old man for whom physical existence has become increasingly burdensome?" (Moltmann, *HTG*, pp. 123-24). As "deeply shocked" as Moltmann was by Rahner's trajectory of thought, so this author is "deeply shocked" that Moltmann would question one's vow of celibacy or one's Order based on a legitimate argument by one who is no longer able to answer such an *ad hominem* line of inquiry.

despite popular opinion, Moltmann's doctrine of God is not as "revolutionary" as it would first appear because his proposals are not actually original alternatives. What one finds with Moltmann is a deceptive ease in the employment of various categories within theological discourse, a tendency that creates both ambiguities and indistinguishable parallels with traditionally problematic formulations. J. B. Webster has stated: "My fear is that Moltmann has not registered sufficiently that he is making some extraordinarily bold moves by applying to God terms such as 'suffering', 'history' or 'experience'. It is difficult to escape the impression that Moltmann finds talk of God fundamentally unproblematic."[105] Part of the present task is to expose the problematic nature of what Moltmann believes to be his unproblematic discourse.

C.1. The Intimate Link between the Cross and the Trinity

As mentioned before, Moltmann wants to argue that the cross and the Trinity cannot be divorced from one another: "The theological concept for the perception of the crucified Christ is the doctrine of the Trinity. The material principle of the doctrine of the Trinity is the cross of Christ."[106] So intertwined are these themes that the logic of one is dependent on the logic of the other: One cannot understand the cross except as a trinitarian event; one cannot understand the Trinity except as the dramatic portrayal of God on the cross. With Lutheran overtones, Moltmann can state: "When the crucified Jesus is called the 'image of the invisible God', the meaning is that *this* is God, and God is like *this*."[107] Moltmann's self-titled "revolution in the concept of God" is precisely this link between the cross and the Trinity. Rather than taking the cross as primarily a soteriologically significant event,[108] Moltmann considers it to have consequences for one's general view of God. Jesus' cry of dereliction, his cry of despair in the words of Psalm 22, creates a trinitarian drama in which the Father's absence is called into question, making this moment of the Son's suffering the apotheosis of all human experiences of "godforsakenness".

Although Moltmann's starting point has some distinct advantages, it is not without some undeniable problems. In the first place, beginning a doctrine of God strictly on the crucifixion limits the cross's significance. Although the

---

[105] J. B. Webster, "Jürgen Moltmann: Trinity and Suffering", *Evangel* 3.2 (Summer 1985), p. 6.

[106] Moltmann, *CG*, pp. 240-41.

[107] Moltmann, *CG*, p. 205.

[108] Moltmann states that the cross's link to soteriology is "by no means" false (although the point is not further elaborated), but he also asserts that this connection is "not radical enough" (*CG*, p. 201). For Moltmann, the radical nature of the cross beckons a reciprocity which has consequences for humans *and* for God, a point that directs one to the assumptions Moltmann makes regarding God's relationship to the world within history.

cross is an important part of both Christian belief and proclamation as to who God is, several themes vital to any doctrine of God are not adequately addressed through Moltmann's trinitarian staurocentrism. In the way Moltmann elaborates the cross as a starting point for the doctrine of God, the most pressing lacuna is an account of creation – and, thus, of the relationship between God and the world as a relationship of creator to creation. Any viable doctrine of God would be remiss were it not to factor this element. Such a practice was not only a key factor of patristic conventions but marks modern theological conceptualities as well.[109]

Second, given a Cappadocian reading of trinitarian economic activity, one can state that the crucifixion is a "trinitarian undertaking"; without the broader narrative contours of the gospel story, however, one cannot appreciate the cross's trinitarian character simply by looking at its instantiation. In other words, the Trinity existed prior to the crucifixion, and acknowledging this prevenience is in part necessary for understanding the roles of the persons at Golgotha. One wonders if Moltmann exaggerates the link between the cross and the Trinity so that the logic of trinitarianism is *limited to* the crucifixion. One of Moltmann's most remarkable lines in this regard is when he states: "The cross stands at the heart of the trinitarian being of God; it divides and conjoins the persons in their relationships to each other and portrays them in a specific way."[110] Such terms appear to suggest that the Trinity reaches a certain sense of actuality through the event of the cross, thereby questioning any logic of the trinitarian relations that is proposed before and beyond the historical event of the crucifixion.[111]

Succinctly stated, Moltmann has no available conceptual resource for safeguarding the transcendence of God, and this third limitation of Moltmann's starting point is perhaps the greatest threat to his project's coherence.[112]

---

[109] As mentioned in Chapter 2 of this study, the church fathers' doctrinal component of *creatio ex nihilo* allowed them to distinguish the Christian God from the pantheon of gods of Greek and Roman antiquity. T. G. Weinandy advances this line of argument convincingly in *Does God Suffer?*, both in Chapters 5 and 6.

[110] Moltmann, *CG*, p. 207.

[111] R. Olson states, "Moltmann makes the bold assertion that the immanent Trinity is not the ground of the economic Trinity but vice versa. Historical events become determinative of God's eternal being" ("Trinity and Eschatology: The Historical Being of God in Jürgen Moltmann and Wolfhart Pannenberg", *Scottish Journal of Theology* 36.2 [1983], p. 217). As Olson notes, Moltmann does not dissolve the distinction, but in elaborating an "interaction" (*Wechselwirkung*) or a "retroactive" effect (*zurückwirken auf*) of the economic upon the immanent, the question is begged as to how the distinction can be maintained.

[112] Ironically, whereas Moltmann does not convincingly secure God's transcendence, he does wish to make this theme do theological work, as when he states: "Understood in trinitarian terms, God both transcends the world and is immanent in history . . . . He is, if one is prepared to put it in inadequate imagery, transcendent as Father, immanent as Son and opens up the future of history as the Spirit. If we understand God in this way, we

Moltmann's "staurocentric trinitarian immanentism" leads him to denounce any speculation of God *in se* as heavenly riddles; one can build a doctrine of God only upon God *pro nobis* as depicted in the cross:

> We cannot say of God who he is of himself and in himself; we can only say who he is for us in the history of Christ which reaches us in our history . . . . In that case we would have to give up the distinction made in the early church and in tradition between the "God in himself" and the "God for us", or between "God in his majesty" and "God veiled in the flesh of Christ", as Luther and Melanchthon put it.[113]

This method, although noteworthy for its emphasis on revelation, fails to appreciate the work such dualities performed for past articulators. The value of an "immanent Trinity" and of a *Deus absconditus* is that they provide the conceptual space for doctrinal articulations and theological safeguards that are not as clearly presented in specific passages of Scripture, including the case of the crucifixion.[114] The previously mentioned example of *creatio ex nihilo* serves

---

can understand our own history, the history of suffering and the history of hope, in the history of God" (Moltmann, *CG*, pp. 255-56). Fiddes finds Moltmann's inconsistency unproblematic in that an implicit need exists for Moltmann to affirm the immanent Trinity in order to avoid pantheism (Fiddes, *The Creative Suffering of God*, pp. 135-36). Given how explicit Moltmann is in advocating the sole importance of the economic Trinity, such implicitness is unjustified.

[113]Moltmann, *CG*, pp. 238-39. Many have followed Moltmann at this point, most notably C. M. LaCugna in *God for Us* (New York: HarperCollins, 1991). Both Moltmann and LaCugna assume they are following Rahner's lead as elaborated in the latter's *The Trinity* (trans. J. Donceel; New York: Crossroad Herder, 1998). LaCugna and others are more careful in interpreting Rahner's axiom than Moltmann, for they openly acknowledge that a strict symmetry cannot be maintained between God *in se* and God *pro nobis* because of the inherent limitations history places on the latter; therefore, an ontological distinction does not exist between these aspects of the duality, but the particularity of the latter's mode of revelation must be acknowledged while maintaining the freedom of the former. Y. Congar remarks: "This self-communication takes place in the economy in accordance with a rule of 'condescendence', humiliation, ministry and 'kenosis'. We have therefore to recognize that there is a distance between the economic, revealed Trinity and the eternal Trinity. The Trinity is the same in each case and God is really communicated, but this takes place in a mode that is not connatural with the being of the divine Persons" (*I Believe in the Holy Spirit* [3 vols; trans. D. Smith; New York: Crossroad Herder, 2000], III, p. 15).

[114] P. D. Molnar demonstrates the importance of a robust account of an "immanent Trinity" when he surveys K. Barth's theology in contradistinction to those who would advocate a strong symmetry within the aforementioned dualities. According to Molnar, the notion of an "immanent Trinity" helps preserve God's freedom, keeps the creator-creation distinction in line, and keeps revelation within the "faith seeking understanding" apparatus. See his "The Function of the Immanent Trinity in the Theology of Karl Barth", *Scottish Journal of Theology* 42.3 (1989), pp. 367-99 and

to prove the point: Although this belief is detectable in Scripture, it does not appear to be as "theologically available" as the narrative progression of a human life leading up to a death that is verified through four gospel accounts. Nevertheless, *creatio ex nihilo* is an important theological constituent of how God relates to the world that theologically qualifies and substantiates the significance of Jesus Christ's life as the Word who created and is re-creating all things. In general, the contributions of these dualities help in underwriting a sense of doctrinal integrity regarding the truth claims of God's self-revelation by safeguarding that revelation through an ontological and epistemological prevenience to human experience.[115]

C.2. A Dubious Ontology

These problems regarding Moltmann's starting point for his doctrine of God indicate an even greater and more general issue: Moltmann's lack of a conceptually sustainable ontology. Moltmann's ontological claims are ambiguous and difficult to interpret. The most sustained effort for underwriting an ontology is detectable in Moltmann's first work of the trilogy, *Theology of Hope*. Given certain moments in *CG*, it is possible that Moltmann elaborates these prior ontological claims within the particularized setting of the crucifixion. From time to time (although perhaps not frequently enough for critics), Moltmann in *CG* reverts to past arguments regarding the future, promissory history, eschatology, and the resurrection.

Even in *Theology of Hope*, however, ontology is not given its due. Although not strictly Blochian or Hegelian, Moltmann's project in *TH* can be viewed as a "foundation" for an ontology, but by no means is this effort fully developed, for Moltmann typically draws pieces from varying constructs while not resolving their obvious dissonance within his proposals. Moltmann's emphases in *TH* on futurity and promise, where God interacts within history from the future, place in significant doubt God's antecedence to the world. Given these eschatological

---

"Toward a Contemporary Doctrine of the Immanent Trinity", *Scottish Journal of Theology* 49.3 (1996), pp. 311-57; see also Molnar's collection of essays *Divine Freedom and the Doctrine of the Immanent Trinity* (London: T & T Clark, 2002).

[115] When Moltmann does speak of the transcendence of God, the tendency is to speak of the future, but such a move, although concurrent with his moves in *TH*, is tenuous because of its underdeveloped conceptual grounding. Without these details, the natural tendency is to grant Moltmann a scheme in which the economic determines the immanent, with the latter being affirmed but not conceptualized to the degree necessary for it to do substantial theological work within this set of issues. As D. B. Farrow mentions of this retroactive futurity in Moltmann's project, "The commitment to retroactivity rather than to 'antecedence' temporalizes God and (in a qualified sense) divinizes creaturely experience of God" ("In the End is the Beginning: A Review of Jürgen Moltmann's Systematic Contributions", *Modern Theology* 14.3 [July 1998], p. 436).

emphases, it is legitimate to ask whether God "is" or if he simply is in a state of "becoming" since the fulfillment of his being rests in the future.[116] For all the fanfare *TH* enjoyed during its first few years in print, there is within its program an insufficient balance between futurity and historicity, immanence and transcendence; critics of this text have been consistent in identifying this omission as a serious limitation.[117]

Although not as suggestive ontologically as *TH*, the programmatic statements of *CG* continue in the vein of this conceptual ambiguity. When on several accounts Moltmann suggests that God's being is absent[118] or must be extrapolated from the event of the cross, the question is begged regarding God's being. Given this underpinning, Moltmann can state: "Anyone who speaks of God in Christian terms must tell of the history of Jesus as a history between the Son and the Father. In that case, 'God' is not another nature or a heavenly person or a moral authority, but in fact an 'event.'"[119] For those who find Moltmann's statement to be detrimental to the personal nature of God, especially with regard to the act of prayer, Moltmann continues that believers do not pray *to* a personal God but pray *in* this event among the persons of the godhead. In a further gesture of similar consequence, Moltmann questions God's being, stating that "the Trinity is no self-contained group in heaven, but an eschatological process open for men on earth, which stems from the cross of Christ".[120]

If Moltmann's ontology is questionable from an eschatological perspective, it certainly is so from a historical one as well. Many acknowledge Moltmann as a "panentheist" because he advocates God's participation within the affairs of the world. Moltmann does not shy away from this label,[121] but it could carry a number of overtones. The role history plays within the being of God is crucial: Does God enter history from a prevenient act of will without determinative consequences to his nature because of this act, or is God in fact constituted in some way by this engagement with the world? Moltmann clearly sides with the

---

[116] This ambiguity is sharply demonstrated when Miller comments that for Moltmann eschatology and ontology are ultimately the same thing (*The Eschatological Ontology of Jürgen Moltmann*, p. 294).

[117] Otto remarks: "More problematic is Moltmann's view of God as having 'future as his essential nature' . . . . On the basis of the ontic-historical reading of history (*Historie*) forwards toward the end, however, this God can never be fully actualized, since this would close the open possibilities and future which are this God's 'essential nature' and confine him to the static 'external present' which Moltmann decries. Thus, Moltmann's God can only be said to exist phenomenologically, not actually" ("Moltmann and the Anti-Monotheism Movement", p. 295).

[118] Moltmann, *CG*, p. 256.

[119] Moltmann, *CG*, p. 247.

[120] Moltmann, *CG*, p. 249.

[121] "A trinitarian theology of the cross perceives God in the negative element and therefore the negative element in God, and in this dialectical way is panentheistic" (Moltmann, *CG*, p. 277).

latter option, in part because of its Hegelian appeal; "The 'history of God'",
Moltmann writes, "cannot be thought of as history in the world, but on the
contrary makes it necessary to understand the world in this history."[122] Given
the place of the cross for the determination of God's being, one can say that
God "acquires a history" on the cross. Once again, the natural progression of
these assertions raises serious questions that Moltmann does not sufficiently
acknowledge. Does God not have a "history" prior to the cross? Does God
require the world for his self-actualization? Is God dissolved into history?[123]

In sum, Moltmann can speak of the triune God as a dialectical event, an
"eschatologically open history" in which the relationship between the Father
and the Son is still incomplete until the Son as Kyrios hands over the world to
the Father.[124] Given such ontological ambiguities, further complexities abound
when Moltmann attempts to account for human activity, for he goes so far as to
state: "We participate in the trinitarian process of God's history. Just as we
participate actively and passively in the suffering of God, so too we will
participate in the joy of God wherever we love and pray and hope."[125] Although
not a process theologian in the proper sense of the term, it is no coincidence
that following this statement Moltmann can refer to Whitehead's famous
characterization of God as the "great-companion – the fellow sufferer, who
understands".

In *CG*, Moltmann attempts an ontological dynamism reminiscent of his

---

[122] Moltmann, *CG*, p. 218. Moltmann has continued this line of thought in *God in
Creation* (trans. M. Kohl; New York: Harper and Row, 1985), where he can say: "An
ecological doctrine of creation implies a new kind of thinking about God. The centre of
this thinking is no longer the distinction between God and the world. The centre is the
recognition of the presence of God *in* the world and the presence of the world *in* God"
(p. 13). Clearly, Moltmann wishes to espouse panentheism (as opposed to pantheism)
because it allows for differentiation; the ambiguity surrounding this move is how
Moltmann maintains this differentiation.

[123] These questions raise the suspicion present in H. U. von Balthasar's assessment of
Moltmann's work as being one of re-mythologization: "Interpretations of this kind, like
all talk of God's suffering, become inevitable wherever the internal divine process,
'procession', is lumped together with the process of salvation history. Thus God is
entangled in the world process and becomes a tragic, mythological God" (*Theo-Drama*
[5 vols; trans. G. Harrison; San Francisco: Ignatius, 1988-1998], IV, p. 322).

[124] Such a portrayal makes the unity of the godhead all the more precarious in
Moltmann's system, for God's unity is not a presupposition but a goal of history. As
O'Donnell remarks in light of Moltmann's quotation above: "In completing his work,
the Son fulfils his mission, and the unification of God is fulfilled in that there is a mutual
indwelling of God and his redeemed creation . . . . The tritheistic danger in this scheme
is seen in Moltmann's reference to Father, Son, and Spirit as three subjects who work
together in history. Classical trinitarian theology vigorously maintained that in God
there is only one centre of consciousness and will. Moltmann implies that there are
three" (*Trinity and Temporality*, p. 150). Once again, Moltmann's ontological limits
pose additional problems for the principal ones in his purview.

[125] Moltmann, *CG*, p. 255.

project in *TH* while securing religious significance within the historical event of the cross. Such moves create a number of conceptual ambiguities, the most pronounced being the blurring of the distinctions and interrelationships among God, history, and the world so that Moltmann's intended "consistent" view of God is frankly quite inconsistent.

C.3. God as Love

Part of the dubious nature of Moltmann's ontology is the way in which he presses the notion that God is love. Of course, to anyone superficially acquainted with the Christian tradition, the notion that God is love appears to be central to its faith claims and worship. As noted in Chapter 2, a modern favoring of the Johannine tradition easily leads to the assertion that God is agapic love and that this love is demonstrated in Jesus' life. In assuming this claim, Moltmann follows not only a convention within popular Christian belief and spirituality but also makes a conceptual move that has grown more popular within systematic theology. Given that in some ways ontology has been displaced by epistemology in the modern period so that terms like "relationality" and "personhood" are more predominant than "essence" and "being", some theologians have felt that ontological categories can be avoided and superseded with the simple acknowledgment that "God is love". This "tyranny of love" in systematics has led to sentimentality and conceptual carelessness on the part of many theologians today in that they presuppose that this assertion is self-explanatory and self-sufficient.[126] Nothing, however, could be further from the truth, for the slippery slope that leads to the Feuerbachian critique is perhaps most perceptible when it is said that "God is love" because the "love" in question usually turns out to be whatever humans find to be amenable to their present values and beliefs.

Moltmann's project in *CG* demonstrates these tendencies with little reservation. At times, one finds a qualifying statement within *CG* or beyond, but for the most part, Moltmann too proceeds as if the notion that "God is love" were uniformly understood by all interested observers.[127] Despite the occasional

---

[126] These presumptions are dangerous, in part because a strict identity statement is not implied; popular convention holds that "God is love", but the statement "love is God" does not quite touch the truth implied by the prior notion. According to H. Jansen, this kind of difficulty suggests that "at least a formal distinction is made between God and love" by Moltmann and others. He continues: "The obvious question that arises then is who or what is the subject of the act [of love], since acts require subjects" ("Moltmann's View of God's (Im)mutability: The God of the Philosophers and the God of the Bible", *Neue Zeitschrift für systematische Theologie und Religionsphilosophie* 36.3 [1994], pp. 293-94).

[127] One of the key issues here is the relationship between love and freedom, a theme Moltmann explores in his reflections on creation. As B. J. Walsh remarks, Moltmann counters Barth's position on these matters by stating "that God is not free in terms of

qualification, Moltmann's view that "God is love" runs the risk of becoming a projection of idealized human love since the checks aimed at avoiding this outcome are all too infrequent in his work.

This tendency is never clearer than when he assumes that the capacity to love includes the capacity to suffer. Certainly, for humans loving also means being vulnerable to the possibility of suffering,[128] but the relevance of this understanding to God's nature is another matter altogether. Does God love the way we do, and if he does, must one say then that God suffers as we do as well? The matter is quite clear for Moltmann and equally is nonnegotiable: "God's being is in suffering and the suffering is in God's being itself, because God is love."[129] What he later terms the "dialectic of human life" is for him the dialectic of the divine life. This unjustified equation on the part of Moltmann and other theologians demonstrates some of the unquestioned and biased tendencies of modern theological speculation.

Because of the interrelationship between human love and suffering and its assumed relevance to the divine realm, Moltmann believes that divine impassibility is inconsistent with the biblical affirmation that God is love. In many ways, this logic leads Moltmann to deride divine impassibility as an unfaithful importation of Hellenistic metaphysics into the Christian portrayal of God. According to Moltmann, it is indisputable that God must suffer because God is (human?) love; he asserts explicitly throughout *TK* that the cross of Christ naturally leads to the notion of God's passion.

This line of thought is oblivious to the patristic understanding of God, which was able to maintain that God could be impassible and could love because of the fullness inherent in the divine nature. The example of Gregory Thaumaturgus comes to mind as one figure who was surveyed in Chapter 2 who could maintain this tension. In the case of Gregory and others, these

---

choosing between being or not-being love. This view of God as love has significant implications for the doctrine of creation because 'if God is love, then he neither will nor can be without the one who is his beloved.' 'In this sense God 'needs' the world and man'" ("Theology of Hope and the Doctrine of Creation: An Appraisal of Jürgen Moltmann", *Evangelical Quarterly* 59.1 [1987], p. 70, with quotes from Moltmann's *TK*, p. 58). Of course, Moltmann wants to maintain the freedom of God and attempts to do so with a phrase like "essential resolve", but the path toward necessity nevertheless is indicated. In "The Function of the Trinity in Moltmann's Doctrine of Creation", *Theological Studies* 51.4 (1990), p. 681, Molnar labels Moltmann's moves here as depicting God as a "prisoner of love", in part because of the latter's apparent approval of C. E. Rolt's view that God has to give and has to love because these constitute his very nature (Moltmann, *TK*, p. 31).

[128] Moltmann acknowledges that this dynamic is a human one: "But the more one loves, the more one is open and becomes receptive to happiness and sorrow. Therefore the one who loves becomes vulnerable, can be hurt and disappointed. This may be called the dialectic of *human* life: we live because and in so far as we love – and we suffer and die because and in so far as we love" (*CG*, p. 253, emphasis added).

[129] Moltmann, *CG*, p. 227.

distinctions rest on subtle semantic connotations that are indicative of important ontological claims and distinctions, and Moltmann on the whole fails to acknowledge the subtlety of the former because of his project's incongruity with the latter.

To summarize this brief appraisal, Moltmann's doctrine of God is lacking on a number of counts despite its instant appeal as one based on revelation and one that takes the contemporary understanding of the human condition seriously. The logical consequences of Moltmann's broad claims are the dismissal of divine impassibility and the other tenets of "classical theism" as well as a neglect of soteriology. Lost also are such pivotal Christian doctrines as the incarnation and the atonement. His staurocentric trinitarian immanentism provides no logical space for transcendent claims about God beyond an ontologically questionable category of the "future", and yet Moltmann wishes to preserve this theme and tries to incorporate it without sufficient warrant. The way he portrays his position makes the fathers oxymoronic in their claims for divine impassibility, and the theological discourse he perpetuates is not checked in its Feuerbachian tendencies. Overall, one does not find in *CG* an account of the tentative quality of theological discourse, particularly when attributing pathic speech to God. Recalling Webster's insightful claim, Moltmann is not sufficiently troubled by the tentativeness of God-talk.

These oversights and many more suggest that Moltmann's doctrine of God is deeply problematic. Rather than offering to contemporary theological discourse a genuine alternative, his doctrine bypasses the developments made by previous articulations in favor of a more modernized and accessible account for contemporary readers. Unfortunately, this accessibility runs the risk of repeating old problems veiled in new forms and categories. The danger is perhaps no clearer within Moltmann's reflections than when he speaks of the Father in relation to the Son's crucifixion.

D. The Role of the Father within the Trinitarian Drama of the Cross

D.1. Must A Loving Father Suffer?

Inherent within the question of what the cross means for God is the question of how the Father relates to the Son's despair and torture during the cruel and vicious ordeal of the crucifixion. The role of the Father in this drama has always been an issue of importance to Christians, whether the matter is located at the Garden of Gethsemane or Jesus' cry of dereliction. When Moltmann poses the issue so that the cross has a bearing on one's doctrine of God, the role of the Father becomes even more important because now one is moving beyond the parameters of Jesus' life and ministry to the godhead itself, thereby requiring a process of theological induction that can be either fruitful or debilitating for trinitarian thinking.[130] Unfortunately, Moltmann cannot incorporate past understandings when engaging the role of the Father in the crucifixion because he has made his project ill-disposed to these alternatives at other turns, whether they be the introduction of negativity/conflict into an apparently "tragic" God or the dismissal of such important themes as sin and salvation. Although Moltmann says he does not devalue the salvific merits of the cross and at times he is willing to incorporate the term (but not the logic) of sin, he cannot speak of the cross in broader ways because of its exclusive centrality in his theological scheme.

Moltmann's depiction of the Father comes very close to being sadistic in nature: "The Son suffers in his love being forsaken by the Father as he dies."[131] This criticism of theistic sadism has been leveled at Moltmann on a number of counts by several figures, including D. Sölle.[132] Why would the Father allow this tragedy to occur to his Son? For Sölle and others, Moltmann does not have an adequate answer to this question, especially in light of the strong statements he makes regarding the Pauline notion of the Father's "delivering up" the Son to suffer and die. At this point, Moltmann engages the term *paradidonai* in its instantiations (e.g., Romans 8:32) where the Father is said to surrender or give up his Son.[133] The overtones at times suggest that the Father is the active agent that "annihilates" or "executes" the innocent Son.[134]

---

[130] "Moltmann gives the impression that there is a tension, a dichotomy between God and God, that God the Father forsakes God the Son, and that God is against God. This view is problematic, especially as he does not see the tension of God-forsakenness as an event that took place once and for all on the Cross of Jesus, but as a permanent event in the very heart of the Trinity" (A. G. Nnamani, *The Paradox of a Suffering God*, p. 177).

[131] Moltmann, *CG*, p. 245. In all fairness, Moltmann also speaks about the Father suffering "in his love the grief of the death of the Son", yet no warrant is suggested as to why Christ was forsaken, much less how the contradiction of God loving on the one hand and forsaking on the other can be maintained.

[132] See D. Sölle's article "Gott und das Leiden", in M. Welker (ed), *Diskussion über Jürgen Moltmanns Buch "Die Gekreuzigte Gott"* (München: Kaiser, 1979), pp. 111-17 and her work *Suffering* (trans. E. R. Kalin; Philadelphia: Fortress, 1975), pp. 26-27.

[133] Moltmann quotes a passage from W. Popkes that he finds agreeable: "To express the idea in its most acute form, one might say in the words of the dogma of the early church: the first person of the Trinity casts out and annihilates the second . . . . A theology of the cross cannot be expressed more radically than it is here" (*CG*, p. 241).

[134] D. W. Jowers observes that as Moltmann emphasizes more God's passion as a starting point for his theology, his tendency has been to invoke greater agony and resistance on the Son's part in facing the crucifixion, as in the case with *TK* ("The Theology of the Cross as Theology of the Trinity", *Tyndale Bulletin* 52.2 [2001], p. 247), leading to the assumption that Moltmann's appeal to God's passion is directly reciprocal to how strong his case is for negativity within the godhead, i.e., the "God against God" motif. Naturally, these gestures fail to account for a point that both von Balthasar and O'Donnell would want to push, namely the eternal double surrender of the Father and Son in the incarnation and crucifixion of the Son, a move that suggests the possibility of complementing passages such as Rom. 8:32 with ones such as Gal. 2:20.

Of course, since Moltmann has not safeguarded adequately the divine transcendence in the way he portrays the matter, it is an "open" question whether the Father could do something to help the Son. Moltmann is entirely "sympathetic" with statements like Horkheimer's denunciation of an omnipotent God in the face of innocent suffering. One sees how the unqualified value Moltmann attributes to innocent suffering alters his doctrine of God, for in line with others (including process theologians and protest atheists), Moltmann essentially questions God's sovereignty and omnipotence because of the high value he attributes to the plight of the innocent sufferer, thereby raising the issue of whether God can actually save the sufferer or redeem her suffering.[135] By elevating the cry of dereliction to the degree that he does, Moltmann attempts to show that God is not oblivious to the "plight of the modern man" since Jesus' death cry echoes the cries of those who have felt forsaken throughout history. As Moltmann claims time after time, the cross is a moment in which God enters in solidarity with the innocent sufferer, thereby historicizing God at this crucial moment of history.

Although Moltmann's suggestions attempt to offer a quasi-soteriological hope in that the Father delivers the Son for humanity's salvation, the matter remains problematic. How can God be sympathetic with the plight of humanity and yet do nothing about its condition? Does not that very sympathy become meaningless or even taunting?[136] These questions once again raise the theodicy issue and point to how Moltmann has not attempted to deal with it directly; rather, he believes that in God's absorption of sin and death one automatically finds comfort in despair and hope in meaninglessness. Nevertheless, the conditions of possibility for this absorption remain elusive to Moltmann. Without safeguarding these conditions, the meaning surrounding such an absorption or solidarity is unavailable and therefore lost.

With these elements in place, including the fact that the Father does not do anything to help the Son – and it is questionable that he can – soteriology is *prima facie* dismissed for the coherence of the cross, innocent suffering is given an unquestionable and nonnegotiable value, and God mysteriously envelops or assumes this forsakenness into his very being. These moves leave Moltmann with only one alternative for the generalized category of suffering: the Father *must suffer* along with the Son if God is to be exculpated before the grand tribunal of modern theodicy. If the Father does not suffer with the Son, then he is a sadist. Suffering with the Son is an act of involvement that questionably stems from Moltmann's scheme, for it implies that God retains some sort of power during the crucifixion. This power, not of overcoming with force but rather of envelopment or sublation, means that God's very being is constituted by suffering and death, and if these conclusions are true, then it follows that the

---

[135] Nnamani, *The Paradox of a Suffering God*, p. 178.

[136] "Whatever pain the Father might suffer from a crime, after all, cannot absolve him of the guilt of allowing it to occur" (Jowers, "The Theology of the Cross as Theology of the Trinity", p. 248).

Father must suffer.[137] As on previous occasions, one can see Moltmann's quasi-Hegelian methodological tendencies in full display at crucial moments in his reflections.

D.2. A Modern-Day Patripassianist?

In advocating the suffering of the Father, however, Moltmann runs the risk of falling into officially renounced heresies of the Christian tradition, especially those surrounding the patripassianist controversies of the third century. Moltmann is quick to find an apparent means by which to bypass this designation,[138] which is to label the suffering of the Father of a different *kind* than the suffering of the Son; rather than suffering pain and death as the Son does, the Father suffers the loss and grief of a dying Son: "The Son suffers dying, the Father suffers the death of the Son".[139] In this regard, Moltmann can speak of the Father's "sympathy" in watching and enduring the death of his Son. By labeling the Father's suffering as qualitatively different from the Son's, Moltmann thinks that he has avoided the patripassianist designation, settling for what could be thought of as an equally problematic alternative, namely "patricompassianism".[140]

If one were to revisit the patripassianist controversy, however, one would see that Moltmann has only partially absolved himself from this heresy. At stake in the patripassianist controversy was whether the Father and the Son were one person. For many Patripassianists, the answer had to be affirmative because of the perceived alternative, namely the existence of polytheism within the logic of the Christian gospel. By attempting to affirm the oneness of God and the divinity of Christ, Patripassianists forced themselves into undesirable

---

[137] The bipolarity of Moltmann's "trinitarianism" is most evident here in that whereas the Father and the Son are said to suffer, little is mentioned of the Spirit. Moltmann acknowledges this oversight at a later juncture, but within *CG* itself, the absence of a true role for the Spirit in the crucifixion significantly questions Moltmann's "trinitarian" view of the cross; as C. Braaten asks regarding Moltmann's project, "Would not a binitarian concept of God work as well?" ("A Trinitarian Theology of the Cross", *Journal of Religion* 56.1 [1976], p. 118).

[138] Braaten wonders why Moltmann does not confront Patripassianism head-on in order "to challenge the old Greek philosophical concept of God" ("A Trinitarian Theology of the Cross", p. 118). The most obvious answer is that Moltmann does not want to associate himself with the modalistic monarchian underpinnings of this heresy, an issue treated with more detail below.

[139] Moltmann, *CG*, p. 243. Moltmann continues: "The grief of the Father here is just as important as the death of the Son. The Fatherlessness of the Son is matched by the Sonlessness of the Father, and if God has constituted himself as the Father of Jesus Christ, then he also suffers the death of his Fatherhood in the death of the Son. Unless this were so, the doctrine of the Trinity would still have a monotheistic background."

[140] This term is explicitly used by Moltmann in *The Future of Creation*, p. 73.

formulations, e.g., that the Father entered Mary's womb and both died and rose from the dead.[141] Many found the instantiating claims of the Patripassianists noteworthy, but such odd conclusions left many to question their proposals in light of Scripture.

When it came to the issue of suffering, however, Patripassianists accommodated a variant that is worth noting in this context. In the case of Praxeas, a duality within the Lord came to be acknowledged (one similar to Adoptionism but admittedly derived from the opposite side of the theological spectrum) in which "the man Jesus was, strictly speaking, the Son, while the Christ, i.e., the divine element (*spiritum, id est deum*) was properly the Father."[142] This bifurcation led Praxeas and others to make claims such as that the Son suffers while the Father co-suffers, a line of reasoning that inspired a flurry of theological activity, including Tertullian's formal addresses on the matter.

In considering the historical details of this heresy more carefully, one can see that the issue for the early church was not simply the modalistic threat when one asserts the suffering of the Father, but more fundamental is the question of how God's trinitarian being maintains its character in light of the Son taking upon himself human flesh. In other words, the early church would wish to affirm the unity of the godhead and its distinction from the world, but the manner in which one safeguards these tenets is just as important as the tenets themselves. Traditionally, the topic of suffering was considered to be one associated with the transience of the material world and so, outside of the incarnation, unsuitable for theological consideration. A differentiation in kinds of suffering for the Son and the Father did not resolve the issue, as the examples of Praxeas and his associates prove. The same must be said for the case of Moltmann's distinction.

The matter is placed into focus if one references the key issues Tertullian posed to Praxeas in the extensive quotation made in Chapter 2 of this study. According to Tertullian, "co-suffering" implies the capacity to "suffer", and so Praxeas and other Patripassianists, despite their efforts in differentiating forms of suffering for the purpose of maintaining the divine unity, fail in avoiding this basic charge, for the early church found it unacceptable to conflate the divine essence with what was perceived to be an occurrence of the material world. Of course, things have changed in the modern theological situation, where God is commonly referred to as suffering. Nevertheless, one wonders if Moltmann's claim to maintain the triune nature of the godhead through a differentiation in kinds of suffering attributed to the Father and the Son sufficiently distinguishes him from the patripassianist designation. He admits that God's very nature is capable of suffering, and the logical conclusion of his other tenets leads to questionable demarcations for preserving the divine unity, characteristics native to the patripassianist agenda.

---

[141] Kelly, *Early Christian Doctrines*, p. 121.

[142] Kelly, *Early Christian Doctrines*, p. 121.

D.3. Maintaining the Impassibility of the Father

Although a "suffering Father" makes sense within Moltmann's quasi-Hegelian system in which death and forsakenness become part of God's very being, it is questionable just how necessary or desirable this notion is apart from these ontological conventions. What religious value does a "suffering Father" have for contemporary believers? Is this notion warranted given past and present ontological tendencies, or is it simply an addendum that stems from the unquestionable value of human suffering?

Biblically, no justification exists for asserting a "suffering Father". In Jesus' ministry, the Father for the most part remains an elusive reference, usually alluded to as his "Father in heaven". Despite this apparent distance, in light of Jesus' confession, the Father is theologically relevant for Christian reflection. Jesus had an intimate relationship with the Father, his ministry was in light of the Father's will, and in seeing him individuals saw the Father. Despite these references, however, the Father himself is not accessible as is the Son through the incarnation. In the all-important moment for Moltmann's project, the crucifixion on Golgotha, Jesus vocalizes his cry, but no response appears; rather, one finds sheer silence and apparent abandonment in the gospels.

In locating the biblical limitations surrounding such a notion as a "suffering Father", one need not entirely close the issue. After all, the human concept of sonship implies fatherhood and *vice versa*, leading to the hypothesis that the Father, because of his intimate link with the Son, would have to be affected by the Son's fate. What this result could be, however, is conceptually inconclusive. The usual Old Testament metaphor in all of these matters, namely Abraham's near-sacrifice of his son, Isaac, does not depict Abraham as grief-stricken and in terror but rather operating obediently within the "fear of the Lord". Of course, many have striven to "humanize" Abraham's condition as he takes Isaac up the mountain and prepares the altar to sacrifice his son.[143] But such moves are addendums to the biblical narrative, one that at crucial moments resorts to silence and mystery, including (and perhaps, most especially) at Golgotha. Could there be a rationale for not having a "suffering Father", who beholds the suffering of his only-begotten Son? Can moments of silence within the canon serve as conceptual boundaries for speech practices aimed at affirming a "suffering" God?

I believe theologically justifiable reasons exist for Scripture's silence regarding the notion of a "suffering Father". Rather than assuming these silences to be missed opportunities, contemporary observers of this state of affairs can argue that Scripture's admissions and reservations about God's suffering leave the notion of God's impassibility conceptually available. Instead of projecting solutions to Scripture's silence, as Moltmann aims to do with his "patricompassianism", one should acknowledge this silence regarding the person of the Father as a theologically significant component of any biblical

---

[143] The example of S. Kierkegaard's *Fear and Trembling* comes to mind as a prominent example of this vein of literature.

trinitarianism. In fact, Scripture's portrayal of the access to the Father as only through the Son's mediation is precisely the kind of (dis)closure or "revelation in hiddenness" one finds in Scripture's account of God's self-communication. In light of this broader biblical and theological framework, several reasons appear for maintaining the impassibility of the Father.

First of all, an impassible Father maintains an operational hermeneutical guideline when assessing God's economic activity. The Father's impassibility grants significance to the Son's incarnational passibility by acknowledging the latter as a *possible* but not *necessary* economic manifestation of the former. If one were to integrate the label of "necessity" at this point, such a move would only serve to undermine the significance of the cross as a true act of agapic love undertaken freely by the triune God for the sake of the world's redemption. Otherwise, the cross would be narrated in some sense as a requisite for God's being. Despite Moltmann's criticisms, Barth supersedes the former's project in this regard by more faithfully representing the Reformed tradition.

Second, affirming a "suffering Father" takes away from the importance of the incarnation itself. The perpetual temptation to "everything or nothing" declarations demonstrates itself at this point, for contemporary theologians, including Moltmann, find that it is not enough to say that the Son, one of the triune persons, suffered in the flesh; rather, if God's taking up creation's suffering is to be valid and efficacious, then "all of God" must suffer. This practice suggests that the incarnation was insufficient to overcome suffering and death and that the work of the Son is limited in that it is undertaken by only "one-third" of God.

The accompanying loss of soteriological categories further complicates the matter because such circumstances prohibit the religious value of stating that the Son came from the Father in the incarnation and returned to him in the resurrection. By devaluing the Son's role within redemption history, Moltmann and other modern-day Patripassianists find that the Father too must suffer if it is to be said that God takes human suffering seriously.

It appears that the religious value of a "suffering Father" occurs only when the Son's suffering is devalued, for the significance of a "suffering Father" apart from this estimation is questionable. In other words, if the incarnation were to be taken seriously as "one of the godhead took upon himself flesh in order to suffer and die for the sins of the world", what could the notion of a "suffering Father" possibly add to the Son's crucifixion? Some·may say – and one finds elements of this argument in Moltmann – that a "suffering Father" absolves him of responsibility for the Son's suffering and death, but this opinion avoids the explicit biblical assertion that the Son voluntarily took upon himself the suffering that he endured: "No one takes [my life] from me, but I lay it down of my own accord. I have power to lay it down, and I have power to take it up again" (John 10:18). When one acknowledges this biblically explicit theme, the Father cannot be blamed for not intervening and stopping the crucifixion; on the contrary, when one acknowledges Jesus' free will in this event, the cross begins to take on a more trinitarian character, not so much in the form of "God against God" as Moltmann states but as "God and God" redeeming fallen creation.

Further, the "silence" one finds concerning the Father in the gospel narratives serves a complementary role to the "audible" voice of Jesus. In other words, the immediacy and availability of the incarnation, a theme that is uncongenial for both Jews and Greeks given their theological tendencies, retain a transcendent quality when pictured within the trinitarian background of the Father as source and end of Jesus' life and ministry. In biblical fashion, the silence of the Father continues the tradition of the "backside of God", the elusive significance of the Tetragrammaton, and the pillar of fire with no form. The transcendent Father preserves a certain mystery and unavailability to one's understanding of the trinitarian godhead. Thus, when one reads Jesus saying that "If you know me, you will know my Father also" (John 14:7), the veracity of the revelation is not questioned but the distinction in persons is not erased either. Although problematic for many throughout its *Wirkungsgeschichte*, the same notions of "mystery" and "trinitarian differentiation" are preserved when one hears Jesus' confession that no one knows the hour of his coming except for the Father (Matthew 24:36); once again, one sees the affirmation that even with the unparalleled immediacy of God in the Son incarnate, God cannot be entirely comprehended in human terms; he cannot be grasped or systematized without reserve; he will not allow himself to be subsumed under critical and empirical valuations and under analyses of modern scientific verification. Such passages, when read within the rubric of making impassibility a possibility for the Father, help secure something that Moltmann sorely lacks: a means of safeguarding analogical discourse in which a likeness (*similitudo*) is suggested at the same time that a greater unlikeness (*dissimilitudo*) is affirmed.[144]

In advocating the mystery and transcendence surrounding the person of the Father within the life and testimony of Jesus, one can consider the Father in impassibilist terms. In characterizing the Father as impassible, one need not assume that the Father cannot love or that he is uninterested within the world's affairs. Rather, stating that God the Father is impassible complements the immediacy of the Son's revelation while preserving an epistemic distance within the events of the crucifixion. In the complete vulnerability to sin and death that the Son shows on the cross, the notion that the Son assumes these conditions out of his power and love stems from the fact that he comes from the Father and returns to him. In this way, the Father is impassible because he is "not affected against his will from an outside source" (to use the definition proposed in Chapter 1), thereby affirming his victory and power over sin and death even during the most brutal and tragic moments of Christ's *via dolorosa*. Without the theological safeguard of affirming an impassible Father, sin and death appear to have certain leverage over God's being, altering the logic of salvation history and God's prevenience and sovereignty in relation to human experience.

Early authorities in the church tended to interpret the Father in precisely

---

[144] J. Tück, "The Utmost: On the Possibilities and Limits of a Trinitarian Theology of the Cross", *Communio* 30.3 (2003), p. 439.

these impassibilist terms, showing themselves attentive to the parameters set by Scripture for theological reflection. Such awareness proved that the church fathers were capable of engaging in a dialectical methodology in which tension-laden tenets of God-talk could be simultaneously held with the goal of averting detrimental heresies and unfaithful speech practices in their understandings of the true God.

D.4. Conclusion

In surveying Moltmann's doctrine of God as begun in *CG*, one realizes that in spite of the suggestive appeal his foundational tenets display, serious problems remain that far outweigh any achieved benefits. In particular, Moltmann's staurocentric trinitarianism assumes that a doctrine of God can be constructed from the cross of Christ without the broader narrative framework of the gospel. This move not only threatens the soteriological implications of the cross but also provides little recourse in substantiating the relationship between God and the world as creator and creation. This ontological vacuum, filled only by a quasi-Hegelian construct lacking in logical flow from start to finish, creates a void naturally filled by precisely that which Moltmann wishes to avoid: the Feuerbachian tendency of projecting unto God those qualities that are most amenable to the *Zeitgeist*. In the case of Moltmann, this projection takes the form of God being unconditionally an "event of love" in which judgment and redemption are replaced with solidarity and sublation.

In assuming too "uncritically" that the cross can give the doctrine of God "public credibility",[145] Moltmann elevates Jesus' cry of forsakenness as paradigmatic of all human moments of suffering, irrespective of the gospels' narrative flow and of the hermeneutical dangers of universalizing a historical event with an existential moment that all humans share. Essentially, in trying to speak to the "modern man" in the contemporary situation, Moltmann has adopted too readily the conditioned speech patterns of modernity with regard to innocent suffering and human tragedy, including those tendencies that suggest one cannot explain these moments as rational so that such irrationality or absurdity must be absorbed rather than re-narrated by God's very being.

These qualities point to dismissing divine impassibility as antiquated and useless; however, apart from this questionable doctrinal construct advanced by Moltmann, impassibility does demonstrate theological relevance when applied to the person of the Father, for through this notion a biblical pattern can be maintained of God's revelation in his hiddenness, his presence marked by an acknowledgment of his absence. Moltmann's project dictates that the Father must suffer, and this consequence proves how flawed his system is in itself; although desirable given the modern traits of comprehensiveness and totality, a "suffering Father" actually takes away from the importance of the Son's incarnation and of the qualified check that must be placed on the Son's

---

[145] Moltmann, *CG*, p. 201.

revelation in which the persons of the Father and the Son must be complementary but not indistinguishable.

In arguing for the impassibility of the Father, allusions to the Son have been maintained throughout, especially when speaking of the Son's availability to human understanding and experience because of the incarnation. Is the Son therefore passible in all ways that humans are, or can the Son also be said to be impassible in some way? These questions are also contentious in a context in which Chalcedon is continually debated. The following chapter aims to relate an impassibilist element to the person and work of Jesus Christ.

CHAPTER 5

The Impassible Christ

A. The Gospel as Subverting Principle

It is difficult not to believe that within the doctrinal realm of christology one finds the most sustained pressure for undermining popular accounts of divine impassibility. Certainly, the Old Testament offers compelling instantiations of theopathic language (as considered in Chapter 2), but Christianity has perpetually struggled with the implications stemming from its faith in an incarnate God. In saying quite casually that the child in the manger was God, that God was crucified at Golgotha, and other quite common statements, Christians throughout the centuries have easily made the leap of saying that "God suffers". If Jesus was God, then all that Jesus did and endured would have to implicate Christianity's understanding of God in some way. If Christ is the truest and most indicative expression of who and how God is, then moments of Christ's suffering (to take the example most pertinent to this study) have to be negotiated within some conceptual theological apparatus for the understanding of divinity in general.

One can assume that this christological thrust is at the heart of those statements quoted above that suggest how divine impassibility runs entirely counter to the central belief system of Christianity. When theologians can state, "That God Almighty can and does suffer in relation to His sinful creatures, – this is a cardinal doctrine of Christianity",[1] or more recently that "The concept of divine suffering is not only the core of [Christian] faith but the uniqueness of Christianity",[2] such claims are made in light of the crucified Christ. When thinkers past and present emphatically deride the notion of divine impassibility, they do so not so much on the basis of historical investigation but on faith commitments revolving around the identity of Jesus.

What one notices in such moves is not so much ill-intentioned motives as a conceptual inattentiveness of a kind that cannot be sustained over time because of its unraveling effects upon God-talk. Certainly, in Jesus we have an invaluable expression of God's self, and yet from Jesus' own testimony we see his constant reference to his Father and his request to his Father to send the Spirit as another "paraclete" unto his disciples. Yes, in Christ's teaching we have a glimpse into what the kingdom of heaven is like, and yet Christ grew weary, slept, ate, and drank as do all finite, limited mortals. In a sense, when

---

[1] White, *Forgiveness and Suffering*, p. 84.
[2] Lee, *God Suffers for Us*, p. 1.

one sees Jesus one sees the Father, but in another, and equally important, sense, when one sees Jesus one sees what true humanity is and should be. Jesus Christ was and is both Son of God *and* Son of Man.

Obviously, these claims are not easy to maintain, and the early church struggled mightily with the implications of the gospel. The identity of the Son was at the heart of the two major phases of conciliar deliberations in the early church: At one point, the relationship of the Son to the godhead was considered (the first and second ecumenical councils), and subsequently, the identity and implications of his incarnation were treated (councils three through seven). From these conciliar achievements, the church developed a grammar or way of speaking that tried to attend to the divinity and humanity of Christ, a move that stood in tension with the sensibilities of the time in which the problem of the One and the Many continued to be assumed. What emerged were habits and patterns of thought and speech that make sense only in light of sustained deliberations concerning the gospel narratives and the faith commitments that emerged from them. The history is complex as it took form within an agonistic climate in which heresy and orthodoxy were in flux and negotiations were being entertained between the broader culture of the era and the particularities of the gospel story.

As part of these negotiations, the role, shape, and influence of divine impassibility played a significant role within emerging orthodoxy. As noted, this axiom was assumed by both heretic and orthodox alike even though that *prima facie* it appeared that the notion favored more the former than the latter. That divine impassibility was assumed by both parties is primarily indicative of the *Sitz im Leben* of early Christianity; that it was often problematized and chastened in a number of expressions suggests that it did not arise out of the fray without significant alterations and accents native to basic Christian claims.

The present chapter will begin with a "thick description" of what christological negotiation regarding this axiom looked like for the early church in relation to the Son's passion. If J. J. O'Keefe is correct in writing that "concerns about impassibility go to the heart of the [christological] controversy itself",[3] then the effort spent delving attentively to this theological discussion should be beneficial for the present endeavor. After this synopsis as well as a summary of its modern reception, the chapter will move to consider what are commonly called the "British debates" concerning divine impassibility, those that took place around the turn of the 20th century. The thesis advanced here will be that the "British debates" demonstrate a sustained moment in which divine impassibility was challenged quite forcefully and dismissively largely because of an inherent Chalcedonian ambiguity within this context's God-talk. In this regard, the "British debates" represent one moment in the history of Christian reflection in which the gospel is taken to subvert popular conceptual discourse – in this case, the assumption of an impassible God. Yet, as is usually the case, if unqualified, the subversion is ultimately unsatisfactory because it

---

[3] J. J. O'Keefe, "Kenosis or Impassibility: Cyril of Alexandria and Theodoret of Cyrus on the Problem of Divine Pathos", *Studia Patristica* 32 (1997), p. 359.

ignores or cursorily treats relevant issues in its wake. In remedying one perceived ailment (in this case, the plight of Hellenistic metaphysical influence upon Christian theological discourse), the cure fails as a panacea to avert other, quite sinister side effects – for example, the pressing need to safeguard the transcendence and so divinity of Christ even at those moments in which Christ is most "humanly accessible". The chapter will conclude with some brief, constructive remarks regarding how impassibility can play a role within the doctrinal realm of christology.

B. Pre-Chalcedonian Considerations

If one is to consider the advantages of maintaining divine impassibility within christological conversations, one must pay heed to its past articulators during the early rise of Christian orthodoxy. Chapter 3 of this study attempted to do just that, but the scope of this chapter fell short of considering the conciliar age. Prior to Nicaea, one notices that the language of divine impassibility is at play, both among individuals who would influence the shape of Christian orthodoxy (Ignatius, Tertullian, Irenaeus, and others) as well as those who came to be deemed as heretics (e.g., Docetists, Gnostics, Modalists, and others) and who often provoked doctrinal refinement. Given the inherent complexity of the matter, the negotiations at play regarding the impassibility axiom were at times subtle, controversial, and ambiguous.

The Arian controversy is an exemplary case of this complexity. Behind Arius' claims of the Son being a creature and that his being was of a different essence from the Father is the underlying conviction that the divine could not change, generate, or suffer as creatures do. His opponents countered his arguments, not with a dismissal of divine impassibility but rather with its qualification through the doctrine of the incarnation. One sees this kind of theological work in Athanasius' *Epistola ad Epictetum*, which elaborates what has come to be designated his "doctrine of appropriation". In this letter, Athanasius is writing after the Nicene Council's deliberations to strengthen further its declarations that the Son was of the same essence of the Father and that the assumed flesh was not coessential to the Word. Athanasius believes that, while "strange", it is perfectly reasonable to state: "He it was Who suffered and yet suffered not. Suffered, because His own Body suffered, and He was in it, which thus suffered; suffered not, because the Word, being by Nature God, is impassible."[4] For Athanasius, the Son retained his identity as God even when he took human flesh; this appropriation implies that "the Body was not the Word, but Body of the Word".[5]

---

[4] Athanasius, *Epistola ad Epictetum*, 6.

[5] Athanasius, *Epistola ad Epictetum*, 6. In elaborating this notion, Gavrilyuk states, "The appropriation of the flesh meant that in the incarnation God acted and suffered in and through the flesh, and did nothing apart from the flesh" (*The Suffering of the Impassible God*, p. 162).

As helpful as this clarification of christological language at this point in the debates was, issues still remained. In particular, the nature of this "assumption" or "appropriation" had to be dealt with in greater detail, for in its crudest form it could imply that the Son simply "wore" human flesh as some sort of attachment. One sees here how Nicaea paved the way for Ephesus and Chalcedon because the claim of a Son who was of the same essence as the Father (the doctrine of God) naturally led to the question of how in the economy one is to understand the identity of this God-man (christology).

C. The Christological Controversy

C.1. Historical Background

When one moves to the christological controversy, modernity has maligned Chalcedon because many believe that the linguistic conventions typified by this council only helped spawn a dualist christology that has been maintained for centuries within the Christian tradition. But this generalization is inaccurate regarding the proceedings of the council itself, for one of the motivations behind it was precisely to curb the tendency to embark upon dualist christologies.

A number of parallels exist between the events and themes leading to Chalcedon and those that led to Nicaea.[6] First, the major factions of the fifth-century council held on to divine impassibility as part of a conventional and nonnegotiable matrix of theological modifiers. The phrase that the Son "suffered impassibly" is usually associated with Cyril of Alexandria, and part of the rationale for Nestorius' project was the defense of divine impassibility at all costs; therefore, two of the major figures enmeshed in the controversy wished to· preserve the term in their discourses. What one finds in these examples is what one finds among Docetists, Arians, and others before: The true issue surrounding divine impassibility was not its viability but its form and extensiveness within each theological formulation.

Another parallel along these lines is the way divine impassibility functioned for the Nestorians, which was very similar to past heretical articulators. As Gavrilyuk states, "Despite fundamental differences in their christologies, there is a peculiar affinity between the Arian and Nestorian conceptualizations of the divine transcendence . . . . We find the same basic impulse [of the Arians] to protect absolute divine impassibility in Theodore and Nestorius."[7] This affinity

---

[6] Cyril himself makes it a point to mark these similarities, no doubt in part because of polemical considerations. See *On the Unity of Christ* (trans. J. A. McGuckin; Crestwood, NY: St. Vladimir's Seminary Press, 1995), p. 51.

[7] Gavrilyuk, *The Suffering of the Impassible God*, p. 141. Although a generalization that must not be pushed too far, O'Keefe remarks that he believes the Alexandrine reading of Scripture (e.g., Cyril) dictated the way philosophy (as a general category) was employed whereas the Antiochene school (e.g., Nestorius and Theodoret) preferred to give

basically rests on the belief that the divine and the material cannot intermingle because that would corrupt, and so diminish, the integrity of the former. Once again, we see the notion of divine impassibility taking a life of its own that is separate from a strong biblical reading of God's capacity and willingness to relate to his creation. Given that the past controversies heightened the need for articulating how the world and the divine interrelate in the Christ-event, Nestorius and his followers resorted to a program in which the basis for all other christological judgments was the nonnegotiable distinction between the human and the divine in Christ. This assumption is a natural result of an overextended notion of the transcendence of God where any relationship of the divine to the material world would threaten God's nature and so God's capacity to save.[8] Christologically speaking, God could not have suffered in the events of the life of Christ because that would mean that God's being would have been irretrievably tarnished.

Such a line of argument shows why one of the principal grievances against Cyril's program was that he was a "theopaschite". Given the alleged linguistic tricks and conceptual chicanery proposed by Cyril and others, the Nestorian camp believed that God's transcendence was compromised and diminished by their opponents since a strict duality was not maintained throughout their arguments. In his reading of Nicaea's second article and of certain biblical passages, such as the "Christ hymn" of Philippians 2, Nestorius believed that there was no warrant to state that the divine essence suffered, for such a claim would be sheer impiety.[9] Essentially, Nestorius believed that the only way to preserve the divine impassibility and to steer clear of theopaschitism was to offer a dual-subject account of the incarnation. Because of this method, Nestorius was favored by certain factions in the East while Cyril was duly charged with doing away with the divine impassibility.[10]

The great irony when one considers Cyril's views is that, although in his

---

primacy in their commitments to such categories as divine impassibility ("Kenosis or Impassibility", p. 359).

[8] Interestingly, even though Nestorius is associated with the Antiochene school that supposedly emphasized the humanity of Christ more than his divinity, O'Keefe remarks that "Nestorius worried far more about the impassibility of God than he did about the humanity of Jesus," as can be seen with his early arguments against the term *theotokos*. See "Impassible Suffering? Divine Passion and Fifth-Century Christology", *Theological Studies* 58 (1997), p. 52.

[9] Nestorius states of the Philippian passage: "Since [Paul] was going to mention the death [in the passage], he posited the title Christ so that no one might imagine that God the Word was passible, for Christ is a term that applies to both the impassible and the passible natures in a single persona. This is how Christ can be said, without danger, to be both passible and impassible; impassible in the Godhead, but passible in the nature of his body" ("Nestorius' Reply to Cyril's Second Letter" in J. McGuckin, *Saint Cyril of Alexandria and the Christological Controversy* [Crestwood, NY: St. Vladimir's Seminary Press, 2004], p. 365).

[10] Gavrilyuk, *The Suffering of the Impassible God*, p. 145.

own day his opponents argued that he advocated theopaschitism, many contemporary readers find him advocating a metaphysically untenable view of God because of his commitment to divine impassibility! Such varied readings from opposite viewpoints indicate that Cyril's position is a complex one that requires careful attention. In the first place, in contrast to Nestorius, Cyril begins from the unity of Christ instead of a dual-subject approach. Through this strategy, Cyril attempts to bypass the minutiae of attributing this detail to one nature or the other by opting instead to emphasize the miracle of the incarnation itself. Some moderns would find this method problematic, especially since Cyril does not attribute suffering to the divine nature *per se*; that consideration, however, is secondary in Cyril's mind. Rather than speculating about the divine nature in itself, Cyril believes that the "narrative of Incarnation, not the notion of divine impassibility, [should drive] his Christology".[11] This kind of negotiation is what leads him to speak in such dialectical terms regarding the nature of the Son's "impassible suffering".

Biblically, Cyril supports his views through a specific reading (among other passages) of the "Christ hymn" of Philippians. Cyril's opponents interpreted the passage to imply two subjects: one in the form of God and the other in the form of a slave, the latter being essentially a "God-bearing man". But Cyril could not hold to such an interpretation because that would imply that Christ was different from other prophets and saints only in matter of degree. Cyril opposes this reading with the belief that in the incarnation, with the corresponding notions of "emptying"[12] and "humiliation", something radically new occurred: the Son took upon himself human flesh, and this same Word was therefore the subject of all the things attributed to Christ. Whereas the Nestorians found their division of natures helpful in maintaining the coherence of christological language, Cyril believes such a move does away with the hopefulness of the gospel in that overcoming the division between God and the world is in reality the miracle of the incarnation.

What Cyril attempted to do was to avoid the "either human or divine" alternative in accounting for Christ's suffering and to make the subject of such experiences one entity: God who took upon himself human flesh. This incarnation took place within the economy and had to be considered in very unique ways that avoided attributing suffering simply to the human nature (which is very much the plight of humans in any case) and the divine nature

---

[11] O'Keefe, "Impassible Suffering?", pp. 50-51.

[12] It is important to note that Cyril did not believe that in emptying himself the Son did away with his divinity; rather, the act of "emptying" himself implies for Cyril that the Son took upon himself human flesh. The same can be said for Cyril's understanding of the Johannine notion that the "Word became flesh" (John 1:14), as he links these passages in *On the Unity of Christ*, pp. 54-55. Cyril clearly states the matter through the following: "And what is this 'emptying out'? It is his life in the form of a slave, in the flesh which he assumes; it is the likeness to us of one who is not as we are in his own nature, since he is above all creation" (*On the Unity of Christ*, p. 86).

alone (which would jeopardize the notion of divine impassibility in particular and the divine transcendence overall).[13] Although Christ was certainly divine, within a particular *kairos* one could move to attribute human characteristics to the divine because of the radical quality of the incarnation. In this way, in contradistinction to Nestorius, "Cyril's starting point was the 'economic' Christ whom we meet in Scripture and in the Church."[14] The alternative, which he saw in Nestorius and others, is to demystify the incarnation and to keep intact the apparently unbridgeable gap between divinity and humanity.

With respect to divine impassibility in particular, Cyril does maintain the theme but in a very different way from his opponent Nestorius. Whereas the latter opts for a notion that is nonnegotiable in its implications for relationality within the economy, Cyril speaks in dialectical terms, implying that Christ suffered impassibly.[15] For some, this move suggests terminological imprecision or (worse) trifling, but Cyril is attempting something very important through such phrasing: "To say that 'he suffered impassibly' deliberately states both sides of the paradox with equal force and absolute seriousness of intent, refusing to minimise either reality."[16] Without this apparent contradiction, the additional paradox involving soteriological claims could not ensue; as Smith suggests of what is at stake in such phrasing: "The Word must be divine in order to free us from death; and . . . the Word must genuinely experience suffering and death in order to conquer death itself, and provide examples for his disciples who would imitate the Lord's passion in their own martyrdom."[17]

The key to Cyril's logic rests in large part on a robust notion of *communicatio idiomatum*, which Weinandy calls "the test of christological orthodoxy".[18] According to Weinandy, underwriting this communication of

---

[13] Of course, one can distinguish the two natures in Cyril's mind, but at this point he would pause to state that the "disunion" is proper only at the conceptual level (see J. W. Smith, "Suffering Impassibly: Christ's Passion in Cyril of Alexandria's Soteriology", *Pro Ecclesia* 11.4 [2002], p. 467). As a constant check of his extensive treatment of the subject, Cyril reminds his readers repeatedly that the union is an utter mystery (e.g., *On the Unity of Christ*, p. 77).

[14] O'Keefe, "Impassible Suffering?", p. 43.

[15] Those moments in which Cyril sounds dualist must be qualified with these dialectical statements in order that his position not be caricatured, as it often is in modern theological discourse. Concessive remarks, as when he states, "So, even if he is said to suffer in the flesh, even so he retains his impassibility insofar as he is understood as God" (*On the Unity of Christ*, p. 117), should not be read as Nestorian.

[16] McGuckin, *Saint Cyril of Alexandria and the Christological Controversy*, p. 185.

[17] "Suffering Impassibly", p. 466. Smith's thesis regarding Cyril applies to many other patristic sources, namely that one cannot overemphasize the relationship of impassibility with soteriology within the patristic testimony: because of the former, the latter is possible; the latter is implied by the former.

[18] *Does God Suffer?*, p. 175. The point cannot be overstated for Weinandy, for he believes that "it was not a proper understanding of the Incarnation which gave rise to the

idioms is a double sense of unity for Cyril: Jesus is "one existing reality or being", and this existential reality of Jesus is the Son of God incarnate.[19] With such considerations, one can then properly make the various linguistic moves one finds in Scripture in which Jesus is given both divine and human attributes because these are being spoken of one person rather than two natures.

When one engages the language of Chalcedon's deliberations, one sees Cyril's position vindicated with the nuanced moves one would anticipate as necessary. Although the language of "one person, two natures" is in part a concession from Cyril's viewpoint, the other qualifiers for this union, including "inconfusedly", "unchangeably", "indivisibly", and "inseparably", all show marks of a Cyrilline position.[20] Through the Council's language of unifying the divine and human natures, Cyril's alternative was declared orthodox when compared to the alternatives of Nestorius and Theodoret. Nevertheless, given that the issue remained unsatisfactory for many who believed such terminology was misleading or unhelpful, Chalcedon and Cyril have been vilified for centuries.

C.2. The Modern Assessment

The scholarly critique of both Chalcedon and Cyril has been part of a general trend to affirm a more dynamic ontological framework generally and a "suffering God" particularly. Although several cases could be used to illustrate this negative reception,[21] Moltmann serves as a convenient possibility as he has been considered earlier in this work.

According to Moltmann's reading, the tradition has had problems considering the forsakenness of Jesus upon the cross to the extent that orthodox christology tended to Docetism.[22] Moltmann believes that this docetic inclination manifests itself through the two-natures doctrine of Chalcedon, and the culprits underwriting this move are antiquity's views of the metaphysical as well as the pious longing for salvation.[23] According to Moltmann and others, both of these factors coalesced in an unhelpful hybridity that dominated the

---

communication of idioms . . . but rather it was the communication of idioms which gave rise to a proper understanding of the Incarnation" (p. 198).

[19] *Does God Suffer?*, p. 191. Weinandy goes on to clarify that this unity exists as one entity but not as one essence or quiddity, a move that avoids the kind of confusion that Nestorius and some believe Cyril to have promulgated (pp. 192, 194).

[20] See Schaff, *The Creeds of Christendom*, II, pp. 62-63.

[21] For a survey of some examples, see G. W. Stroup, III, "Christian Doctrine: I, Chalcedon Revisited", *Theology Today* 35 (1978), pp. 52-64. A work often referenced in this vein is J. Hick (ed), *The Myth of God Incarnate* (London: SCM Press, 1977).

[22] "Traditional christology came very near to docetism, according to which Jesus only appeared to suffer and only appeared to die abandoned by God: this did not happen in reality" (Moltmann, *CG*, p. 227).

[23] See Moltmann, *CG*, pp. 227-28.

early church, especially in its conciliar era.

In treating Cyril's position, Moltmann acknowledges that the Alexandrian father pushes for the unity of Christ considerably, and yet the latter falls short of stating that the suffering of Christ affected his divine nature, thereby conceding to the *apatheia* axiom once again, as many had done before and continued to do after. Essentially, Moltmann counters the doctrine of appropriation that Cyril took from Athanasius and discredits it, for it comes short of stating what Moltmann already insists is necessary, that the divine nature, and not simply the human nature, suffered. Any other response or suggestion to the contrary falls short of the implications Moltmann wishes to find in the cross of Christ for human suffering today.

Given the historical reading attempted in this chapter, it appears that Moltmann's view of Cyril is both accurate and inaccurate. It is true that Cyril, when pushed, would concede that Christ suffers in his human nature but not in his divine nature since the latter is not capable of suffering. This perspective, however, obscures Cyril's main point, which is to affirm the unity of the person of Christ. From Cyril's point of view, the distinction of natures and the ensuing negotiation of appropriations is first and foremost a baffling mystery of revelation. Cyril's perspective as a whole suggests that the unity of Christ's person prevails over what he occasionally makes of the natures themselves.

Moltmann's misreading of Cyril is nefarious if for no other reason than that he misses the key motives for Cyril's christological program. Moltmann himself states that one must begin christology from the totality of the person of Christ, a move that Cyril would not find problematic. Nevertheless, Moltmann believes that this "totality" is missing in the Chalcedonian formulation because of what he finds to be a dualist ontological scheme, i.e., one in which suffering cannot be attributed to the godhead apart from the flesh assumed by Christ. Webster has countered this curt dismissal of Chalcedon when he remarks: "However much [the two-natures doctrine] may be open to abuse, in its sophisticated forms it is by no means dualist. Indeed the whole thrust of the Chalcedonian definition is that an adequate Christology has to regard as axiomatic the unity of the person of Christ as 'one and the same Son'."[24] Webster continues, "The doctrine of the two-natures is intended to emphasise that in the God-man Jesus we have to do with one logical subject with an integrated identity."[25]

Webster's remarks are suggestive for a couple of reasons. First, he notes that what Moltmann originally rejects about the doctrine is in fact that which it was originally framed to avoid. As dualistic as "two-natures" may sound, the doctrine, especially when understood against its Cyrilline backdrop, aims at maintaining the unity of Christ's person.[26] Second, Webster is not oblivious to

---

[24] Webster, "Jürgen Moltmann: Trinity and Suffering", p. 5.

[25] Webster, "Jürgen Moltmann: Trinity and Suffering", p. 5.

[26] As Fiddes remarks, "We cannot isolate experiences and attributes within sealed compartments labeled 'divine' and 'human', and still present Christ as 'one person'" (*The Creative Suffering of God*, pp. 26-27).

the doctrine's potential abuse, and the history of Christianity proves the case. Although accounts exist that attempt to live up to the aims associated with the use of the two-natures, others have moved from this doctrine to affirm a duality; therefore, one sees that Moltmann has taken as determinative the history of Chalcedon's misinterpretation rather than its best representations that live up to its original purposes.

Equally problematic is Moltmann's intolerance of any view that falls short of stating that God suffers in his being. Rather than seeing what the ancients found untenable in such declarations, Moltmann believes that this notion is a tenet for viable Christian faith, thereby attributing a nonnegotiable value to suffering in itself as a category of self-deriving meaning. Not only does this move apotheosize human suffering, but it creates deep christological difficulties in considering the *communicatio idiomatum* and the parameters for christological language. In pushing the barriers of what the tradition has found acceptable, Moltmann in essence has lost a grasp of christological speech, a symptom that runs rampant throughout history, especially in modern Christian thought. Quite simply, the theological implications stemming from the identity of the one called Jesus of Nazareth are absent from Moltmann's program as it is articulated in his speculative doctrine of God; an account of the incarnation that would have created greater coherence and exchange between divinity and humanity within Christ's person is sorely missing in his project. In this instance, as in others, Moltmann has lost an opportunity to claim and to be claimed by the tradition with its original parameters and warrants.

C.3. Conclusion

From this brief consideration of the christological controversy and its reception, one notices that this controversy aimed to establish a way of speaking and thinking of Christ that would maintain the integrity of his divine and human identity.[27] In the debates between Cyril and Nestorius, one sees two approaches to impassibility as it relates to the Son: a dual-subject approach (Nestorius) and a single subject approach that then incorporates a doctrine of appropriation. History has named Cyril the representative of orthodoxy because of his dialectical approach to the issue, and yet many have continued to be dissatisfied with his work. Moltmann and others have found Cyril's position to be inherently contradictory rather than dialectical or paradoxical, a view that has

---

[27] As a means of expressing this point, reference will be made to "Chalcedonian reasoning". This term is used rather than something akin to the popular phrase "Chalcedonian Definition" for reasons spelled out in S. Coakley's chapter "What Does Chalcedon Solve and What Does it Not?" in S. T. Davis, D. Kendall, and G. O'Collins (eds), *The Incarnation* (Oxford: Oxford University Press, 2002), pp. 143-63. Although Coakley rejects thinking of Chalcedon as a "language rule" on anachronistic grounds, her proposals of *horos* (horizon) and the idea of a "regulatory *grid*" are not all that different from what is being espoused presently.

led many to offer alternatives to both his work and the accomplishments of Chalcedon.

Once again, this time within the realm of christology, the interrelationship between the divine and suffering raises questions about the propriety and fittingness of God-talk as it pushes the limits of language. In reaching these limits, the issue can either be painstakingly qualified and nuanced or it can be allowed to remain unproblematized so that the conventions of a given era can determine the nature of the interplay. What follows is an assessment of a moment in historical theology where it seems that the latter occurred, the so-called "Anglican debates" regarding divine impassibility.

D. The British Debates

By the early twentieth century, divine impassibility came under significant scrutiny in what can be termed the "Anglican" or "British debates" regarding the issue.[28] In fact, Mozley's *The Impassibility of God* was commissioned by the Archbishops' Doctrine Commission in 1924 precisely because the issue had reached such a fevered pitch during the early decades of the past century. British thinkers at this time began to deride the importance of divine impassibility in a collective and sustained front. The difficult appraisals alluded to above (namely that "theology has no falser idea than that of the impassibility of God"[29] and that "the doctrine of the impassibility of God, taken in its widest sense, is the greatest heresy that ever smirched Christianity"[30]) stem from this agonistic climate.

This context was significantly inflected by a number of factors that in turn influenced the shape of the impassibility debates. With the publication of *Lux Mundi* in 1889 and the popularity of H. Bushnell's *Vicarious Sacrifice* in 1891, one sees a changing of the tide in which higher criticism of the Bible, a move to affirm a particular view of the incarnation, and a sympathetic view of kenotic christology came to the fore of the discussion. Needless to say, what was largely at work in these commitments was a "christology from below" that was subsequently used to underwrite a "christology from above".[31] Additionally,

---

[28] Although the phrase "Anglican debates" is often used because of convention, it is important to note that the phrase is inaccurate: A. M. Fairbarn and P. T. Forsyth were Scottish Congregationalists, and a number of American influences were prominent at this time as part of north, trans-Atlantic cross-pollination. For general surveys, see Mozley, *Some Tendencies in British Theology*; A. M. Ramsey, *An Era in Anglican Theology* (New York: Charles Scribners' Sons, 1960); and J. Dickie, *Fifty Years of British Theology* (Edinburgh: T & T Clark, 1937).

[29] Fairbairn, *The Place of Christ in Modern Theology*, p. 483.

[30] White, *Forgiveness and Suffering*, p. 84.

[31] Obviously, within such a contested milieu, certain figures arose who attempted to defend traditional orthodoxy and the conventional place divine impassibility had retained within this framework. It is evident where Mozley's sympathies were, and

this "christology from below" was maintained alongside the Protestant assumption that Christ is the most faithful and lasting representation of who God is. Since Christ demonstrated suffering love to us by descending and being crucified, these characteristics must be determinative of the divine nature as a whole from eternity on. As Fairbairn states prior to the passage quoted above: "From [the incarnation], therefore, comes, first, the *complete* revelation of God. God as He is in Himself and to Himself stood disclosed to man."[32] From this move one can answer logically the famous question *Cur Deus Homo?* by stating that God always suffered pains because of his creation, thereby precipitating the self-giving event of sending his Son to die for humanity.[33] These pains are principally due to the loss of relationship between God and humanity on account of the effects of human sin. According to W. Temple: "If the God who forgives suffers under the impact of sin in a fashion that requires Gethsemane and Calvary for its manifestation, it is impossible to say that He forgives through indifference."[34] Particularly telling in this quotation is the absence of a detailed differentiation between the life of Christ on earth and the godhead in general; rather than seeing a trinitarian interplay at Gethsemane and Calvary, Temple and others assumed that the events of Christ's life could be generalized quite sweepingly to the godhead itself.

Such commitments naturally lead to the attribution of suffering to the Father, and in this regard (as in others), the "British debates" theologically predate the contemporary inclinations toward patripassian tendencies. Once again, Fairbairn is helpful here when he remarks: "There is a sense in which the Patripassian theory is right; the Father did suffer, though it was not as the Son that He suffered, but in modes distinct and different."[35] The parallels are striking in their similarities to Moltmann and others who have written recently on the Father's relationship to the suffering of the Son, and such a move suggests that contemporary sensibilities deem it insufficient to attribute suffering only to the Son, for "all of God" had to suffer if God's solidarity with humanity was to be effective and sufficiently extensive.

Finally, these debates allow one to see the notion of love intertwined with the notion of suffering in inseparable correlation. This move, one of the most

---

others such as F. von Hügel (*Essays and Addresses on the Philosophy of Religion* [second series; London: J. M. Dent and Sons, 1926-1930]) and B. Brasnett (*The Suffering of the Impassible God* [London: SPCK, 1928]) offered similar endeavors.

[32] Fairbairn, *The Place of Christ in Modern Theology*, p. 483 (emphasis added).

[33] Expressive of this view is C. A. Dinsmore's comment: "There was a cross in the heart of God before there was one planted on the green hill outside of Jerusalem" (*Atonement in Literature and Life* [New York: Houghton Mifflin, 1906], p. 232).

[34] W. Temple, *Christus Veritas* (London: Macmillan, 1962), p. 260. Another similar passage from Temple is: "The revelation of God's dealing with human sin shows God enduring every depth of anguish for the sake of His children. What is portrayed under the figure of physical suffering and literal blood-shedding is only a part of the pain which sin inflicts on God" (p. 269).

[35] Fairbairn, *The Place of Christ in Modern Theology*, p. 484.

characteristic of today's passibilist climate, has its theological antecedent in these British debates. To quote White again, "to us the crucial point is that [God] is love. Now love is passible; and if God is love, God is passible."[36] One also sees this idea with the popular musings of G. A. Studdert Kennedy: "If the Christian religion means anything, it means that God is Suffering Love, and that all real progress is caused by the working of Suffering Love in the world."[37] For a summary of this argument, one can turn to the statement of G. B. Stevens, a contemporary of these discussions: "If Christ gave his life in utmost sacrifice for men, it is because there is in the being of God himself the possibility of vicarious suffering which, so far from marring his blessedness, is one of the elements of that matchless perfection whose name is love."[38] Essentially, in ways reminiscent of contemporary authors, the belief among many within these debates was that "if God's love be infinite, then He can suffer infinitely too".[39]

From these salient tendencies one notices an absence of any sort of Chalcedonian reasoning that would temper or alter some of these claims. It is easy to anticipate that Chalcedon would pose difficulties for such patterns of thought and speech, so it is no surprise that within such contexts this ecumenical council would be derided. For example, Temple says that, "The formula of Chalcedon is in fact a confession of the bankruptcy of Greek Patristic Theology",[40] an expression that shows obvious distaste for the conciliar outcome.

Why would Chalcedonian reasoning not fare well in such discussions, especially in light of a context in which the incarnation, the christological notion of kenosis, and other important claims were present? A push to the experiential and to the immanent over and against the transcendent is detectable in many of the musings of the age, a feature that coincided with the rising influence of continental Protestant liberalism upon English theology. Additionally, when Studdert Kennedy's work was so welcomely received – work that stemmed from his experience as a chaplain during the First World War – it is easy to see that the violent times were calling for a different expression, one that would take into consideration the massive suffering that was being witnessed in Europe at the time.

In summary, the "British debates" concerning divine impassibility represent a pivotal moment in which the axiom was derided and critiqued in a sustained and extensive manner. The general difficulty one finds among many who argued for the passibilist position within these debates is the loss of Cyrilline or Chalcedonian reasoning. In its place is a discourse that all too easily conflates

---

[36] White, *Forgiveness and Suffering*, p. 83.

[37] G. A. Studdert Kennedy, *The Hardest Part* (2nd ed.; London: Hodder and Stoughton, 1918), p. 41.

[38] G. B. Stevens, *Christian Doctrine of Salvation* (New York: Charles Scribner's Sons, 1905), p. 446.

[39] White, *Forgiveness and Suffering*, p. 84.

[40] As quoted in Mozley, *Some Tendencies in British Theology*, p. 42.

the human and divine in Christ so that suffering becomes not only a real experience of Christ's human life but also by extension part of the triune God's experience and life as well. The category of suffering is assumed rather than extensively engaged so that it has an eternal permanence akin to divine love, and in fact both suffering and love are depicted as two sides of the same coin, one naturally implying the other. This apparently attractive alternative served well for the post-World War I era; it is no wonder that it was continually promoted and accepted within a post-World War II/post-Holocaust one as well.

E. Divine Impassibility in the Flesh

With the double testimony of the Hebrew Scriptures and the gospels' depiction of a suffering Christ, there is no question that divine impassibility as it existed in the wider Hellenistic world is untenable for Christians. Perhaps more than any other facet of Christian faith, the notion of a crucified Jesus questions an unproblematic appropriation of impassibilist language within Christian theological discourse. It is no wonder that this question has resurfaced time and again throughout the history of Christian theology, often in the shape of the pious versus the speculative.

It is the contention of this study that divine impassibility has a role to play in current theological discourse, even within the locus of christology. Without a sense of transcendence, a notion that the Son of God was in the midst but also beyond that which he was facing and suffering in the ordeal leading up to Golgotha, the gospel ceases to be "good news". Certainly, one aspect of the hopefulness depends on the way the Son took upon himself the human condition: in that respect, both Moltmann and those associated with the "British debates" have made a formidable case for the humanity and vulnerability of Christ. Nevertheless, any account that stops at this point falls short of the equally important dynamic of Christ's identity as the one of the Trinity who took on human flesh.

Because of this feature, a case can be made that Christ "suffered impassibly", as contradictory and difficult as such phrasing sounds. Too much is at stake to let go of one side of the continuum. Whatever arguments one could make about the language of Chalcedon, there is a sense in which Chalcedonian reasoning is at the very core of what Christians profess about who Christ is and what he did. In order to elaborate this possibility, a tendency detected early in Ignatius' letters will serve what follows. As these epistles show, Ignatius could account for Christ's (im)passibility on the basis of the narrative logic of incarnation, crucifixion, and resurrection.

In what follows, the ancient *exitus-reditus* scheme associated with the narrative of Christ's life will be considered in order to pose the argument that any vibrantly theological account of the identity and work of Christ has to take shape within a framework that values the key moments within the Christ event. In contradistinction to the different strands of staurocentric emphases within contemporary passibilist alternatives, the following suggests that there is a sense in which the crucifixion has become domesticated and ridden of its status as a theological corrective within the contemporary scene, especially since the reality and value of suffering are nonnegotiables within contemporary theodicies. Given the present post-Holocaust sensibilities prevalent in theology today, it may be more formidable, and therefore theologically more suggestive, to argue for the merits of the incarnation and resurrection alongside the apparently more accessible notion of crucifixion.

E.1. Divine Impassibility and the Incarnation

H. McCabe was of the opinion that "the temptation to hold that it is in the nature of God to suffer arises because of a weakening hold on the traditional doctrine of incarnation".[41] Given the present theological landscape, it is hard to disagree with such an analysis. Especially among those who opt for christologies "from below" and espouse the crucifixion as the defining event of the Christ event, the tendency is to humanize Jesus and domesticate the cross to such a degree that the question remains as to how human suffering touches God. Without a vibrant account of the incarnation, one could fall into making the subsequent move of attributing suffering to God, and as it has been noted, such an affirmation is quite acceptable within the contemporary context.

Simply beginning with the incarnation, however, is an inadequate safeguard of the divine transcendence since many within the "British debates" also emphasized the incarnation as a way to disestablish the possibility of divine impassibility. What is desirable within an account of the incarnation that opens the possibility for impassibility is one that can coincide and be shaped by Chalcedonian reasoning. Certain views of the incarnation are believed by their espousers to be in tension with Chalcedon, and so the task is not necessarily an obvious or natural one. One of the key challenges is the Son's *kenosis* or "self-emptying" that leads to what are commonly denominated as "kenotic christologies".

The tension at play between Chalcedon and kenotic christologies revolves around the perception that in the former the divine nature is fully present in Christ whereas the latter admits of a certain "divestment" or "self-limitation" in the incarnation. Both possibilities tend to emphasize diametrically opposed themes, that of fullness and limitation. As with so many issues in theological reflection, one's starting point often veils the possibilities of other, relevant markers. One senses as well that significant in such a configuration are some of the basic issues inherent to the christological debates, namely the nature and display of the divine within the economy of creation.

The subtext of these discussions is the "Christ hymn" of Philippians 2:5-11 and its famous use of the concept of *kenosis* to speak of the Son's "self-emptying". As noted, both Cyril and Nestorius found it important to incorporate this passage in their debates leading up to the Council of Chalcedon. At play in

---

[41] H. McCabe, *God Matters* (Springfield, IL: Templegate Publishers, 1987), p. 46.

these discussions are the rationale and shape of the *kenosis* itself. Although long-standing discussions have occurred throughout history regarding these themes,[42] at first blush, the "Christ hymn" preserves an *exitus-reditus* logic.[43] There is a narrative progression from preexistence, solidarity/sharing, to exaltation, irrespective of how the details are further teased out. The narrative display at work in the "Christ hymn" implies both historical and theological data in an integrated fashion that informs the identity and significance of Christ's life and work.

In demarcating the particulars of the *kenosis* itself, several difficulties immediately present themselves. One of the more challenging issues involved with this theme is the way that God and humanity are usually juxtaposed as two competing and ultimately incompatible entities. From such an assumption, one sees the difficulty of Chalcedon's language of "two natures" in that it is obvious to anyone that divinity and humanity are not the same thing and in fact are diametrically opposed to one another on a number of specific issues. Divinity is infinite, eternal, and omnipotent (just to take a sampling of attributes) whereas humanity is finite, temporal, and vulnerable. How these two can be found in Christ lies at the heart of the many controversies that ensued after Chalcedon and that continue today.

In order that Chalcedonian reasoning be preserved within an incarnational, specifically kenotic, christology, several steps are in order. First, it is important to note that given a vibrant account of creation, divinity and humanity need not be considered diametrically opposed realities. As humans are created in God's image, a continuum is at play, one with a specific direction no less, in which humans stem from and are called and capacitated to turn back to their origin and end. One cannot help but wonder how much this oppositional line of thinking is indebted to the problem of the One and the Many and/or to an overbearing account of the fall. Chalcedon, as an extension and culmination of the christological accomplishments of the patristic age, does not suggest that these "natures" are so much opposed as complementary to the point that they can co-exist in the person of Christ.

With this last remark, it is worth mentioning as a second point that the language of "natures" is very problematic when one assumes that it suggests self-standing, independent, and competing entities. W. Pannenberg relates the difficulty when he states: "The problem results from speaking of 'two' natures as if they were on the same plane. This poses the pseudotask of relating the two natures to one another in such a way that their synthesis results in a single

---

[42] These occurrences include the famous debates between the schools of Giessen and Tübingen in the 17th century and the work of Thomasius and others in the 19th.

[43] While commenting on verse six of this passage, Barth states: "This equality of Christ with God is, so to speak, the fixed, *ultimate* background from which his road sets out and to which it returns" (*The Epistle to the Philippians* [trans. J. W. Leitch; Louisville: Westminster John Knox, 2002], p. 61).

individual in spite of the hindrances posed by the idea of a 'nature'."[44] The aim of the language of "natures" was to suggest that "true divinity" and "true humanity" were at play in the person of Christ; unfortunately, such terms tend to indicate that divinity *simpliciter* and humanity *simpliciter* were somehow joined in Christ, as if those concepts could be postulated and entertained without any conceptual difficulty and without the oppositional underpinnings they imply. Such reasoning sounds very close to Nestorian, and it is no wonder that many churches in the East opposed the language espoused by the Fourth Ecumenical Council.

In Cyrilline fashion, it would seem unhelpful to speak of the *kenosis* as a "giving-up" or a "perpetual self-limitation" of certain divine properties.[45] Obviously, in "journeying into the far country", the Son took up the form of a slave, and in doing so subjected himself to finite conditions of human existence, but such claims do not rest so much on speculative achievement (a process that would probably lead to different conclusions if left to its own devices) but on divine self-disclosure within the economy. The shape of the life and work of Christ keep a check on speculative endeavors, and here one is reminded of the conclusions reached in Chapter 3 of this study related to relational/act and metaphysical/abstract attributes where the former were considered as more determinative and helpful than the latter in relating God's personal nature. The great value in Cyril's viewpoint is that the scandalous particularity of Jesus' life has the potential for keeping speculative God-talk grounded in historical contingency so that finite, temporal, and vulnerable humanity becomes the mirror and gateway to infinite, eternal, and powerful divinity.

Rather than approaching the incarnation as a restriction, one can then see that the God-man is the expression of divine expansiveness. The Son embodied both extremes of the continuum alluded to above and in doing so demonstrated his sovereignty and power over all things. As Barth remarks, "The Christian theological tradition has always been in agreement that the statement 'The Word was made flesh' is not to be thought of as describing an event which overtook Him, and therefore overtook God himself, but rather a free divine activity, a sovereign act of divine lordship, an act of mercy which was necessary only by virtue of the will of God Himself . . . God is always God even in His humiliation."[46]

In light of the specific notion of divine impassibility; Chalcedonian reasoning suggests the Cyrilline notion of "suffering impassibly" on grounds

---

[44] W. Pannenberg, *Jesus – God and Man* (2nd ed.; trans, L. L. Wilkins and D. A. Priebe; Philadelphia: Westminster, 1977), p. 322.

[45] Unfortunately, many of the debates surrounding kenotic christology strive to delineate these matters so that much of what results tends to the speculative because of its inherent unverifiability.

[46] Barth, *CD*, IV/1, p. 179. L. J. Richard says of Barth's position that rather than being a sign of weakness, *kenosis* becomes the highest affirmation of God's transcendence (*A Kenotic Christology* [Washington, D.C.: University Press of America, 1982], p. 162).

that in Christ's suffering we see *historically* a genuine human who suffers in a true way, and yet *theologically* the nature of this suffering takes the double aspect of 1) being assumed voluntarily 2) for the purpose of redemption. The incarnation thus represents a pivotal step within the economy of God showing his impassibility "in action". God's constancy and eternal resolve to reach out to humanity is given a wondrous expression as a child born in the humblest and most vulnerable of circumstances. In harkening back to the point made by Gregory Thaumaturgus, God demonstrated his impassibility precisely in his passibility.

E.2. Divine Impassibility and the Crucifixion

In considering the cross and the specific issue of atonement, one moves from the person of Christ to his work and its significance. The early church managed to reach some ecumenical consensus when it came to the identity of Christ, but the issue of his work was more elusive, resulting in no conciliar demarcation of what Christian orthodoxy believes surrounding the efficacy of Christ's work outside of general remarks found in the creeds. When one analyzes the biblical literature, it is easy to see why: there are no fewer than "five constellations of images"[47] that the Bible employs to elaborate the work of Christ for those who believe in him, and if one were to select only one of them, the scope and extent of meaning of subsequent theological expressions would be constricted as a result.

The atonement and the cross of Christ more generally can and often do play a role within passibilist alternatives. For instance, one sees that the "British debates" refer time and again to the importance of the atonement for all subsequent reflection about who God has revealed himself to be in Christ. At play in these and other instantiations are the commitments alluded to above that make talk of a "suffering God" all too facile and potentially saccharine. Issues such as the unquestioned link between love and suffering, the tendency to project the historical contingencies of Christ's life and death unto the godhead more generally, and others come into play specifically because of the way the image of the crucified Christ is used in these discussions.

As mentioned above, modern staurocentric endeavors find the image of Christ crucified quite appealing because it creates the possibility for an interplay between divinity and suffering. Many, including Moltmann, have found a certain hopefulness in such imagery in that God can be said to not be indifferent or unconcerned for the plight of humanity. In this sense, Christ enters into "solidarity" with the human condition by taking its condition upon himself in faithfulness unto death. The additional "cry of dereliction" in the

---

[47] This phrasing is found in J. B. Green and M. D. Baker, *Recovering the Scandal of the Cross* (Downers Grove, IL: InterVarsity, 2000), p. 23. The five constellations are the court of law, the world of commerce, personal relationships, worship, and the battleground.

synoptic accounts of Matthew and Mark only adds to this specific reading of Golgotha. The category of "godforsakenness" can be used as a way to assure those who feel "godforsaken" in specific situations that such a feeling is not out of God's reach, that it is actually part of the divine experience of suffering.

The difficulty of this staurocentric line of reflection is that it does not suggest a traditional account of the atonement. In depicting Jesus as the "fellow-sufferer who understands", this understanding can bypass the difficulty of the theodicy question by keeping it intact in its modern form, namely by leaving the category of suffering as an a priori matter that is unquestioned, not situated within a meaning-generating schema, accepted, and given a nonnegotiable value. From these basic assumptions, no need presents itself to account for suffering and sin in a theological manner. What follows from these methodological choices is an account of Golgotha independent of a soteriological framework.

Granted, in many instances, the soteriological push does much in the way of moving too quickly to resolution, to justifying the suffering of Jesus as a means of achieving something else. Such attempts to sidestep the offense that is the cross are egregious in that they fail to recognize how scandalous it is to say that the Son of God suffered and died. Nevertheless, from the other side of the spectrum, it is equally difficult to abandon any account of soteriology, for at such a point the theological rationale for contextualizing Christ's cross would be lost. Jesus' suffering is not simply an end in itself: its importance lies in its subject (the one who is suffering) and its rationale (what such suffering points to or suggests).

Christ was not simply another victim in the long list of humans who have been persecuted, beaten, and killed unjustly; Jesus was the Son of God who faced the powers of sin and death and provided the means by which others could live victoriously in spite of the ongoing influence of such powers. The continuity of incarnation-crucifixion-resurrection suggested here plays out at this point in that a Chalcedonian kind of reasoning along Cyrilline lines would suggest that Christ, the God-bearing-man, was the one who died on the cross at Golgotha that day, a declaration that would qualify any notion of victimization with the equally important move of God's freedom to love and reach out to humanity in the most difficult of circumstances.

Essentially, what such negotiations imply is that passibility and impassibility are worth noting at the crucifixion for the same reasons that Christ's humanity and divinity require substantiation at all points of christological reflection. Current theologians have maintained an important front against a flaccid account of the crucifixion that domesticates and justifies it as a means to an end, instead moving the point of focus to God's sharing or koinonia in the sufferings of humanity. Yet, such a move requires an impassibilist perspective in order that such sharing has a goal or end in sight that springs from a steady resolve inherent in the very character of God. God's "reaching out" is in order to "lift up" humanity from its fallen condition, and so God's solidarity or passibility has to be complemented by his transcendence/impassibility in order that such an act of solidarity can be a hopeful, redemptive, and ultimately glorifying expression of God's love.

Of course, such broad strokes are intentionally offered in order to allow different models of the atonement to fit within them. Whichever biblical model is chosen (including the five constellations alluded to above), the dynamic of solidarity and efficacy are at play. Christ undergoes and endures the fallen human condition in order to overcome it for those seeking to be God-like. For these reasons, it is important to keep an impassibilist perspective even at the most passibilist moment of Christ's life, his crucifixion. To cite Barth once again, "He acts as Lord over this contradiction even as He subjects Himself to it."[48]

E.3. Divine Impassibility and the Resurrection

The resurrection completes the three-fold pattern adopted in this chapter to characterize the life and significance of the Christ-event. In today's context, there is a clear movement to the crucifixion that results in an unfortunate neglect of the resurrection. Lamentably, it seems that such staurocentric emphases contribute to a situation in which the cross is much more palatable than the resurrection.

Of course, the topic of resurrection has always been offensive, given its supernatural underpinnings, and yet there is a sense in which it has played a significant role in the church's understanding of the gospel. The Apostle Paul could state to the Corinthians, "and if Christ has not been raised, then our proclamation has been in vain and your faith has been in vain."[49] Contrary to some of the remarks surveyed in this study, von Balthasar can agree with Paul that, "Had Christ not arisen, there would have been neither Church nor faith",[50] yet Christians and skeptics alike have debated its historicity and significance to the Christian faith. As much of a "stumbling block" as the cross of Christ has been throughout the ages, one cannot help but wonder if the resurrection poses an equal if not more apparently "foolish" obstacle to faith.

The tendency within a work advocating divine impassibility could be to move swiftly to the resurrection as an expression of God's redemptive and ultimately victorious stance against suffering in order to then make the subsequent soteriological and eschatological move of suggesting that all will be settled, justice served, and God vindicated at the end times. Biblical and patristic sources warrant such a move, and the present work does not seek to counter this claim directly. However, such statements could lead to the kind of triumphalistic insensitivity that has marked the church for much too long regarding such matters so that indifference, rather than empathy, could ensue from such theological commitments. Perhaps in beginning with the ending,

---

[48] Barth, *CD*, IV/1, p. 185.

[49] 1 Cor. 15:14.

[50] H. U. von Balthasar, *Mysterium Paschale* (trans. A. Nichols; San Francisco: Ignatius Press, 2000), p. 191.

Christians often lose sight of the important progression of Christ's life and work that led up to the resurrection. A staurocentric corrective undoubtedly would and has helped such circumstances so that a more humane, humble, and moral perspective can ensue regarding the plight of those who struggle to see the "first fruits" of their redemption.

A way forward from this difficulty could be the structural attempt of A. E. Lewis to offer a "theology of Holy Saturday".[51] Citing the many christological controversies that have erupted because of the apparent incompatibility of "from above" and "from below" approaches, Lewis advises that an expedient possibility could be to dwell on the thirty-six-hour interval between Christ's death and resurrection as a "border" or "limit" that extends the possibility of both differentiation and transition within the biblical narrative. Lewis perceives that the rush to resolve the crucifixion (or make it null) in light of the resurrection or to suspend the resurrection because of the crucifixion are both equally perilous moves that have a bearing on christology. Lewis urges that the reader approach the paschal narratives with a Ricoeurian "second naiveté" in order to see the first of the *triduum* as "the end", which was how the first witnesses must have experienced pre-Easter, a move that would only "throw into sharpest relief the *resurrection* gospel"[52] as a continual development of this unfolding drama, this "linear chain of homogeneous episodes".[53]

The interplay of crucifixion and resurrection is no better illustrated than in the Johannine depiction of the resurrected Christ in which explicit reference is made to Christ's resurrected body as continuing to bear the marks of the crucifixion, a reality that further confirmed his identity to his followers (John 20:24-28). Rather than taking this pericope and its details as incidental, one could draw from this imagery of Christ's resurrected body, as both wounded and transfigured, a moment of paused transition, one in which the great eschatological tension of the "already/not yet" is depicted in a dramatic way. From such a vantage point, Pannenberg can say that in Jesus' resurrection appearances, "the eschatological future was nearer then than at any time since".[54] What the disciples encountered was a foretaste of eschatological fulfillment, one that is encroaching gradually as Christ's return draws nearer.

The point generated from this perspective is that rather than considering impassibility as the more accurate or conceptually refined characterization of God's being, one can see that the way Christ's resurrected body appears to his onlookers is of such a nature that the passibilist moments are not eradicated or cancelled out but continually a part of the logic and reality of resurrection hope. God continues to be in the resurrected Christ nothing less than *pro nobis*, the God who "suffered impassibly" so that we can have hope in participating in such relational and passionate impassibility. Undoubtedly, a tension exists within this dynamic, but rather than a strictly *theo*logical tension, one sees here

---

[51] A. E. Lewis, *Between Cross and Resurrection* (Grand Rapids: Eerdmans, 2001).

[52] Lewis, *Between Cross and Resurrection*, p. 40.

[53] Lewis, *Between Cross and Resurrection*, p. 58.

[54] Pannenberg, *Jesus – God and Man*, p. 108.

an eschatological interplay that foreshadows in the *triduum* the fate of all creation.

E.4. Conclusion

The Christ event is only meaningful within the interplay of passibility and impassibility because at the heart of this dialectic is the narrative logic of incarnation, cross, and resurrection. By affirming divine impassibility before, during, and after the moment of the cross, Christ's sufferings *pro nobis* retain a level of meaning that distinguishes his life from others who die as martyrs or political rebels. Christ was neither of these because of his identity as the Son of God, the one person of the triune God who went "into the far country".

Given the contemporary state of divine impassibility, it is clear that much of the fervor for divine passibility rests on an account of the crucified Christ. In attempting to maintain the scandal and foolishness of the cross, many passibilists rightfully note that impassibility can threaten basic claims surrounding what God has done in Christ. Nevertheless, such perceptions have to be nuanced to show that for many ancient sources, Christ represented not only the second Adam who identified himself with us but also God who appeared for the purposes of restoring his fallen and alienated creation. To secure the latter, the ancients often resorted to impassibilist language, a move that certainly requires a particular kind of sensibility, but a worthwhile one given the way that the modern theodicy formulation tends to "naturalize" suffering. In today's context, one could say that the folly and scandal of the cross have been domesticated when accounts of Jesus portray him as an innocent sufferer who has been "godforsaken" by God in a moment that has its parallels with all other moments of torture and extreme suffering. Such a discourse suggests quite a bit but ultimately not enough as Jesus was not just one among three crucified men on Golgotha at that moment but truly the Son of God (Mark 15:39).

In concluding this study, the burden is left to account for divine impassibility's relevance to the life of the believer – considerations that tend to the pneumatological and ecclesial. In what follows, divine impassibility will serve as an attribute and reality that is generalizable to the whole of Christian discipleship. As counterintuitive as it may appear, the task that follows will attempt to show how disciples of Jesus are to be "apathetic" in accordance with the *apatheia* that theologically inflects the self-revelation of the triune God.

CHAPTER 6

Impassibility and Discipleship

As noted earlier in this study, when the theme of divine passibility is broached and actively promoted, usually the biblical and doctrinal witnesses most prominently used to underwrite the project are the Old Testament portrayal of God in covenant relationship with Israel and the person and experiences of Jesus Christ, especially the passion accounts culminating in Christ's crucifixion. Because of these emphases, often little mention is made in these discussions of the role and function of the Holy Spirit and the subsequent implications such considerations would have for the nature and task of Christian discipleship.

Of course, such negligence of the Spirit is not only limited to passibilist conversations but to broader trinitarian ones as well. As one can note of Moltmann's early project in *CG*, a nominally trinitarian account of God and suffering does not necessarily lead to a robust pneumatological perspective. Even in today's context, alongside a trinitarian revival of sorts there has occurred a growing interest, especially popularly, with the person and work of the Holy Spirit; however, plenty of ambiguities and reservations remain regarding the identity and nature of the Spirit's role within creation, and often such explorations are left to those traditions that actively promulgate and identify with Pentecostal or charismatic themes.

Additionally, Chapter 3 argued that if divine impassibility is to have any relevance as a divine attribute in contemporary theological discourse, then it has to be considered not simply as a *being*-attribute but as an *act*-attribute that demonstrates God's character in action within the created order. By being the latter, i.e., an attribute manifest within the *oikonomia* of divine self-disclosure, divine impassibility can resist its categorization as a tenet of "classical theism" and serve God-talk as more than simply an apophatic qualifier. Certainly, a case can be made for the apophatic function, but, especially given the shape and significance of Christ's life, one sees that impassibility can be narrated as integral to the logic of salvation history. As one who voluntarily took the human condition upon himself, moving from impassibility to passibility, the Son suffered willingly and truthfully for the purpose of redeeming the created and yet fallen order so that believers may be joined with him in his divine impassibility signaled by the resurrection. In this depiction, suffering is not inherent to the human condition as originally intended but something foreign and troublesome that needs nothing less than vanquishment. The inbreaking of God's kingdom, as indicated by the Christ event, points to this reality, especially with Christ's resurrection as a direct defiance of suffering's natural conclusion: death. In this light, impassibility can be thought of not simply as something characteristic of God but as a way of life possible for the follower of Christ.

What ensues is a pneumatological approach to divine impassibility with the aim of underwriting a particular account of Christian discipleship. It is my contention that followers of Christ truly follow and obey their Lord when they suffer as Christ suffered, namely, voluntarily and out of love, for the purpose of testifying to the hope of the resurrection grounded in the triune God. This call, as daunting as it is *prima facie*, can only occur through the empowering and vivifying work of the Holy Spirit, the *vinculum amoris* who unites us to the crucified and risen One. Such proposals, however, need to be prefaced with a consideration of the theodicy project within modernity, especially as it relates to themes raised thus far in this study.

A. Living Amidst Mysteries

A.1. Giving Sin Its Due

One of the long-standing tendencies in the Christian debates concerning divine (im)passibility – and suffering more generally – is the desire to explain. Even in contemporary pastoral settings, the desire and felt-need to explain why bad things happen to good people lead to a myriad of responses that often promote more harm than good in that their "hard rationality" often elide the human element of suffering. As mentioned above (especially in Chapter 3), authorities throughout history have tried to explain suffering as pedagogic or punitive (among other alternatives) because the category of the "innocent sufferer" was nonviable for them.[1] As E. Pagels notes, humans "would rather feel guilty than helpless",[2] and inexplicable suffering initially implies a disorderly aberration in what is thought to be the ordered creation of God's handiwork so that feeling responsible or at fault is easier in the "search for meaning" than accepting that no certain, empirically verifiable answers exist.

One also notes that theological propriety within this discussion would suggest that sin has to be involved in this discussion somehow. If soteriology is to be a viable schema for understanding the church's proclamation of justice and freedom to the victim, then sin must be granted its rightful place in accounting for the present human condition. In other words, suffering and sin are integrally related in that the former is a reflection of the fallen condition of

---

[1] B. Bobrinskoy is right to caution: "It is difficult to speak of beneficial suffering . . . . It is dangerous to speak of suffering as a divine means of salvation. Great discernment, tact, compassion, and prayerful and loving sharing are needed in order not to objectify the suffering of others into a divine law or a necessary pedagogy" (*The Compassion of the Father* [Crestwood, NY: St. Vladimir's Seminary Press, 2003], pp. 64-65).

[2] E. Pagels, *Adam, Eve, and the Serpent* (New York: Random House, 1988), p. 146.

all things. By stating the matter in this way, direct causality need not be implied, i.e., one's specific moment of suffering is not necessarily due to one's specific sin. Nevertheless, sin must be considered as ultimately tied to the phenomenon of suffering in order for the latter to be situated within its proper theological place.[3] Part of the church's proclamation implies that without sin there would be no suffering;[4] if such were not the case, creation would not have been "good" prior to the fall and there would have been no need for the act of "re-creation" implied by God's redemptive activity.[5]

The matter is all the more difficult when one analyzes the complexity of human agency and behavior. In many cases, no empirically verifiable relationship exists between one's decisions, actions, or choices and the plight one endures. Yet, in a very basic sense, the category of the "true victim" is difficult to sustain over time. For instance, testimonies stemming from concentration camp life, to take a prominent example, tell of even apparent "victims" occasionally participating in acts of brutality and abuse in relation to other, "lesser victims"; humans often are not simply executioners, victims, or spectators, but sometimes all three at once, leading Surin to say, "But if each one of us is simultaneously victim, executioner and spectator, then solidarity with victims will not on its own be sufficient to overcome oppression and

---

[3] Obviously, much is contested and at stake in phrasing the matter this way. Perhaps due to abusive linkages between "sin" and "suffering" in the past, J. Swinton uses a constellation of terms that includes "suffering", "evil", and "tragedy" to describe his proposals for a "practical theodicy" (see *Raging with Compassion* [Grand Rapids: Eerdmans, 2007]). The inherent difficulty of using a category such as "evil" is that it begs for differentiation from "suffering", thereby warranting the need for a category such as "tragedy" to fill a further void that is occasioned by such terminological preferences. This strategy leads Swinton to say that suffering is not inherently "evil" but could cause "evil" if it initiates "a crisis of faith that draws people away from God" (p. 55). On the same page, however, Swinton goes on to say that "*crushing suffering* such as the Holocaust is *inherently evil*, partly because it is clearly a deliberate violation of human beings who are made in the image of God and loved by God beyond all things" (emphases added). From these examples, it appears that Swinton is nuancing the term "evil" on the basis of theological rationales when the term "evil" itself is theologically inadequate to account for what is wrong with the world. I try to avoid these difficulties by privileging hamartiological language, all the while acknowledging that by such usage I am maximally extending the connotative spectrum for the categories of "sin" and "fallenness".

[4] This relationship is implied by the link between sin and death found in such biblical passages as Rom. 6:23 and 1 Cor. 15.

[5] I make such claims with a certain level of temerity; I do not believe that eschatological hope necessarily dampens the shock of historical experience; however, I can sympathize with W. Farley (*Tragic Vision and Divine Compassion* [Louisville, KY: Westminster John Knox, 1990]) and others who find that past interactions have tended to explain away or even trivialize moments of suffering. It seems that when this dynamic does occur that it has a way of minimizing not only suffering but hope as well.

injustice."[6] As much as onlookers would want to help in difficult situations, "true solidarity" is impossible because the present human condition is mired within the present fallen state of creation; in this specific sense, Augustine was right to maintain how much the present human experience is plagued by the sin-laden condition of the world.

A.2. The Mystery of Christ's/Our Passion

Sin and suffering only form one cluster of mysteries that grip human beings to their very core as they search to understand themselves and their surrounding world. Another great mystery, of course, is God, especially as self-revealed in the life and work of Christ. As an extension of this mystery, a running question is why God in his freedom would redeem his fallen creation by assuming the corruptible state of affairs it brought upon itself. Whereas the "innocent sufferer" does not have a choice to accept or avoid suffering, Christians believe that the Son freely chose to assume the plight of the human condition for a broader purpose. That purpose is the kernel of truth at the heart of what makes the gospel "good news". Surprisingly, the God of Abraham, Isaac, and Jacob appeared in the flesh to reveal Godself and to redeem. The rationale and shape of God's action in Christ are great mysteries of the faith that many have tried to answer. Certainly, soteriological considerations come into play at this point, but this notion does not express the rationale for the means and mode as much as it relates their results.

Since Christ's suffering was assumed by one not tarnished by the world's fallenness,[7] the knowledge available to the believer that God in Christ suffered the pains and torture of "true" innocent suffering is a way forward through the recast theodicy question of modernity. This understanding leads to an experience that is both different from and in solidarity with – the former providing the conditions for the latter's possibility – what humans naturally experience or "suffer". As Surin suggests, "The only religiously available deity in situations of extreme affliction is a God who can share the sufferings of his tormented creatures . . . . Any other God can only be the moral source of atheism."[8] The gospel speaks of God's capacity and willingness to realize concretely this desire by sharing the plight of humanity within the stringencies of fallen creation. As G. Rossé elaborates, "The abandonment of Christ on the cross presents itself as the response of God to the scandal of man's suffering, of the death of the innocent, of anxiety, and of all the 'why's' that have no answer. It is the definitive 'yes' of God to fallen man, to man estranged from God."[9]

---

[6] Surin, *Theology and the Problem of Evil*, pp. 120-121.

[7] In this regard, K. J. Vanhoozer is right to link divine impassibility with Jesus' impeccability; see *First Theology* (Downers Grove, IL: InterVarsity, 2002), p. 93.

[8] Surin, "Theodicy?", p. 241.

[9] G. Rossé, *The Cry of Jesus on the Cross* (trans. S. W. Arndt; Eugene, OR: Wipf and Stock, 1987), p. 115.

By no means does this admission signify that one must abandon the notion of divine impassibility in all its dimensions, for the theme is precisely what theologically substantiates these christological statements. The belief that an omnipotent, immutable, and impassible God took upon himself powerless, conditioned, and suffering humanity implies that God's power has been revealed in human weakness, not for God's sake but for the redemption of suffering humanity itself. In this act, God's self-revelation on the cross is his "self-justification"[10] in the midst of human suffering. Yet, this "self-justification" is also a judgment against sin and suffering, a judgment that does not simply come from above but from within the fallen creation in order to show how both sin and suffering are ultimately incompatible with who God is and what God desires the creation to be. On both counts, "the believer who takes the atonement seriously has no real need for theodicy" because the latter becomes superfluous in light of the former's suggestion that God has acted through Christ on behalf of the world.[11]

A.3. A Multi-Faceted Apophaticism

The mystery of human suffering coincides with the mystery of God,[12] but the situation may arise that these mysteries are pursued in ways that lead to their disassociation and potentially even subsequent opposition or mutual exclusion. Because these mysteries are so fundamental to the ways humans think about themselves and existence in general, the manner in which these mysteries are ordered and substantiated condition the shape of subsequent discourses that potentially follow. In other words, it matters which mystery is privileged over the other.[13] As noted of popular modern theodicies, the mystery of suffering

---

[10] Surin, "Theodicy?", p. 244; Moltmann makes a similar point: "The cross of Christ then becomes the 'Christian theodicy' – a self-justification of God in which judgment and damnation are taken up by God himself, so that man may live" (*Hope and Planning*, [trans. M. Clarkson; New York: Harper and Row, 1971], p. 43).

[11] Surin, "Theodicy?", p. 244.

[12] D. Ford compellingly suggests that one can speak of a "double mystery, the dark mystery of evil and the bright mystery of goodness" (*Theology: A Very Short Introduction* [Oxford: Oxford University Press, 1999], p. 76).

[13] I am very sympathetic to M. C. Felderhof's reservations in using the language of "mystery" to speak of both God and evil as Ford does above. Felderhof finds it difficult to speak of evil as a "mystery" because the latter term suggests that evil may be contemplated and never properly fathomed or grasped, thereby making action futile. Felderhof opts for considering evil as something to be "resisted" (see "Evil: Theodicy or Resistance?", *Scottish Journal of Theology* 57.4 [2004], especially pp. 408-409). My continual use of the term stems from the desire to preserve the resistance to explain as well as to acknowledge that such gestures as "banality", "senselessness", and "challenging" still do not adequately "do justice to the full impact that such events have on the victims" (p. 409). In other words, I can see Felderhof's point that considering evil

often precedes and conditions the mystery of God, and positive and negative consequences stem from such an ordering; on the one hand, suffering is given a legitimate space conceptually without the need for or recourse to shortsighted explanations and rationales, and yet such a move also questions the very role of God in the world and what that role would suggest of God's very nature. I propose the opposite alternative, that the mystery of suffering be encapsulated within the mystery of God, not only because it is the orthodox ordering of the matter but also because it avoids a number of pitfalls that are inherent to the formulation of modern theodicy.

One of the major examples of such difficulties is presented by McCabe, who suggests that if one begins with human suffering and moves to the mystery of God (while not allowing the former mystery to be altered by the latter), one ultimately returns to one's starting point.[14] Such is the case because humanity cannot formulate or muster a legitimate hope to inspire, alter, or ultimately redeem itself. Therefore, the order in which these mysteries are pursued is all-determinative for how divine (im)passibility plays out within the notion of God relating to the world. Since by their very nature these mysteries eventually defy strict concretization, once the order is established, theology can only do so much to explain or situate these mysteries into workable "concepts" or "thoughts". Because of this challenge, theological method must give way to a reverent apophaticism in light of both themes.[15]

As modernity has been prone to emphasize, human suffering is one of the great mysteries of existence, and no humanly contrived answer will suffice to explain or justify its scope and degree. When explanations are thought to be found, they eventually are lacking because they fail to console and make the pain any more bearable. For this reason, as difficult as it is to do within certain theological schemas, the category of the "innocent sufferer" ought to be maintained. If a reason exists for such suffering, theologians and believers alike are best served in guarding silence in reaction to the temptation to explain.[16]

---

as a "mystery" has its limits, but it is questionable what would constitute "moral propriety" (p. 404) in such instances. My alternative to Felderhof would be an apophatic/doxological approach, which I do not think he would find disagreeable. For a work that considers the "problem of evil" from a specifically doxological stance, see R. D. Crews, *The Praise of God and the Problem of Evil* (PhD thesis, Duke University, 1989).

[14] This suggestion comes from *God Matters*, p. 41.

[15] By the term "reverent apophaticism", I am hinting at the context of worship, where mysteries and silence are viable categories and where theological "knowledge" can give way to "ignorance" in a justified way. McCabe eloquently states: "What we need is to be taken up by God himself, to share in his knowledge of himself, a sharing that to *us* must just look like darkness. So that our faith seems not like an increase of knowledge but, if anything, an increase of ignorance. We become more acutely aware of our inadequacy before the mystery as we are brought closer to it" (*God Matters*, p. 20).

[16] Sölle here powerfully proposes the image of "mute suffering" when "no discourse is possible any longer, in which a person ceases reacting as a human agent" (*Suffering*, p.

Rather than running the risk of being rationalists like Job's friends, those who witness and experience massive and unwarranted suffering would do well to maintain silence before the mysterious plight of the human condition. At a certain visceral level, the suggestion that "suffering precedes thinking" is a compelling consideration, making Sölle's remark apropos: "Respect for those who suffer *in extremis* imposes silence."[17]

As was the case with the mystery of human suffering, the mystery of God's ways of relating to human beings also invites silence at choice moments. Because God and his dealings with humanity are ultimately mysterious, a reverent apophaticism should be observed as well when God himself appears silent during impending circumstances.[18] Certainly, it is a great mystery as to why God allows certain horrors like Auschwitz to occur, but narrating God's silence in such a way as to implicate him is itself an act of theological presumption when excessively sustained. One senses these kinds of moves in contemporary theology; for instance, Moltmann remarks, "It is precisely in this experience of anguish that we find a great solidarity between Christians and atheists. In it, faith suffers from the God who has *withdrawn his presence*"[19] or later, "The paradox is found in the fact that, in spite of his being . . . the Son of God, he *was not heard*."[20] Although it is true that Jesus' cry admits of being forsaken by the Father, does this admission imply that the Father and the Spirit of love between them had withdrawn so that Jesus' cry was not heard by God? A more coherent way to describe the drama of the cross is that the Father had hidden but not withdrawn his presence, for one could say that the bond between the Father and Son was maintained throughout in the person of the Holy Spirit. Certainly, as true life came into contact with hopeless death, the bond was

---

68). In this regard, theodicies generally are unhelpful because of their inherent rationality based upon foundationalist epistemologies. For an effort that extends this argument historically, see T. W. Tilley, *The Evils of Theodicy* (Washington, DC: Georgetown University Press, 1991), especially Chapter 9. For a recent work that attempts to read the book of Job as a deconstructionist, *post*-theodical work, see D. B. Burrell, *Deconstructing Theodicy* (Grand Rapids: Brazos, 2008).

[17] Sölle, *Suffering*, p. 69. It should be mentioned that the "muting" should be of the observer rather than the sufferer. Muting the sufferer would in fact be morally objectionable.

[18] Again, my use of the term "reverent apophaticism" is an attempt to limit the temptation to explain through a specific doxological manner. Denys the Areopagite brings such a sensitivity to light when he remarks, "We worship with reverent silence the unutterable Truths and, with the unfathomable and holy veneration of our mind, approach that Mystery of Godhead which exceeds all Mind and Being" (Dionysius the Areopagite, *The Mystical Theology and The Divine Names* [trans. C. E. Rolt; Mineola, NY: Dover Publications, 2004], p. 54).

[19] Moltmann, *Hope and Planning*, pp. 32-33 (emphases mine).

[20] Moltmann, *Hope and Planning*, p. 35 (emphases mine). Despite Moltmann's citation of von Harnack's "correction" of Heb. 5:7, no text-critical warrants exist for assuming that the verse needs emendation.

stretched and called into question, but it would seem that too much is at stake theologically to say that the bond was broken. Such a move would occasion the envelopment of the mystery of God by the mystery of suffering, thereby calling into question the purpose and outcome of such an event. As Fiddes notes, "To speak of hiddenness is to indicate presence and not absence,"[21] and a rigorous trinitarianism can accommodate the possibility of hiddenness within the *oikonomia* that at the same time maintains a unity of will and action that is required for God's work on the cross to be intentional as well as effectual.

Divine silences, therefore, need not imply divine absences, and these require of faith a corresponding silence as well – a silence that is epistemologically viable given that human thinking and endeavoring are not *sub specie aeternitatis*. By taking a more loquacious stance, as when they push for a christology that reflects a "from below" cadence, many contemporary passibilists miss what would appear to be the complementary feature of a God who veils himself in his unveiling; in other words, the revelatory implications of a crucified God must be coupled with the motif of God's hiddenness so that a *theologia crucis* can be sustained legitimately over time.

In that God the Father did not abandon Christ, Christians have the hope that they are not abandoned in their trials. In Lutheran terms, God may very well be hidden, but the other side of the continuum exists as well for believers in that they are joined to the (im)passible Christ: As Paul dramatically asks, "Who will separate us from the love of Christ? Will hardship, or distress, or persecution, or famine, or nakedness, or peril, or sword?"[22] If the incarnation is taken as an initial orienting framework for a Christian understanding of suffering, then believers can say that there is no single point in human experience at which one would achieve a state of total godforsakenness. Quite the contrary, the privilege in sharing in the *koinonia* of Christ's sufferings in the power of the Holy Spirit brings with it the hope of participating in the power of the resurrection.[23]

B. Taking Up Our Cross in the Power of the Spirit

In light of the belief that God and suffering are mysteries that should be ordered in such a way that the former conditions the latter, the inevitable *practical* question is, What is the Christian response to suffering in all of its varied and multiform expressions? If theodicy is unhelpful because of its sheer speculative rationality, then what ought Christians to do in a fallen world? Swinton compellingly suggests that this question is the appropriate one in light of the

---

[21] P. Fiddes, "The Quest for a Place which is 'Not-a-Place': The Hiddenness of God and the Presence of God" in O. Davies and D. Turner (eds), *Silence and the Word* (Cambridge: Cambridge University Press, 2002), pp. 43 and 45.

[22] Rom. 8:35.

[23] Phil. 3:10.

inadequacy of our knowledge of such matters,[24] leading him to offer a *pastoral approach* to the problem of evil. Before moving to this very important point, however, one should consider an equally important question, namely: what is the ground for Christian action toward suffering? Christ was mentioned previously in Chapter 5 as that ground, but now a further trinitarian consideration is in order, one that entertains how the (im)passible Christ was the "Spirit-imbued" and "Spirit-empowered" God-man.

B.1. Spirit-Christology

A feature of christology that can be lost in discussions relating to Chalcedonian forms is the role and work of the Spirit in Christ's life. Recently, various studies have endeavored to correct this oversight by offering "Spirit-christologies" that attempt to account for how Christ's life and work were significantly tenored by the Holy Spirit. As M. Welker remarks, "The Synoptic writers explicitly connect Jesus' birth, baptism, temptation in the wilderness, and healings and exorcisms with the Spirit of God, with the action of the power of God."[25] Such textual evidence has led to a number of recent monographs and studies,[26] thereby suggesting that a Spirit-christology may prove fruitful for modeling the shape and life of the church after Jesus' way of suffering. In other words, a Spirit-christology can help in the constructive formulation of divine (im)passibility as a way of life for Christ's body.

Part of the value of a Spirit-christology rests on the manner the Spirit is said to be involved in the fulfillment of Christ's mission and calling. If Christ brought salvation to the world by taking on the fallen human condition, then one can say that he did so in the power of the Holy Spirit. The birth narratives of Matthew and Luke show that the Spirit was at play in the events leading up to Christ's life, and the Spirit's ongoing work in Christ not only signals broader trinitarian commitments but also highlights the historical shape of Christ's life and ministry, a point that is important if Christ is to be a model for the Christian life. Such a perspective elevates certain *kairos* events[27] like Jesus' baptism (the point at which Jesus was anointed by the Spirit for fulfilling his calling) and temptation (an ordeal that Jesus endured because of the Spirit's leading) as key moments in the historical unfolding of Christ's mission. These moments show that Jesus' dependence on God's power was real and continual so that his obedience was perfected over time. In accordance with a robust account of the

---

[24] Such inadequacy leads Swinton to argue compellingly against various theodicies within Christian reflection; see *Raging with Compassion*, Chapter 1.

[25] M. Welker, *God the Spirit* (trans. J. F. Hoffmeyer; Minneapolis: Fortress, 1994), p. 186.

[26] For a survey of some of these approaches, see R. Haight, "The Case for Spirit Christology", *Theological Studies* 53 (1992), pp. 257-87.

[27] I am indebted to Y. Congar for the use of this language with these themes; see *The Word and the Spirit* (trans. D. Smith; London: Geoffrey Chapman, 1986), pp. 87-88.

imitatio Christi, such obedience is intrinsic to what Christians are called to embody, and without the Spirit's enabling, capacitating, and consoling work, it is difficult to see how Jesus' life and ministry can subsequently be a template for Christian existence.[28]

Specifically, for purposes of this study, a Spirit-christology suggests that Christ, who "suffered impassibly", did so in the power of the Holy Spirit.[29] The dialectical tension at play in such Cyrilline phrasings retains a paradoxical (but not contradictory) quality because of the presence and work of God's Spirit in the life of Jesus. Jesus experienced temptation but did not succumb, was persecuted but was not defeated, felt doubt but did not relent, and died but did not remain in the tomb because his life – although in solidarity with us as a real, human life – was also the incarnate life of the Son who came from the Father under the anointing of the Spirit.

Christ's impassibility, therefore, is an indication of the Spirit's work and presence in his life. The Holy Spirit is the "impassibilist Spirit" in the sense that Christ's sufferings, his *pathe,* were undertaken, sustained, and overcome in the power of the Spirit. Such narrations present salvation as the work of the triune God as well as indicate that the "two hands of God" (Irenaeus) within the economy are entwined in the interplay of passibility and impassibility. The line of reflection also suggests that as the "Spirit of Christ", this "other Paraclete" may serve an analogous function in the life of Christ's body, the church.

B.2. Impassibly Bearing Suffering

Part of the benefits of salvation as conceived by many in the early church was a

---

[28] As C. Pinnock remarks, "It is important to recognize that Jesus was dependent on the Spirit. He had to rely on the Spirit's resources to overcome temptation. . . . He suffered real attack in the temptations and was not play-acting. It was not through confidence in his own power that he put himself at risk. .·. . Jesus surrendered himself in trust and conquered the powers of evil by the Spirit, as we all must (*Flame of Love* [Downers Grove, IL: InterVarsity, 1996], p. 88).

[29] Naturally, the importance of Heb. 9:14 is marked here; in relation to this notion, Moltmann relates that the Spirit "is the power that makes [Christ] ready to surrender his life, and which itself sustains this surrender" (*The Spirit of Life* [trans. M. Kohl; Minneapolis: Fortress, 1992], p. 63). Such considerations and the work of D. L. Dabney (in English, see "*Pneumatologia Crucis*: Reclaiming *Theologia Crucis* for a Theology of the Spirit Today", *Scottish Journal of Theology* 53.4 [2000], pp. 511-24) lead Moltmann to think in terms of a *pneumatologia crucis* where the "Spirit of God is the spirit of kenotic self-surrender" (p. 64). This line of thought is certainly suggestive as extensions of the Spirit's work of consoling, comforting, and "helping" (Rom. 8:26), and yet I still would want to nuance the way this "kenotic self-surrender" is understood along the lines of what has been considered christologically in Chapter 5. In other words, I see in the first quote the Spirit working both "within" and "from beyond" in such a way that a case can be made for both passibilist and impassibilist features.

status of human impassibility that marked the road of perfection and blessedness. This expectancy was especially the case when the early church was being persecuted and many within the fold were being martyred. One of the prominent rallying points during the impending trials of those who would be martyrs for the faith was the hope that as they pursued a form of suffering very similar to Christ's own suffering, they could at some point also participate in Christ's resurrection and impassibility. As Gavrilyuk notes, "In the theology of martyrdom impassibility acquired the special sense of a state enjoyed by the blessed after the resurrection in which, according to St Paul, 'corruptible is changed into incorruptible' and all persecution and unjust suffering comes [*sic*] to an end." [30] Impassibility was a state worth pursuing because it meant being free from the perturbations of life and the sufferings of this world that ultimately lead to death. As part of Christ's re-creative activity, impassibility meant that humans could be free from their slavery to corruption and death in order that they could participate in the divine being. In this regard, the work of the Spirit is of utmost importance because it is this Spirit who can minister to those who are afflicted by keeping the resurrected Christ, and so the soon-coming King, in purview. By the gracious communication of Christ's work among believers today, the Spirit in a very real sense capacitates and empowers believers to endure suffering with the hope that suffering, and thus corruption and death, do not have the final word. As Christ was resurrected on the third day, Christians can hope that their mortal bodies will be redeemed and that they will participate in the impassibility that is promised to those who are in Christ.

But for this impassibility to be truly analogous to Christ's impassibility, then the suffering in question is not simply something that is endured as one's fate but the kind of suffering that is undertaken voluntarily for a greater purpose. [31] Within the contours of a broad, trinitarian-conditioned soteriology, there was something at work in Christ's sufferings that went beyond their immediate environs. Endured suffering, although indicative of solidarity, had to be undertaken in a way and with a rationale that served a greater purpose in order that redemption could follow. Such is the christological pattern.

Just as Christ took on human suffering voluntarily, his followers are called to do the same in the power of his Spirit. The nature of this "co-suffering" is only possible through the work of the Spirit, who recalls both Christ's crucifixion and resurrection. In a mysterious sense, the Spirit's consolation and empowerment enable believers to suffer with those who suffer and to mourn with those who mourn because the character of this consolation is one that can relate to the situation at hand (passibility) and offer a "presenced-hope" that is directed to the eschaton (impassibility). In this regard Christians, in light of the example of Christ, are called to be both passible and impassible in the

---

[30] Gavrilyuk, *The Suffering of the Impassible God*, p. 70.

[31] Of course, the issue of motive here is very important, especially this side of the biting Nietzschean critique. For a consideration of varying motives for martyrdom in ancient sources, see J. W. Smith, "Martyrdom: Self-Denial or Self-Exaltation?", *Modern Theology* 22.2 (April 2006), pp. 169-96.

consolation they offer to those in need. The capacities to relate and help those who are suffering stem from the pneumatological anamnesis of Christ's life. Because of the Spirit's capacitating role, Christians can be fellow-sufferers without being fellow-victims; while the latter suggests despair and meaninglessness, the former keeps open the possibility of vindication and blessedness.

B.3. Post-Theodical Community

In this light, the Christian community is called to be a fellowship of "fellow-sufferers" so that what is endured collectively by Christ's body is not simply that which is one's lot but that which is indicative of the mode of cruciform discipleship that Jesus' followers are called to embody and live out as an active form of resistance and defiance of suffering in this world.[32] Just as mysteries persist in life as to the shape of suffering and the role God plays in it (undertaking suffering for a season), so Christ's body is called to offer hope and be a sign of the coming reign of Christ through the *koinonia* of one another's sufferings.[33] Such a move problematizes suffering in a way that is often overlooked; as Weinandy remarks, "Because much contemporary theology has failed to recognize the christological and soteriological significance of Christ's suffering, it has in turn failed to grasp the unique ecclesial significance of suffering, that is, that those who now suffer in Christ, as members of his body, suffer and experience suffering in a radically different manner than those who have not come to faith in him."[34]

With such a statement, Weinandy does not intend to diminish or explain away suffering, but the remark does serve to suggest that suffering can be renarrated in light of Christ's suffering, and by being so, suffering can be

---

[32] S. Hauerwas makes a similar point in *Naming the Silences* (Grand Rapids: Eerdmans, 1990) when he suggests that traditionally Christians have not had a solution to the problem of evil but rather a means of resisting it by the practices enacted by the community gathered in Jesus' name (pp. 52-53).

[33] J. D. G. Dunn speaks of the integral relationship that exists between death and life for Paul in 2 Cor. 4:7-5:5 in a way that relates to the present discussion: "Death must have its say in the believer's experience *in order that* the life of Jesus may come to visible expression also; *the life of Jesus manifests itself precisely in and through the dying of the body*; life and death are two sides of the one process" (*Jesus and the Spirit* [Philadelphia: Westminster, 1975], p. 328). Dunn goes on to elaborate another Pauline passage, Rom. 5:2-11, and how suffering is part of a trajectory that produces hope. In both cases, the thrust of these thoughts leads one to consider how suffering plays a vital role in vibrant discipleship so that what is endured in this world can become moments in which God's presence and power become all the more real in the life of the Christian fellowship. Such reasoning fits within the Pauline dialectic of considering the manifestation of divine power in human weakness (p. 329).

[34] Weinandy, *Does God Suffer?*, p. 173.

something different for Christians than it is for others. Suffering need not be avoided at all costs until one inevitably succumbs to it at its most pressing and all-inclusive end; rather, when shared and collectively endured by the body of Christ, suffering can point to the hope of redemption, the hope that God will sustain, comfort, and ultimately vindicate.

Given these commitments, there is something to be said for the suggestion that Christians cannot subscribe to the theodicy project. Christians cannot "justify" God in light of all the pain and suffering in the world; God does not provide his body with the kind of answer that any "objective observer" would want. But God does present the church with a crucified person and calls his followers to be a cruciform community with the expectation that at some point in eschatological time the depiction of Revelation 7:17 will be realized: "For the Lamb at the center of the throne will be their shepherd, and he will guide them to springs of the water of life, and God will wipe away every tear from their eyes."

B.4. Conclusion

Divine impassibility points to God's power, wisdom, and love that are prior, contemporaneous, and subsequent to moments of humanly embodied suffering. Although affirming divine impassibility does not explain away the mystery of evil, which ultimately requires eschatological resolution, it does affirm by faith the mystery of God in whom the former will be resolved. Since pain and suffering surround us while it is in God that creation lives, moves, and has its being,[35] the two mysteries must be maintained.

If one is to take the *imitatio Christi* seriously as a way of discipleship, then it is clear that the Son's taking on the human predicament freely and out of love is a paradigm for Christian existence. As the synoptic verse suggests, the call of discipleship suggests that believers deny themselves, take up their cross, and follow Christ.[36] The path of discipleship implies cruciformity but not victimization. As Christ "suffered impassibly", believers too are called to "suffer impassibly" with one another as a way of pointing to the world that sin and suffering do not ultimately determine the value and significance of existence. Rather than lives of fate, peril, and demise, Christians can lead lives of meaning, hope, and eschatological victory. In this regard, impassibility is not simply a divine attribute but a characteristic of Christ's body wherever the present fallen order is endured, confronted, and overcome. Such is the relevance and hope of divine impassibility.

---

[35] Acts 17:28.

[36] Matt. 16:24; Mark 8:34; Luke 9:23.

Bibliography

All ancient Christian sources are taken from the *Ante-Nicene* and *Nicene Fathers* editions published by Hendrickson unless otherwise noted

Althaus, P.; *The Theology of Martin Luther* (trans. R. C. Schultz; Philadelphia: Fortress, 1966)

Apostolic Fathers (3rd ed; trans. M. W. Holmes; Grand Rapids: Baker, 2006)

Anselm of Canterbury: The Major Works (eds. B. Davies and G. R. Evans; Oxford: Oxford University Press, 1998)

Aquinas; *Summa theologica* (5 vols; trans. The Fathers of the English Dominican Province; Allen, TX: Christian Classics, 1948)

Aristotle; *The Basic Works of Aristotle* (ed. R. McKeon; New York: The Modern Library, 2001)

Athenagoras; *A Plea for the Christians*

Augustine; *City of God*

— *On Free Choice of the Will*

— *On Patience*

von Balthasar, H. U.; *Theo-Drama* (5 vols; trans. G. Harrison; San Francisco: Ignatius, 1988-1998)

— *Mysterium Paschale* (trans. A. Nichols; San Francisco: Ignatius Press, 2000)

Barth, K.; *Church Dogmatics* (14 vols; eds. G. W. Bromiley and T. F. Torrance; Edinburgh: T & T Clark, 1936-1975)

— *The Epistle to the Philippians* (trans. J. W. Leitch; Louisville: Westminster John Knox, 2002)

Bauckham, R.; "'Only the Suffering God Can Help'; Divine Passibility in Modern Theology", *Themelios* 9.3 (1984), pp. 6-12

— *Moltmann: Messianic Theology in the Making* (Basingstoke: Marshall Pickering, 1987)

— *The Theology of Jürgen Moltmann* (Edinburgh: T & T Clark, 1995)

Birch, B. C., W. Brueggemann, T. E. Fretheim, and D. L. Peterson; *A Theological Introduction to the Old Testament* (Nashville: Abingdon, 1999)

Bobrinskoy, B.; *The Compassion of the Father* (Crestwood, NY: St. Vladimir's Seminary Press, 2003)

Bonhoeffer, D.; *Letters and Papers from Prison* (New York: Touchstone, 1997)

Braaten, C.; "A Trinitarian Theology of the Cross", *Journal of Religion* 56.1 (1976), pp. 113-121

Brasnett, B.; *The Suffering of the Impassible God* (London: SPCK, 1928)

Brueggemann, W.; *Theology of the Old Testament* (Minneapolis: Fortress, 1997)

Burrell, D. B.; *Deconstructing Theodicy* (Grand Rapids: Brazos, 2008)

Calvin, J.; *Institutes of the Christian Religion* (2 vols; ed. J. T. McNeil; trans. F. L. Battles; Philadelphia: Westminster, 1960)

Camus, A.; *The Rebel* (trans. A. Bower; New York: Vintage, 1991)

Childs, B. S.; *Old Testament Theology in a Canonical Context* (Philadelphia: Fortress, 1985)

Cohn-Sherbock, D. (ed); *Holocaust Theology: A Reader* (New York: New York University Press, 2002)

Congar, Y.; *The Word and the Spirit* (trans. D. Smith; London: Geoffrey Chapman, 1986)

— *I Believe in the Holy Spirit* (3 vols; trans. D. Smith; New York: Crossroad Herder, 2000)

Copleston, F.; *A History of Philosophy* (9 vols; New York: Image, 1993-1994)

Creel, R. E.; *Divine Impassibility* (Cambridge: Cambridge University Press, 1986)

Crews, R. D.; *The Praise of God and the Problem of Evil* (PhD thesis, Duke University, 1989)

Cyril of Alexandria; *On the Unity of Christ* (trans. J. A. McGuckin; Crestwood, NY: St. Vladimir's Seminary Press, 1995)

Dabney, D. L.; "*Pneumatologia Crucis*: Reclaiming *Theologia Crucis* for a Theology of the Spirit Today", *Scottish Journal of Theology* 53.4 (2000), pp. 511-24

Davies, O. and D. Turner (eds); *Silence and the Word* (Cambridge: Cambridge University Press, 2002)

Davis, S.T., D. Kendall, and G. O'Collins (eds); *The Incarnation* (Oxford: Oxford University Press, 2002)

Dickie, J.; *Fifty Years of British Theology* (Edinburgh: T & T Clark, 1937)

Dinsmore, C. A.; *Atonement in Literature and Life* (New York: Houghton Mifflin, 1906)

Dionysius the Areopagite; *The Mystical Theology and The Divine Names* (trans. C. E. Rolt; Mineola, NY: Dover Publications, 2004)

Dostoevsky, F.; *The Brothers Karamazov* (trans. R. Pevear and L. Volokhonsky; New York: Farrar, Straus, and Giroux, 1990)

Dunn, J. D. G.; *Jesus and the Spirit* (Philadelphia: Westminster, 1975)

Eckardt, B. F., Jr.; "Luther and Moltmann: The Theology of the Cross", *Concordia Theological Quarterly* 49.1 (1985), pp. 19-28

Eichrodt, W.; *Theology of the Old Testament* (2 vols; trans. J. A. Baker; Philadelphia: Westminster, 1961-1967)

Enron, L. J.; "You Who Revere the Lord, Bless the Lord!", *Journal of Ecumenical Studies* 18.1 (1981), pp. 63-73

Fairbarn, A. M.; *The Place of Christ in Modern Theology* (New York: Charles Scribner's Sons, 1899)

Farley, W.; *Tragic Vision and Divine Compassion* (Louisville, KY: Westminster John Knox, 1990)

Farrow, D. B.; "In the End is the Beginning: A Review of Jürgen Moltmann's Systematic Contributions", *Modern Theology* 14.3 (July 1998), pp. 425-47

Felderhof, M. C.; "Evil: Theodicy or Resistance?", *Scottish Journal of Theology* 57.4 (2004), pp. 397-412

Fiddes, P.; *The Creative Suffering of God* (Oxford: Clarendon, 1988)

Ford, D.; *Theology: A Very Short Introduction* (Oxford: Oxford University Press, 1999)

Forde, G. O.; *On Being a Theologian of the Cross* (Grand Rapids; Eerdmans, 1997)

Fretheim, T. E.; *The Suffering of God* (Philadelphia: Fortress, 1984)

Fritsch, C. T.; *The Anti-Anthropomorphisms of the Greek Pentateuch* (Princeton: Princeton University Press, 1943)

Frohnhofen, H.; *Apatheia tou Theou* (New York: Peter Lang, 1987)

Gammie, J. D.; *Holiness in Israel* (Minneapolis: Fortress, 1989)

Gavrilyuk, P. L.; *The Suffering of the Impassible God* (Oxford: Oxford University Press, 2004)

Goetz, R.; "The Suffering God: The Rise of the New Orthodoxy", *Christian Century* 103.13 (1986), pp. 385-89

Goldingay, J.; *Old Testament Theology* (2 vols; Downers Grove, IL: InterVarsity, 2003)

Grant, C.; "Possibilities for Divine Passibility", *Toronto Journal of Theology* 4.1 (1988), pp. 3-18

Green, J. B. and M. D. Baker; *Recovering the Scandal of the Cross* (Downers Grove, IL: InterVarsity, 2000)

St. *Gregory Thaumaturgus, Life and Works* (trans. M. Slusser; *The Fathers of the Church*, vol. 98; Washington, D.C.: Catholic University of America Press, 1998)

Griffin, D. R.; *God, Power, and Evil: A Process Theodicy* (Philadelphia: Westminster, 1976)

— *Evil Revisited* (Albany, NY: State University of New York Press, 1991)

Gunton, C.; *Act and Being* (Grand Rapids: Eerdmans, 2002)

Haight, R.; "The Case for Spirit Christology", *Theological Studies* 53 (1992), pp. 257-87

Hallman, J. M.; *The Descent of God* (Eugene, OR: Wipf and Stock, 2004)

Hart, D. B.; "No Shadow of Turning: On Divine Impassibility", *Pro Ecclesia* 11.2 (Spring 2002), pp. 184-206

Hauerwas, S.; *Naming the Silences* (Grand Rapids: Eerdmans, 1990)

Haynes, S. R.; "Christian Holocaust Theology: A Critical Assessment", *Journal of the American Academy of Religion* 62.2 (1994), pp. 553-83

Hegel, G. W. F.; *Faith and Knowledge* (trans. W. Cerf and H. S. Harris; Albany: State University of New York Press, 1977)

Henning, L. H.; "The Cross and Pastoral Care", *Currents in Theology and Mission* 13.1 (1986), pp. 22-29

Heschel, A.; *The Prophets* (2 vols; Peabody, MA: Prince, 1999)

Hick, J. (ed); *The Myth of God Incarnate* (London: SCM Press, 1977)

Hippolytus; *Against the Heresy of One Noetus*

— *The Refutation of All Heresies*

Horkheimer, M.; *Die Sehnsucht nach dem ganz Anderen* (Hamburg: Furche Verlag, 1970)

Hou, D.; "The Infinity of God in the Biblical Theology of Denys the Areopagite", *International Journal of Systematic Theology* 10.3 (July 2008), pp. 249-66

von Hügel, F.; *Essays and Addresses on the Philosophy of Religion* (second series; London: J. M. Dent and Sons, 1926-1930)

Hume, D.; *Dialogues and Natural History of Religion* (Oxford: Oxford University Press, 1998)

Hunsinger, G.; "The Crucified God and the Political Theology of Violence: A Critical Survey of Jürgen Moltmann's Recent Thought: I", *Heythrop Journal* 14.3 (1973), pp. 266-279

Ignatius of Antioch; *To the Romans*

— *To the Smyrneans*

— *To the Ephesians*

— *To Polycarp*

Irenaeus of Lyons; *Against the Heresies*

Jaeger, W.; *The Theology of the Early Greek Philosophers* (trans. E. S. Robinson;

Eugene, OR: Wipf and Stock, 2003)

Jansen, H.; "Moltmann's View of God's (Im)mutability: The God of the Philosophers and the God of the Bible", *Neue Zeitschrift für systematische Theologie und Religionsphilosophie* 36.3 (1994), pp. 284-301

Jonas, H.; "The Concept of God after Auschwitz: A Jewish Voice", *Journal of Religion* 67.1 (1987), pp. 1-13

Jowers, D. W.; "The Theology of the Cross as Theology of the Trinity", *Tyndale Bulletin* 52.2 (2001), pp. 245-66

Justin Martyr; *Apology*

Kelly, J. N. D.; *Early Christian Doctrines* (revised edition; San Francisco: HarperCollins, 1978)

Kierkegaard, S.; *Fear and Trembling* (trans. A. Hannay; New York: Penguin, 1985)

Kuyper, L. J.; "The Repentance of God", *Reformed Review* 18.4 (1965), pp. 3-16

— "The Suffering and the Repentance of God", *Scottish Journal of Theology* 22.3 (1969), pp. 257-77

LaCugna Mowry, C.; *God for Us* (New York: HarperCollins, 1991)

Lambrecht, J. and R. F. Collins (eds); *God and Human Suffering* (Grand Rapids: Eerdmans, 1989)

Lee, J. Y.; *God Suffers for Us* (The Hague: Martinus Nijhoff, 1974)

Lewis, A. E.; *Between Cross and Resurrection* (Grand Rapids: Eerdmans, 2001)

von Loewenich, W.; *Luther's Theology of the Cross* (trans. H. J. A. Boumen; Minneapolis: Augsburg Publishing House, 1976)

Luther's Works (55 vols; eds. J. Pelikan and H. T. Lehmann; Saint Louis: Concordia; Philadelphia: Fortress, 1958-1986)

McCabe, H.; *God Matters* (Springfield, IL: Templegate Publishers, 1987)

McGrath, A. E.; *Luther's Theology of the Cross* (Grand Rapids: Baker, 1990)

McGuckin, J.; *Saint Cyril of Alexandria and the Christological Controversy* (Crestwood, NY: St. Vladimir's Seminary Press, 2004)

McWilliams, W.; *The Passion of God* (Macon, GA: Mercer University Press, 1985)

Meeks, M. D.; *Origins of the Theology of Hope* (Philadelphia: Fortress, 1974)

Metz, J. B.; *The Emergent Church* (New York: Crossroad, 1987)

— "Suffering unto God", *Critical Inquiry* 20 (1994), pp. 611-22

Miller, E. L.; *Questions that Matter* (4th ed; New York: McGraw-Hill, 1984)

Miller, J. A.; *The Eschatological Ontology of Jürgen Moltmann* (PhD thesis, Emory University, 1972)

Molnar, P. D.; "The Function of the Immanent Trinity in the Theology of Karl Barth", *Scottish Journal of Theology* 42.3 (1989), pp. 367-99

— "The Function of the Trinity in Moltmann's Doctrine of Creation", *Theological Studies* 51.4 (1990), pp. 673-97

— "Toward a Contemporary Doctrine of the Immanent Trinity", *Scottish Journal of Theology* 49.3 (1996), pp. 311-57

— *Divine Freedom and the Doctrine of the Immanent Trinity* (London: T & T Clark, 2002)

Moltmann, J.; *Theology of Hope* (trans. J. W. Leitch; New York: Harper and Row, 1967)

— *Hope and Planning* (trans. M. Clarkson; New York: Harper and Row, 1971)

— "The 'Crucified God': A Trinitarian Theology of the Cross", *Interpretation* 26.3 (1972), pp. 278-99

— *The Future of Creation* (trans. M. Kohl; Philadelphia: Fortress, 1979)

— *God in Creation* (trans. M. Kohl; New York: Harper and Row, 1985)

— *History and the Triune God* (trans. J. Bowden; New York: Crossroad, 1992)

— *The Spirit of Life* (trans. M. Kohl; Minneapolis: Fortress, 1992)

— *The Church in the Power of the Spirit* (trans. M. Kohl; Minneapolis: Fortress, 1993)

— *The Crucified God* (trans. R. A. Wilson and J. Bowden; Minneapolis: Fortress, 1993)

— *The Trinity and the Kingdom* (trans. M. Kohl; Minneapolis: Fortress, 1993)

— *Experiences in Theology* (trans. M. Kohl; Minneapolis: Fortress, 2000)

— *A Broad Place: An Autobiography* (trans.; M. Kohl; Minneapolis: Fortress, 2008)

Moltmann, J. (ed); *How I Have Changed* (Harrisburg, PA: Trinity Press International, 1997)

Moore, J. F.; "A Spectrum of Views: Traditional Christian Responses to the Holocaust", *Journal of Ecumenical Studies* 25.2 (1988), pp. 212-24

Morris, T.V. (ed); *Philosophy and the Christian Faith* (Notre Dame: University of Notre Dame Press, 1988)

Mozley, J. K.; *The Impassibility of God: A Survey of Christian Thought* (Cambridge: Cambridge University Press, 1926)

— *Some Tendencies in British Theology* (London: SPCK, 1951)

Ngien, D.; *The Suffering of God according to Martin Luther's "Theologia Crucis"* (Eugene, OR: Wipf and Stock, 2001)

Nnamani, A. G.; *The Paradox of a Suffering God* (New York: Peter Lang, 1995)

O'Donnell, J. J.; *Trinity and Temporality* (Oxford: Oxford University Press, 1983)

O'Keefe, J. J.; "Impassible Suffering? Divine Passion and Fifth-Century Christology", *Theological Studies* 58 (1997), pp. 39-59

— "Kenosis or Impassibility: Cyril of Alexandria and Theodoret of Cyrus on the Problem of Divine Pathos", *Studia Patristica* 32 (1997), pp. 358-365

Olson, R.; "Trinity and Eschatology: The Historical Being of God in Jürgen Moltmann and Wolfhart Pannenberg", *Scottish Journal of Theology* 36.2 (1983), pp. 213-227

Ott, M. R.; *Max Horkheimer's Critical Theory of Religion* (Lanham, MD: University Press of America, 2001)

Otto, R.; "Moltmann and the Anti-Monotheism Movement", *International Journal of Systematic Theology* 3.5 (2001), pp. 293-308

Pagels, E.; *Adam, Eve, and the Serpent* (New York: Random House, 1988)

Pannenberg, W.; *Basic Questions in Theology* (2 vols; trans. G. H. Kehm; London: SCM Press, 1971)

— *Jesus – God and Man* (2nd ed.; trans. L. L. Wilkins and D. A. Priebe; Philadelphia: Westminster, 1977)

Pelikan, J.; *The Christian Tradition* (5 vols; Chicago: University of Chicago Press, 1971-1989)

Philo; *The Works of Philo: New Updated Edition* (trans. C. D. Yonge; Peabody, MA: Hendrickson, 1993)

Pinnock, C.; *Most Moved Mover: A Theology of God's Openness* (Grand Rapids: Baker, 2001)

— *Flame of Love* (Downers Grove, IL: InterVarsity, 1996)

Pinnock, C., R. Rice, J. Sanders, W. Hasker and D. Basinger (eds); *The Openness of God* (Downers Grove, IL: InterVarsity, 1994)

Pinnock, S. K.; *Beyond Theodicy* (Albany, NY: State University of New York Press, 2002)

Plato; *Five Dialogues* (trans. G. M. A. Grube; Cambridge: Hackett, 1981)
— *Timaeus and Critas* (trans. D. Lee; Middlesex: Penguin, 1983)
Prestige, G. L.; *God in Patristic Thought* (London: SPCK, 1952)
Rahner, K.; *The Trinity* (trans. J. Donceel; New York: Crossroad Herder, 1998)
Ramsey, A. M.; *An Era in Anglican Theology* (New York: Charles Scribers' Sons, 1960)
Richard, L. J.; *A Kenotic Christology* (Washington, D.C.: University Press of America, 1982)
Rist, J. M.; *Stoic Philosophy* (Cambridge: Cambridge University Press, 1969)
Rossé, G.; *The Cry of Jesus on the Cross* (trans. S. W. Arndt; Eugene, OR: Wipf and Stock, 1987)
Rubenstein, R. L.; *After Auschwitz* (2nd ed; Baltimore: Johns Hopkins University, 1992)
Runyon, T. (ed); *Hope for the Church* (Nashville: Abingdon, 1979)
Sarot, M.; "Auschwitz, Morality and the Suffering of God", *Modern Theology* 7.2 (1991), pp. 135-52
Schaff, P. (ed); *The Creeds of Christendom* (3 vols; Grand Rapids: Baker, 1993)
Schleiermacher, F.; *The Christian Faith* (eds. H. R. Mackintosh and J. S. Steward; Edinburgh: T & T Clark, 1999)
Schwöbel, C.; *God: Action and Revelation* (Kampen: Kok Pharos, 1992)
Seneca; *Moral Essays* (ed. J. Henderson; trans. J. W. Basore; Loeb Classical Library, vol. 1; Cambridge, MA: Harvard University Press, 2003)
Sia, S.; "The Doctrine of God's Immutability: Introducing the Modern Debate", *New Blackfriars* 68 (1987), pp. 220-32
Simon, U. E.; *A Theology of Auschwitz* (London: Victor Gollancz, 1967)
Smith, J. W.; "Suffering Impassibly: Christ's Passion in Cyril of Alexandria's Soteriology", *Pro Ecclesia* 11.4 (2002), pp. 463-483
— "Martyrdom: Self-Denial or Self-Exaltation?", *Modern Theology* 22.2 (April 2006), pp. 169-96
Sölle, D.; *Suffering* (trans. E. R. Kalin; Philadelphia: Fortress, 1975)
Steinmetz, D. C.; *Luther in Context* (2nd ed; Grand Rapids: Baker, 2002)
Strelan, J. G.; "Theology Crucis, Theologia Gloriae: A Study in Opposing Theologies", *Lutheran Theological Journal* 23.3 (1989), pp. 99-113
Stroup, G. W., III; "Christian Doctrine: I, Chalcedon Revisited", *Theology Today* 35 (1978), pp. 52-64
Studdert Kennedy, G. A.; *The Hardest Part* (2nd ed.; London: Hodder and Stoughton, 1918)
Surin, K.; "The Impassibility of God and the Problem of Evil", *Scottish Journal of Theology* 35.2 (1982), pp. 97-115
— "Theodicy?", *Harvard Theological Review* 76.2 (1983), pp. 225-47
— *Theology and the Problem of Evil* (Oxford: Blackwell, 1986)
Swinton, J.; *Raging with Compassion* (Grand Rapids: Eerdmans, 2007)
Tatian; *Address to the Greeks*
Temple, W.; *Christus Veritas* (London: Macmillan, 1962)
Tertullian; *Against Praxeas*
— *Against Marcion*
Theophilus; *To Autolycus*
Thiel, J. E.; *God, Evil, and Innocent Suffering* (New York: Herder and Herder, 2002)
Tilley, T. W.; *The Evils of Theodicy* (Washington, DC: Georgetown University Press, 1991)

Tück, J.; "The Utmost: On the Possibilities and Limits of a Trinitarian Theology of the Cross", *Communio* 30.3 (2003), pp. 430-51

Vanhoozer, K. J.; *First Theology* (Downers Grove, IL: InterVarsity, 2002)

Vercruysse, J. E.; "Luther's Theology of the Cross at the Time of the Heidelberg Disputation", *Gregorianum* 57.3 (1976), pp. 523-48

Wakefield, J. L.; *Jürgen Moltmann: A Research Bibliography* (Langham, MD: Scarecrow, 2002)

Walsh, B. J.; "Theology of Hope and the Doctrine of Creation: An Appraisal of Jürgen Moltmann", *Evangelical Quarterly* 59.1 (1987), pp. 53-76

Webster, J.B.; "Jürgen Moltmann: Trinity and Suffering", *Evangel* 3.2 (Summer 1985), pp. 4-6

— *Holiness* (Grand Rapids: Eerdmans, 2003)

Weinandy, T. G.; *Does God Suffer?* (Notre Dame: University of Notre Dame Press, 2000)

Welker, M. (ed); *Diskussion über Jürgen Moltmanns Buch "Die Gekreuzigte Gott"* (Münschen: Kaiser, 1979)

— *God the Spirit* (trans. J. F. Hoffmeyer; Minneapolis: Fortress, 1994)

White, D.; *Forgiveness and Suffering* (Cambridge: Cambridge University Press, 1913)

Wiesel, E.; *Night* (trans. M. Wiesel; New York: Hill and Wang, 2006)

Willis, W. W., Jr.; *Theism, Atheism and the Doctrine of the Trinity* (Atlanta: Scholars Press, 1987)

Woollcombe, K. J.; "The Pain of God", *Scottish Journal of Theology* 20.2 (1964), pp. 129-48

Zizioulas, J. D.; *Being as Communion* (Crestwood, NY: St. Vladimir's Seminary Press, 1993)

— *Communion and Otherness* (New York: T & T Clark, 2006)

Index